Outward Bound

OUTWARD BOUND

SCHOOLS OF THE POSSIBLE

ROBERT GODFREY

PREFACE BY HENRY TAFT

ANCHOR PRESS / DOUBLEDAY
GARDEN CITY, NEW YORK 1980

The Anchor Press edition is the first publication of *Outward Bound*. It is published simultaneously in hard and paper covers. Anchor Press edition: 1980.

Library of Congress Cataloging in Publication Data

Godfrey, Bob, 1941–
   Outward Bound, schools of the possible.

   Includes index.
   1.   Outward bound schools—United States.
2.   Outward Bound, Inc.   I.   Title.
GV200.53.G62   796.5   77–82942

ISBN: 0–385–12270–5
Library of Congress Catalog Card Number 77–82942

CONTENTS

PREFACE   vii

CHAPTER ONE: The Southwest Outward Bound School   3

CHAPTER TWO: The North Carolina Outward Bound School   43

CHAPTER THREE: The Hurricane Island Outward Bound School   95

CHAPTER FOUR: The Northwest Outward Bound School   147

CHAPTER FIVE: The Colorado Outward Bound School   179

CHAPTER SIX: The Minnesota Outward Bound School   213

CHAPTER SEVEN: The Dartmouth Outward Bound Center   249

APPENDIX   265

INDEX   267

PREFACE

"It is wrong to coerce people into opinions," said Kurt Hahn, "but it is our duty to impel them into experience."

I remember once watching a seventeen-year-old girl hesitate at the top of a cliff. I could hear the tremor in her voice as she asked a question to postpone the inevitable. I held my breath as she leaned back over the void in her first rappel and then walked backward down the cliff, joy in her face as she realized she was actually doing it—a tremendous personal achievement in the face of fear and doubt, made even more meaningful by the cheers and smiles of her friends waiting below.

That is the stuff of Outward Bound, and that is what Bob Godfrey gives us so well in this book—not the philosophy, not the pedagogic theory, but the experience itself. Here is Outward Bound from the point of view of the student, complete with all the difficult, wonderful, tedious, painful, joyful, demanding, and rewarding things that happen during an Outward Bound course.

Bob Godfrey has chosen to tell the story of Outward Bound by recounting his actual experience with a group of students at each school. His remarkable odyssey begins in the dry heat of the Gila Wilderness Area in New Mexico. From there he moves to the lush, damp greenness of North Carolina, to a pulling boat off the coast of Maine, to the Presidential Range of New Hampshire, to the snow peaks of the North Cascades in Washington State, to a North canoe in the Boundary Waters Canoe Area, and finally, to Colorado in the depth of winter.

In choosing this approach, Godfrey has come as close to the experiential core of Outward Bound as any attempt with pen and camera can come. His perspective is a contemporary cross section of the reality of Outward Bound, a reality vested in people, in their relationships, and in their experiences in magnificent wilderness environments—unquestionably what Outward Bound is all about.

The first goal of Outward Bound is self-confidence, the central strength that flows from knowing you have actually done things that seemed impossible. In today's world young people are often urged to do something because it is easy.

Outward Bound says, "It's difficult, but we know you can do it. And when you've done it, you can be really proud of what you've accomplished."

Until you feel comfortable with yourself, it is hard to open up to others. The second goal of Outward Bound is to get you to do so. There is something about wilderness travel that leaves no choice. You must share with your companions; you must contribute to the common effort; you must carry your own weight and reach out to help others when the need arises; otherwise the whole enterprise founders. In the woods, in the mountains, on the sea—this lesson is clear.

It is strange that much of our educational system still resists the idea of learning through experience, still rejects whatever is not academic. Almost none of our eighteen years of education deals with our fears and emotions, our feelings of self-worth, our motivation, our relations with other people. These are the lessons of Outward Bound and the source of its deep effect on young people. In this sense Outward Bound is a complement to traditional education.

Of course there are many other aspects of an Outward Bound course. Service, for example. Hahn taught that helping others was an important part of a young person's education, and most Outward Bound courses provide just such an opportunity. It might be as simple as a community building project in one course or trail maintenance or fire fighting or as dramatic as a search and rescue operation off the coast of Maine. The point is to experience the satisfaction that comes from going beyond yourself to serve others.

What about wilderness skills? Can you learn to climb or canoe white water or camp in the winter on Outward Bound? Yes—at least you can get an introduction to the wilderness: to rock-climbing, rafting, sailing, and backpacking; to knots, first aid, and protection of the environment; to traveling through wild country on your own. Learning about the wilderness is an intense, demanding, and beautiful part of Outward Bound.

But you thought Outward Bound was a survival course? Tough it out in the wilderness with three matches and no toilet paper? No, that is not what it is—except metaphorically, as an experience that teaches you to survive in the wilderness of life: "If I can do this, I can do anything."

How did it all start, this unconventional educational movement called Outward Bound? Although the concept is English in flavor, the founder and spark was Kurt Hahn, a prolific German developer of new educational concepts and a political activist.

Hahn was the founding headmaster of the boarding school of Salem in southern Germany, the precursor of Outward Bound. Hahn's outspoken criticism of Hitler led to his being jailed and escaping to Scotland. There, in 1934, Hahn founded Gordonstoun, a private school attended by several members of the British royal family, including the present patron of Outward Bound in England, Prince Philip.

At Gordonstoun, Hahn developed his concepts under the "Moray Badge" scheme, described by the London *Times* as a "system of athletic standards for every boy to reach." As England became acutely aware of the dangers brewing in Europe and the need to prepare their youth for extraordinary challenges ahead, the Moray County scheme spread to the whole nation. "It fills a gap for which our educators should be repenting," said the *Times*. "It attempts to provide for the little man of our towns who begins earning his living at 14 an opportunity of experiences in which he can win self-respect, exhilaration, and the feeling of achievement in the difficult years of adolescence when his part in the world often seems so insignificant and meaningless."

Building on this recognition, Hahn organized an experimental program in Wales in the summer of 1940. It was a three-week course "of study and progressive physical and mental work." The *Times* went on to say that "the claim of the advocates of the County Badge training that it draws out and develops latent powers, was certainly justified on this occasion."

The Welsh program was the first Outward Bound course. Hahn established the first permanent school in Aberdovey, Wales, in 1941 under the leadership of Jim Hogan and with the great encouragement and support of shipping magnate Lawrence Holt.

From this beginning, six Outward Bound schools developed in the United Kingdom, sponsored and controlled by the Outward Bound Trust in London. The movement soon spread to Europe and wherever the English had been: Kenya and West Africa; Singapore, Hong Kong, Australia, and New Zealand; Canada and the United States. Today there are thirty-four Outward Bound schools around the world and more in the planning stage.

The first Outward Bound School in the United States was founded in Colorado in 1962. Among the prime movers were Joshua L. Miner, then teaching at Phillips Academy in Andover, and F. Charles Froelicher, then headmaster of Colorado Academy in Denver. Today there are six: Colorado, Minnesota, Hurricane Island, Northwest, North Carolina, and Southwest, plus the Dartmouth Outward Bound Center. Although Outward Bound in this country was inspired by Outward Bound in England and remains related to it both philosophically and through staff exchanges and trustee visits, there are no direct ties.

Outward Bound, Inc., a tax-exempt, nonprofit institution, is responsible for chartering schools and supporting the Outward Bound movement in the United States. The schools are independently organized, are bound together as a federation, and have agreed to abide by joint policies, particularly in the areas of safety and curriculum.

During 1979 more than 7,500 students attended the seven facilities in the United States, and there are now almost 70,000 alumni of Outward Bound in this country. The largest school is Colorado, with about 2,400 students a year, followed by Hurricane Island with about 1,400. Minnesota, Northwest, North Carolina, and Southwest have about 600 to 900 students annually, and Dartmouth has about 200 public students plus 600 more in special courses for students at Dartmouth College. With more than half the students taking the standard twenty-one to twenty-six-day course and the balance in short courses (fourteen-day, ten-day, seven-day) and contract courses, the annual total of student days now runs to about 130,000.

In its early days Outward Bound in America was designed for adolescent boys, as it was in England. However, it soon began to react to the broader needs of this society, including the women's movement. The first Outward Bound courses for women in the United States were run a decade ago, and today women represent 40 per cent of the students and a substantial proportion of staff as well. One of the great experiences in Outward Bound is to watch a group of macho males learn that their female instructor is not only more sensitive but also tougher and infinitely more competent in the wilderness than they are.

The advent of women was not the only change in American Outward Bound. The average age of students crept from the early teens to about twenty-one; today's typical Outward Bound student is in college rather than high school (although a few courses are still run for fourteen- to sixteen-year-olds). Just as significant was a growing demand for the experience from people in their thirties and forties or older. Only recently, with the popular success of *Passages*, have we come to understand that there are profound transitions at every age. The rites of passage that Outward Bound provided for teenage boys approaching manhood now help older women whose children have left the nest and who are searching for their identities, businessmen who are trapped on the treadmill, and adults who are seeking renewal, inspiration, and perspective. Courses have been designed for a variety of special audiences: managers, women over thirty, educators, families; and we have instituted other courses with special content: leadership skills, mid-life career changes, wilderness skills. Typically, the standard courses appeal to younger people who can take three weeks during the summer, whereas adults find the shorter courses more practical year-round. A glance at the current course schedule shows 300 different courses offered at the seven schools in every month of the year.

It has been a conviction of Outward Bound from the beginning that a mix of ethnic, economic, and social backgrounds adds important depth and dimension to the experience of each student. From this conviction has sprung our continuing effort to provide enough scholarship funds so that no qualified student is turned away; 25 per cent or more of all Outward Bound students receive scholarship aid.

No description of Outward Bound would be complete without a mention of some of the special populations served. For the past several years the Minnesota Outward Bound School has been experimenting with Outward Bound courses for the handicapped, including the blind, the hearing-impaired, and persons with a variety of other physical disabilities from paraplegia to cerebral palsy. The pilot programs have demonstrated to professionals in the rehabilitation field that people with severe disabilities are far more capable than was previously supposed. The impact on able-bodied students and instructors has also been extraordinary. To watch a man without legs climb a rock face is to burn in your memory an inspiration for a lifetime.

Another large population for which Outward Bound has proven useful in breaking the pattern of failure is delinquent youth, a broad spectrum ranging from so-called court-acquainted youth to prison inmates. Work with inner-city youths and delinquents fits in very well with Outward Bound's desire to be of service to the society as a whole, not simply to the privileged middle class, but it has also been frustrating work, with uneven success. The whole concept of Outward Bound is remote from the backgrounds and life-styles of most inner-city minorities, and the questions of motivation, orientation, and follow-up loom very large.

There are several ongoing programs for young people in trouble, including a contract program run by the Hurricane Island Outward Bound School for the state of Florida, a year-long group-home program for adjudicated youth established by the Colorado school, and a number of programs for prison inmates in various states for which Outward Bound has provided the inspiration and consultant help.

This pattern—providing the concept and consultant advice—has been a fundamental part of Outward Bound from the start. Long ago it was obvious that we could not achieve a maximum impact simply by running standard Outward Bound Schools; even at the current level of seventy-five hundred students a year, it would limit the impact to a tiny elite. The solution has been a long-term outreach effort to show others how to use Outward Bound methods and how to adapt them to their own institutions. Thousands of educators have taken a course themselves, and several hundred schools and colleges now incorporate some aspect of the Outward Bound process in their curriculum.

Such programs come in endless variations, from direct imitations of Outward Bound to distant cousins concentrating on some particular aspect, such as wilderness skills, group process, fitness, or simply travel adventure. Most have merit, and as long as safety is respected, we encourage them as worthwhile, even though we have spawned a thousand competitors. If Outward Bound can feel responsible in part for these new developments, it can take satisfaction in the fulfillment of its motto: To Strive, to Serve, and Not to Yield.

No one associated with Outward Bound, whether staff or student, remains untouched. In the seven years since I left the business world, my personal life has been affected more than I could have imagined. In my relationships with other people, my marriage, my values and priorities about my physical self, and my feelings about the natural world, Outward Bound has worked its magic.

Bob Godfrey has caught some of that magic here.

Henry W. Taft
President,
Outward Bound, Inc.

THE OUTWARD BOUND SCHOOLS

Chapter One

THE SOUTHWEST
OUTWARD BOUND SCHOOL

The day starts deceptively. Our camp is low against the long flank of a hillside, shaded from the morning sun. There is a shiver in the air. Nine others are relishing the coolness, moving slowly. Talking quietly. Packing. It is early morning in the desert; there is an air of anticipation, of suppressed eagerness.

Our valley is broad, U-shaped. Our protector, the long hillside, lies completely in shade. Opposite, behind our camp, the sun moves toward us with practiced stealth. Watching, I find that I am involuntarily holding my breath. My eye cannot detect the shadow move, but it does. Relentlessly. Delicately. Disrobing each stunted juniper and tall-standing piñon pine. Each is exposed to the harsh glare of the desert day. Do they feel embarrassed, naked without their protective shadow mantle?

One of our group, Joe Collins, wanders off into the bushes, following a faint trail, carrying a short-handled digging spade. The role of toilet paper garlanding its handle proclaims his destination.

On the drive in, three very full days earlier, Joe had sat next to me as we slammed our way along fifty miles of rutted dirt roads in a bouncing Outward Bound van. Twenty-four years old, soft-spoken, but with a precise and focused intensity, Joe was obviously nobody's fool. Less obviously, he was a classic city slicker. Joe comes from Boston, a graduate student in education at Boston University.

"My idea of roughing it," he confessed with a twinkle, "up to now has been a cheap room at the Ritz."

We talked for a while about values and choice points in life, about what mattered and what didn't. Joe had come to Outward Bound, he said, as part of an ongoing process of trying to sort out some life priorities for himself.

I grunted and watched a magpie flapping its wings crazily, abandoning a juicy morsel of blacktop carrion, to descend again behind us before the van's dust had settled.

Joe did not seem to notice the magpie. He seemed lost in his own thoughts, preoccupied.

Following the shore of the Gila River.

Now, watching Joe head for the bushes, I realize that I have not kept close contact with him. He looks weary and somewhat puzzled. He drags a little as he heads into the bushes, and his pants are baggy. The desert does that, gets you baggy and dusty in no time flat. Your system takes awhile to adjust to dry heat and the energy demands of putting one foot in front of the other on a long day's hike.

For the past three days we have trekked through the canyons of the Gila Wilderness Area of New Mexico to reach our camp on the bank of the Gila River. There are ten members in our group, in the care of an Outward Bound instructor. For most of us it is a radically new experience. We have spent the past two days struggling through a torturously narrow canyon where, in places, we were able to touch both walls with our outstretched arms. The canyon walls towered two hundred feet high. At constrictions, *narrows* as they are called, we had resorted to lowering our packs on ropes and occasionally wading chest-deep in cold water through murky pools. Yesterday evening we emerged into more open terrain and camped in the shelter of a grove of cottonwoods. Everyone in our group found the going demanding, an abrupt contrast to our normal routines.

The time is now 8:00 A.M. Jeanette, in the shade of a cottonwood tree, is packing the backpack used in the Outward Bound program. Built around a lightweight frame of aluminum tubing, it weighs little more than a pound and is designed in curves to conform to the natural contours of the back, spine, and hips. It is strong enough to support a rhinoceros. The pack itself is of durable green ripstop nylon. One large compartment is for clothes, food, cooking gear, and the like, and two side pockets are for smaller items. One's sleeping bag, groundsheet, and foam insulating pad are rolled together into a tight tube that is strapped to the outside of the frame below the main pack. Our pack is our most intimate companion on the expedition—friend and foe, necessary for survival, but malicious as a medieval torturer, rubbing us sore as we struggle along.

Jeanette is faced by a not unusual problem: Her pack is full to the top, but on the sand beside her remain a flashlight, a plastic bag containing spare clothes, and sundry other small items. With a rueful shrug, she lifts out larger items and gamefully presses the contents down, readjusts, and endeavors to fit everything in.

Jeanette comes from Albuquerque. She works as a "full-time secretary and part-time soldier" in the Army Reserves. For five days each week she is interred in the basement office of a military complex. She is twenty-seven years old, the mother of a two-and-a-half-year-old daughter. Outward Bound is part of the process of putting herself together after her divorce, she explained to the group on the first day.

Since then Jeanette has kept to herself. It is obvious that the physical demands of the experience are taking a heavier toll on her than she had expected. I feel sure that she is reassessing her involvement, questioning her ability to continue, and perhaps considering withdrawal. From what we know of the activities ahead of us today, I suspect that it will be a testing time.

The sun's shadow has now moved down the hillside and is only a hundred or so feet above the campsite. Soon it will be on us; shortly we will sweat. I savor the last few cool moments.

Down by the river four other members of the tribe (as Southwest Outward Bound calls its groups) are filling water bottles, brushing teeth, reluctantly preparing to sever contact with the stream that has been our companion for the past three days. This watercourse, the Gila River, is the main liquid artery through the Gila Wilderness Area. It is a broad river, shallow, clear, and with a fine mosaic of clean gray gravel for its bed. Yesterday we had crossed it in the late afternoon, knee-deep, enjoying its cool rush after a full dirty day through the canyons.

The Gila Wilderness sprawls in the southwestern corner of the state of New Mexico, close to the Mexican border. The Gila, sixty-five miles by a hundred miles of canyon country, is a desert. Rainfall can be as little as twelve inches in a dry year, as much as twenty-eight in a wet one. Although it is arid, a glance at a topographic map shows a lot of green. There are trees almost everywhere in the Gila: ponderosa pine, limber pine, Engelmann spruce, stands of piñon juniper, oak, and cottonwood along the watercourses. It is a rolling country, lacking the precipitous grandeur of the more spectacular canyon lands, but with its own delicate charm. The Gila feels gentle.

The sun *is* hot. It *is* dry. The aridity cannot be denied. There are the customary spiky, spiny, slithery, stingy inhabitants: the cactus, the thornbush, the scorpion, and the rattlesnake; the countless bugs: the solpugids (hairy-bodied, spiderlike, tan-colored creatures, hiding under stones and in crevices by day, appearing at night to chomp on the rest of the insect world with their four-section, pointed, tooth-edged beaks, the most formidable set of jaws in the animal kingdom), the centipedes, the millipedes, the tumblebug, the vinegarroon (the whip scorpion, that arthropodal skunk, with its characteristic habit of expressing indignation with a squirt of malodorous vinegar-smelling liquid), the mutillids (buffalo ants, cute little hairy fellows looking much like a moving mass of colored fuzz), and the tarantulas (less venomous than commonly supposed and sometimes kept as pets by the confident). All these call the Gila home, as does the fabled (dreaded?) Gila monster. But all these are, for the main, timid creatures who prefer to give humans (the real monsters of the desert) a wide berth. As we become accustomed to our desert surroundings, rather than feeling repulsed, we respond with interest, curiosity, and a feeling of special privilege if we are fortunate enough to stumble across any of these little fellows in their natural habitat.

Hiking trails commonly follow the canyon bottom along the watercourses. The cottonwood is the most common shade tree and is abundant. Soft sandy havens—in which to spend a few horizontal moments—are occasionally found within earshot of trickling water.

Once the jangle of man-made rhythms has been left behind, the body begins to adapt to the special rhythm of the desert. It is a rhythm that says, "Go slow; go light; travel when it's cool; rest when the sun is high." We were learning, but not quickly enough. Today we would treat the natural ordinances of the desert with less than due consideration, and we would suffer.

"Tra-la-la!"

Jimbo!

Squatting on his haunches, bandy-looking, a Mack Truck driver's broad-beak cap shading a long, thin face, Jimbo peers at his brood from atop a small hillock.

"Tra-la-la," he repeats in a not unmusical tone.

Beside him, looking tight, efficient, and ready to go stands a well-organized backpack!

"Hey, people. Let's do it. Huh?"

There is a gentle urgency in Jimbo's proddings.

The sun is way up now; already its glare hurts.

Jimbo is our instructor, one of Southwest Outward Bound's finest. A true desert rat. He even looks sandy. His wispy beard is blond, the color of the lighter variety of desert slickrock. His skinny frame, Ichabod Crane of the canyons, is patinaed with sun and dust. Restraint is his consistent quality. There he squats, very together, very organized, watching but not moving, a creature very much at home in his chosen place. He could be a scaled lizard poised motionless. As a lizard's tongue twitches, Jimbo clucks—again—"Tra-la-la." As he squats, quite still, his eyes beadily rove the campsite.

Dan Peavy, thirty-six, a dentist from San Antonio, Texas, moves his languid packing into a higher gear. "Hey, you guys, let's get going," he hollers to the canyon. The camp hustles, but it is still twenty more minutes before our ragged group is assembled and ready to head out.

Jimbo has remained motionless on his hillock, surveying the scene.

The group jostles. There are fundamental questions to be answered. Where are we going? Who leads? Is everyone ready? Has the camp been thoroughly checked and cleaned? Is the fire out, and has its scar been completely obliterated? Is there any trace left of the latrine?

Granny Mountain is the destination, that much is known. The previous evening Jimbo had drawn the group together around a topographic map, following from lessons in map reading during the past three days, and had traced a route through its contour lines with a wisp of dried grass.

It had seemed so simple then. Our campsite on the bank of the Gila River was at an altitude of 5,000 feet. The top of Granny Mountain, the map told us, was 7,752 feet and about five miles away. On the map an intermittent black dotted line joined our camp to the summit, a trail. And hadn't Jimbo yesterday made us wise in the mysteries of the compass? We could find north, adjust for magnetic variation (*declination* to the expert), figure bearings, and orient ourselves to our surroundings. With these tools, map and compass, we were fully in charge of our immediate destiny and should be able to chart our

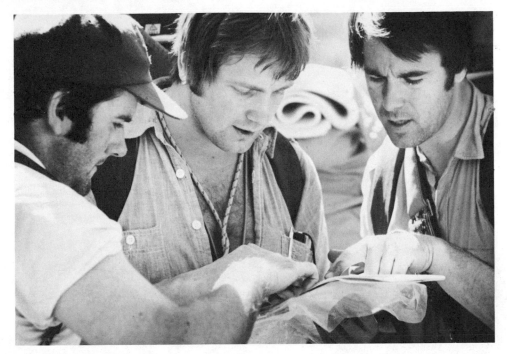

Map reading.

passage through the scrub and cactus with all the assurance of astronauts backed by the NASA computers.

It takes half an hour to make the first two decisions: Who is going to lead, and just where does the Granny Mountain trail begin?

The decision-making process is agonizing. A democracy of nine. Jeanette, as usual, remains withdrawn. Joe also stays in the background. Most of the action is between three people, the rest of the group interjecting occasional comments. Dentist Dan is verbally well organized and confidently pushy. He knows map and compass and trusts them.

"My compass bearing says over there," he proclaims, pointing toward a clump of dense trees.

"This isn't the kind of place that a compass is going to be much use," responds the youngest of our group, Sara Berkley, an outspoken young woman of twenty-two from Coe College, Iowa. "We should circle out from camp and try and intersect with the trail."

"How you going to know it's the right trail?" interjects Ron Gray. Ron is a businessman from Chicago with his own machine tool company. At forty-three years of age he is the father figure of our group, with a no-nonsense Chicago abruptness in his manner. "How you gonna know it just ain't some game trail or something? How you gonna know it's the right trail?" he demands with firm emphasis on the word *right*.

The Gila River.

There is a lengthy pause. I think all of us are aware of Jimbo's eyes coolly appraising the interaction.

"Because," responds Sara in a controlled voice, "we don't just blindly follow the first trail we come to. If we find one that looks right, we follow it for a little way and check the contours on the map and the compass to see if it's going the right way and if the ground features look right."

This commendable logic makes sense to the group.

People begin shouldering packs.

"Hey, wait a minute!" Ron again, sounding chagrined. "You mean to tell me we're all gonna load up these goddamned heavy packs and blunder around in the bushes there for the next half hour. What is this? Some kind of circus?"

"Ron's right." This time it is Joe adding his quiet contribution. "There's no point in all of us setting off until we know where we are going." His controlled Boston tone is persuasive. "One of us should check first and shout if he finds it."

"Two," responds Sara. "Jimbo said there should always be two of us if we go wandering off—in case something goes wrong," she finishes somewhat hesitantly.

It is clear that the group feels that this interpretation of Jimbo's instruction is too literal in the obviously safe surroundings of the campsite.

"Well," Sara continues, but less confidently, "you never know. You might step on a snake or something."

Dan cuts through the ensuing uncomfortable silence. "I'll go look. Who's coming with me?"

"Me," answers Ron. "Anything to get moving."

The pair trots off in the assumed direction of Granny Mountain and disappears into the bushes.

The group goes into repose, and minutes tick by.

"I'm worried," confides Joe, now sprawled on the ground, his head resting on a dead log. "It's almost nine o'clock. At this rate we're going to be doing the last pull up to the top in the heat of the afternoon sun, and these packs are not getting any lighter."

No one replies.

"Tra-la-la," intones Jimbo from his perch.

An uncomfortable silence descends on the group. It is clear that Joe is right. Jimbo, in his own inimitable way, has underscored the fact. We are late, and moments gone are moments gone for good.

"Hullooo."

Dan's voice.

"I think we found it," he shouts.

The group stirs. Packs are shouldered. Dan in the lead, Ron second, the others following in single file, we shamble off, up the easy-angled hillside, through sage and piñon juniper, dead twigs crackling under our feet, heading for the trail.

The situation we have just emerged from holds a time-honored place in Outward Bound, and Jimbo has played the classic Outward Bound instructor role with studied perfection. During the three days that have preceded this morning's scenario we have received ample basic instruction in the gentle art of desert living and travel. Jimbo has spent time with us on the intricacies of map and compass. We have received instruction in the important elements of first aid and emergency care in case of a desert accident. We have been advised on what to do and what not to do from the dual points of view of survival and comfort in this new environment. Most important we have had three days of observing Jimbo, of being able to attend to the manner in which he moves through the desert.

But, of course, we have not yet learned.

This morning, for the first time, we are on our own, and already we have blown it. We had risen late and dawdled over breakfast. And the process of organizing ten individuals into a cohesive whole has taken longer than it should— by almost a factor of three.

But it is neither laziness nor lack of concern that has kept Jimbo silent, watching us from his brooding haunches this morning. It is design, part of the Outward Bound process. The ball has been passed to us. It is our task to go with it. There will be lots to talk over this coming evening at the end of what is certainly going to be a long, hot day.

The hillside we are trudging up this early morning is a hard, dusty, clay-baked thing. It feels solid underfoot. A thick layer—difficult to say exactly how thick, perhaps an inch or so—of unconsolidated dust lies on its surface. Each time the foot is placed, the dust acts as a lubricant, thin enough to cause the foot to slide and rotate but not thick enough to cushion. Wind-deposited, never wet enough to solidify or provide a breeding ground for soil-making organisms, the dust sits there, waiting. Waiting to be stirred by a passing foot or a rasping wind.

Our hosts, *Pinus edulis*, the piñon pine, elder statesmen of the slickrock, impassively observe our progress. These grand old fellows are the commonest species of tree in the southwestern desert, able to survive on microscopic amounts of water, one of the most drought-resistant and slow-growing of trees. *Pinus edulis* has desert living down to a fine art: Don't do much, and then do it real slow. Therein lies the wisdom of the sand country.

I pause for a moment and take a close look at one particularly fine specimen. He pokes himself to a grand thirty feet high. He's been here for a long, long time. Not your typical transient. Three hundred years might be a complimentary estimate of his age. A blushing youth on the desert time scale. His bark is deeply furrowed into scaly ridges and gives off a musky, resinous scent. But more than scent, he is a gourmet provider. The French may savor their truffles, but every autumn the Indian and Spanish-American dwellers of the Southwest harvest in excess of a million pounds of ripe piñon nuts, *piñones*, for the delicatessen markets of the American big city. These little delicacies, with their charactcristic oily, slightly bittersweet taste, make a crunchy snack or the basis of a full meal if nothing else is available.

From my position at the rear of the line I can see nine green packs bobbing their way slowly up the trail. Jeanette is having trouble. She is going very slowly, unable to keep up with those ahead of her. Our party is now divided. The four at the front of the line are some two hundred yards up the hillside; next comes Jeanette, shuffling along, followed by the remaining five. Sara is immediately behind Jeanette.

"How're you doing?" I hear her inquire.

Jeanette stops.

"Not good. Not good at all."

"Hey, you guys," Sara shouts to the group ahead, "hold up there. Jeanette's having problems."

"I need a drink. I feel real hot. Just let me sit down for a minute."

Sara and Joe help Jeanette take her pack off and guide her into the shade beneath a piñon tree. Slumped, partly exhausted, she drinks deeply from a proffered water canteen.

The four who have been ahead have dropped their packs and retraced their steps to join us.

Jimbo is conspicuous by his absence.

We have been hiking for an hour and a half and are only a quarter of the way to Granny Mountain. The packs feel heavier with each step, and the sun's intensity jabs at us.

Prior to the course, Jeanette had written, "Friends thought I was out of my mind to pay to go through the pain of facing disappointment, injuries, and

Jeanette, close to exhaustion, on the grueling hike up Granny Mountain.

Negotiating an obstacle in the narrows of the Gila River.

depriving myself of comfort items." As she slumps in the shade, experiencing her aching limbs and parched throat, she questions her participation. "The lazy in me kept saying you can get out of this course somehow. . . . What's the next few days going to be like if you're having such a time of it so far," she later wrote of the experience.

As Jeanette contemplates ways out, the others discuss the situation.

"At this speed we're never going to get there today," states Ron, a note of aggravation in his voice. He prides himself on being in good physical shape for his age and clearly feels the slow pace set by Jeanette is holding him back. He wants to be personally extended physically, and it isn't happening.

Today Ron's challenge is, not how well he can respond physically to the hike up Granny Mountain, but rather how he can successfully respond to Jeanette's predicament, adjusting his own priorities and providing support and empathy to a weaker member of the group.

Outward Bound generates these situations systematically and deliberately. It is a given that in any Outward Bound group there will be diversity. Participants come for different and sometimes conflicting motives. To be extended physically is a common reason, but the group can only travel at the speed of the slowest member. Today that person is Jeanette, and Ron has to adjust his priorities to cope with a frustrating situation.

Jeanette's predicament affects not only Ron but the group as a whole. Sara and Dan stand separate from Jeanette, quietly discussing the situation.

"I'm worried," says Sara.

"I know," responds Dan. "We still have an awful long way to go today."

"Hey, Ron, come over here for a minute, will you," Sara calls.

Ron joins them.

"Look," she exclaims, "at this speed we're just not gonna make it."

Ron looks at her quizzically. "Do you have something in mind?" he asks.

"Well, one thing we could do is lighten Jeanette's pack. We could each take some of her stuff. A few pounds extra for each of us wouldn't make all that much difference, but it would make all the difference in the world to Jeanette."

Ron and Dan exchange glances and ponder Sara's suggestion. Ron is the first to respond.

"Sure, I'm up for it. Why not? I'm going fine. A few extra pounds aren't going to make that much difference."

Dan looks a little put out at the suggestion. The packs are already heavy enough to be uncomfortable, and the sun's heat is increasing as the morning progresses, but he concurs.

Sara moves over to Jeanette.

"Hey, Jeanette. How's about if we take some of your load, lighten your pack a bit, so you can move easier."

Jeanette glances up at Sara, mixed emotions registering. She struggles for words.

"No. No—I couldn't let you do that." But it is clear that the offer is tempting.

"Look, I know how you must be feeling," interjects Ron. "But if we don't do it, we're just not gonna make it today, and camping out for the night on this hillside with no water isn't gonna do any of us much good."

Others of the group enter the discussion and gently add voices of persuasion. It is clear to all that dividing up Jeanette's load is the only practical solution to the problem. Jeanette, close to tears, is in conflict. Either way her pride will be hurt. If she refuses, she will slow the group down, with the inevitable serious consequences. If she agrees, she will have to hike for the rest of the day knowing that her companions, already loaded, will be additionally burdened on her behalf.

"Jeanette." Joe's quiet voice. "You have to let us help you. That's what this is all about. It's not just who's strongest or who's weakest. That's not very important. It's all of us working together, as a group, supporting each other, to get the thing done."

Jeanette blinks, clearing her eyes. "I guess," she responds, shrugging. "I guess that's what I have to do."

"Right," adds Ron. "This *is* what it's all about. You're in trouble; we help out." And he reaches over to give Jeanette's shoulder a friendly squeeze.

Dan takes Jeanette's foam sleeping pad and groundcloth. Ron stows her food into his already bulging pack. Other members of the group systematically share out the majority of her possessions, and in five minutes her pack is almost empty except for one or two personal items, sun cream, and water canteen. The group is ready to move on up the trail again. The time is eleven-thirty.

Unwitnessed, Jimbo has arrived and for the past few minutes, in his perennial squat, has been observing the interaction. He does not comment directly on what has taken place, merely exchanges pleasantries as the group walks by. There is, though, I think, a satisfied expression on his face. He watches us steadily, eyes calm, and I sense his approval of what has transpired. The group faced a major problem and handled it well.

The next five hours are demanding for the whole group. Keeping together is the name of the game. The faster ones have to modulate their pace to that of the slowest. We endeavor to maintain an even pace, keeping sight of each other; but as concentration diminishes, the group straggles, divides, and loses its cohesiveness. Jeanette, now traveling light, still finds the going tough and stops frequently to curl in the shade of a broad-limbed choya cactus or an overhanging outcrop of rock. As we ascend, the stops become more frequent. Tempers are becoming short. Pack straps rub sore spots on tender hips and shoulders. At one point the trail runs out.

"Over there, to the left," Ron points.

"Don't think so," responds Dan. "That'll put us way off where we want to be."

A discussion follows. No one has a clear sense of direction. One opinion seems as good as another. It seems as though the loudest voice will win.

It is Ron's. "It's gotta be to the left, just gotta be," he insists, shouldering his pack. And with a stubborn, "Well—I'm tired of arguing," he sets off.

Taking the course of least resistance, the group shoulders their packs and follows.

The next thirty minutes are spent vainly thrashing on a steep, trailless hillside, exchanging blows with clumps of dense thornbushes. It does not take long to figure out that the thornbushes are winning.

"I've had this," grumps Dan. "Wherever the trail is, it isn't here."

The group draws together, drops their packs onto the ground, and slumps. Jeanette looks pale. She lies beside her pack, embracing a small patch of shade, flat on her back in the dirt, arms and legs sprawled loosely, panting gently, eyes closed, half asleep.

Sara is the first to summarize the situation. "This is useless, ridiculous. We're getting nowhere."

"All right," snaps Ron peevishly, "what do *you* suggest?"

"What we did this morning. We'll all stay here with the packs while two of us circle out and see if we can't cut across the trail."

Within ten minutes two searchers have found the trail. The group again shoulders their packs and moves slowly upward.

We are now at seven thousand feet. The vegetation is thinning, and we can see the meandering valley that cradles the Gila River far below. The time is three in the afternoon. The hillside faces directly into the afternoon sun. The heat is blistering.

For most of us the final hour of hiking to the top draws on reserves of strength and endurance that have long lain dormant. At a snail's pace, still at Jeanette's speed, we approach the top. At four in the afternoon we arrive. No exultation, no glory, just deep-down weariness, sore feet, and aching backs. Packs are discarded, water bottles produced, and food. For forty minutes conversation is minimal; the group lies sprawled in the shade of a small grove of pine trees, just below the summit, dozing, resting. Sweat-stained bodies in repose.

Sara says to Dan, "I've reached physical limits before, in swimming, but never anything like this."

Joe, a little way off by himself, sprawls, tired but content, singing quietly to himself, "Ye banks and braes . . . I'll be in Scotland afore ye."

Near my feet are a pair of elegant flowering desert plants, eight inches tall, on slender stems, succulent orange fingers cupped into a tuliplike cluster: the Indian paintbrush.

A dumpy cactus, quite small, only inches across, its hemispherical outer surface crisscrossed with a tight mesh of small, sharp spikes—it is known locally as Indian eggs—attracts my idle attention.

Someone starts a small fire from dry twigs, and before long hot water is available. It seems strange to drink hot tea and hot chocolate with the temperature close to a hundred degrees and the sun still blazing down, but parched bodies welcome the refreshments, and the hot liquid seems to energize us more than the lukewarm water in our canteens.

"Take it easy on the liquids," cautions Ron. "We still have a ways to go before we reach Miller Spring."

Miller Spring, our camping site for the night and the next water hole, lies four miles to the northwest, but downhill.

"Time to get moving," someone announces.

The four miles down to Miller Spring take us almost five hours. We leave the top of Granny Mountain at five o'clock. Darkness overtakes us. We blunder downward, attempting to stay with the trail through confusing minor ridges, gullies, stands of pine trees, cacti, and clumps of low bushes. At eight the moon comes up and helps make sense of the shadows. Jeanette is staggering slightly. Others are lurching slowly along, feet aching, muscles sore.

A strange noise ahead captures our attention. We hear the sound of many throats in rhythmic unison.

"Croak, croak, cr-cr-cr-croak."

"Frogs!" Sara exclaims.

"Water!" someone shouts.

We pick up speed, round a corner, and see the moonlight glinting on the surface of a small body of water, a pond surrounded by reeds.

Joe, at the front, pauses for a moment.

The group catches up, and thirsty eyes drink in the scene.

"Oh, my lord," intones Ron, "I don't believe it. For the past two hours I've been convinced that I've been in hell and my punishment was to keep on walking forever."

A tumbledown cabin sits beside the water. Packs are discarded; sleeping bags are unrolled. A fire is started. As close to exhaustion as they have ever been, some of our small group disappear into their sleeping bags immediately, without waiting for food or a hot drink.

Later, lounging next to glowing embers of the evening fire, Jimbo and I are the only two remaining.

"Well, buddy?" I inquire. "What do you think?"

"They did OK," acknowledges Jimbo. "Considering that only four days ago they'd probably have got in their cars to drive half a dozen blocks to the supermarket, they didn't do half bad today, not half bad at all."

The next day's dawn is a peaceful affair. Jimbo is not in a hurry. No one else is either. Someone starts a fire in the circle of stones next to the cabin. Breakfast is desultory. Sara and Ron act as chefs and serve up a proud supply of pancakes with syrup. People emerge sporadically from their sleeping bags, unable to resist the aroma of hot food. The area is a wreck. Sleeping bags are littered in all directions. In the fatigue of the previous evening's arrival, no one had bothered to erect a shelter. Personal gear, sweaters, socks, shirts, underwear, plastic bags, odds and ends, compasses, climbing ropes, packs, food bags lie strewn. The frogs are silent, respectful of the cool morning. Joe has been having problems keeping food in his stomach throughout the trip. He nibbles a pancake, ingests syrup, and heads for the bushes. The others listen sympathetically to the sound of his gagging. He returns a few moments later, white-faced, shaking his head in refusal at the offer of more food.

"Sorry. Just can't keep anything down."

Lunch break.

"How about something to drink, coffee or tea perhaps?" Sara inquires.

"Maybe some weak tea," he replies.

By now everyone is up and about. It is eight-thirty or thereabouts, according to the sun.

"Hey, folks," Jimbo calls, "let's get together for a few minutes under the trees." He points to a shady glade behind the cabin.

"Well," Jimbo starts when we are assembled, "let's spend a few moments going over what happened yesterday. Let's see if we can't learn something from what we did."

There is an air of anticipation in the group. We are all aware that follow-up discussion of the activities is an integral part of the Outward Bound experience, but no one is quite sure of the ground rules. Are we in for an Esalen-style encounter session, probing for deep emotions? Is Jimbo going to lecture us in schoolteacher or military officer manner? Perhaps an est brainwashing diatribe is to be the order of the day, though it is difficult to imagine Jimbo in the role of tongue lasher. Perhaps we will all contemplate our navels, interacting essentially on a nonverbal level.

"Well," Jimbo reiterates persuasively, "let's get things rolling with some individual reactions to yesterday. How do you feel about what happened?"

Jeanette is the first to respond. She is seated straight-legged, her back propped by a pine tree, broad-brimmed hat shading her face. "I'm astonished that I did it. There were times yesterday when I was as near to dying as I've ever been on this earth—at least that's what it felt like."

There is a lengthy moment of appreciative silence. No one responds directly to Jeanette, but there is an unmistakable air of pride in the group. Now everyone looks at her, and the expressions on people's faces say clearly that they understand what she has been through and respect her for it. Jeanette gives a little grin and looks down.

"Yea, Jeanette," someone says softly.

"Yea, all of you," responds Jeanette. "I wouldn't be here now if you all hadn't got in behind me, helped with my stuff, and given me all that support."

Joe is next. "I'm disappointed in myself. There were times yesterday when I was close to blowing my cool, I was getting mad—at myself as well as at what was going on. We were disorganized. We were late. Our leadership was fragmented. I still can't believe we ended up climbing that goddamn hillside in the afternoon sun."

Ron continues, "I really felt the pressure. I mouthed off too much. Look, all of you, you don't have to take much notice of me when I get like that. It's just my way. I've got to blow off steam when things get rough. I can't keep it pent up. If I hurt anybody's feelings yesterday, well, I'm sorry—but that's just the way I am."

Pam, the smallest member of our group, a plucky, blonde-haired young woman who works in an aerobics program in Dallas, answers, "That's OK, Ron—well, I mean—yes—there were times yesterday when I found myself getting irritated by you. But at the same time I kind of wish that I could sometimes let myself

Ridge hiking in Zion National Park, a fabulous desert environment used by the Southwest Outward Bound School.

go like that. I keep my feelings bottled up all the time. I hardly say a word, and it leaves me feeling pent up inside."

There is another silence. The discussion has moved into the potentially disturbing area of interpersonal feedback. No one seems immediately willing to take it a step farther.

I glance at Jimbo. The expression in his eyes convinces me that he, too, is very aware of the direction we are heading. I wonder if he will nudge us farther in that direction or let the discussion evolve in intimacy at its own natural rate.

One of the characteristics of the Outward Bound experience is the way in which a diverse group of individuals from broadly varied backgrounds are immersed in a situation that *automatically* generates a high degree of intimacy and an unavoidable interdependency. Depending to a large extent on the personal style of the particular Outward Bound instructor, this intimacy and dependence can remain confined to spontaneous day-to-day activities and interactions, or it can be highlighted and explored in postactivity discussion groups. Over the years this has been a loaded topic and the subject of some disagreement in Outward Bound. Some Outward Bound staff—the "touchy-feely" ones, as they are sometimes humorously referred to—come experienced in group and individual counseling skills and deliberately facilitate interpersonal sharing. At the other end of the spectrum is the staff member whose main strength lies in his or her expertise in the technical skills of the wilderness environment, the archetypical

nonverbal backwoods person. The majority of Outward Bound instructors have strength in both these areas—they have to—and are chosen for these reasons. Each day of every program they must act as guide and mentor to a complex group of people, guiding them through a variety of situations designed to generate powerful reactions. There are inevitably powerful emotional reactions, and they have to be dealt with. One of the most common reactions at the conclusion of an Outward Bound course is, "I did more than I ever thought I could do." In order for this reaction to be stimulated, as it was in Jeanette yesterday, the group is involved in activities which demand that they draw upon inner resources, reserves of determination, stamina, and the capacity to support weaker members of the group, that many have forgotten they possessed. The degree to which this process is enhanced or inhibited by verbalization of the experience is a vital ingredient in the effectiveness of a particular instructor.

Jimbo remains motionless while the group ponders Pam's remarks about the effect of Ron's behavior on her. For a while no one speaks.

Sara jumps in and moves us back to discussion of more concrete matters. "We were too disorganized yesterday, particularly in the thornbushes. We ended up going in all different directions."

Jimbo asks, "What would you do differently next time?"

Dan Peavy responds, "We need to be clear about which one of the group is acting leader at any particular time and make sure we all give support."

Ken Goldsmith, one of the quieter group members, a social worker from California, adds, "When things got rough yesterday, at moments of crisis, we all wanted to make decisions, but nobody wanted to take responsibility."

"Yep," comes back Dan, "that hits the nail right on the head. That's what I was getting at. We need to give our ideas to the leader but then make the best decision we can and stick with it."

During these interchanges the atmosphere in the group is warm and caring. Yesterday's experience, despite occasional hard words expressed during moments of stress, has brought the group together. Jeanette's triumph has earned her the respect of the group and has also clearly given her a different view of herself and her capabilities. During the hour-long discussion she makes no mention of leaving. It is also apparent that her need has stimulated supportive reactions among other members of the group and that they feel good about having provided this support.

The discussion continues awhile longer. Jimbo guides gently, occasionally summarizing, sometimes asking leading questions. He does not push the group toward greater intimacy than they are ready for. But his manner indicates that this is part of the agenda if and when the group is ready for it.

Now it is eleven o'clock, and already it is hot. We move from the shade of the pines and organize the shambles. By noon we are ready to go. The afternoon's hike is a mellow, laid-back affair compared with the trials of yesterday. We are heading due north, following a well marked trail that lazily contours its way through open stands of pines. The ground is flat; glades and meadows are plentiful. This is different country from the sandy ravines and scrubby, steep

Zion, desert country of contrasts: airy openness interspersed with precipitous narrow canyons.

hillsides we have battled for the past four days. We are on top of an undulating plateau. It is not large, only a few miles across, an island amid steep canyons. We enjoy it, suspecting that it is but an interlude preceding further tussles with the slickrock.

Outward Bound started in America in 1962 in Colorado. Originally, in those early days, programs were centered on a permanent facility, a base camp providing sleeping accommodations, dining room, and a variety of activities in the immediate environment. The pattern of the program during those early days was based on the "dunk 'em and dry 'em" philosophy of Kurt Hahn, the founder of Outward Bound. A group of participants would typically spend the first three or four days of their program in residence at the school base, receiving instruction in a variety of wilderness skills. These would include elementary map and compass, first aid, fire fighting, wilderness search and rescue techniques, basic rock-climbing, and knots and rope work associated with rock-climbing. The group would also begin to move through physical conditioning activities: exercise, running, and the shock of an early morning run followed by a plunge into an icy stream, designed both to jar participants psychologically and to develop their physical resistance to wet, cold conditions. These first days were usually followed by a first expedition into the wilderness lasting three to four days. The group would cover anywhere from ten to thirty miles, depending on the terrain. The skills that had been taught in the first few days would be exercised. The group would also learn more of campcraft and wilderness navigation while at the same time improving in physical fitness. The group would then return to the school base for three or four more days of intense activity, including further technical rock-climbing and rappelling, the mountaineer's way of descending a steep rock face, or, in the case of a sea school, further instruction in seamanship, plus land-based activities on the island used by the school as headquarters. Then a longer wilderness expedition would follow, lasting up to eight days. Typically called the Alpine expedition, the group would complete an extended distance and attempt a major objective necessitating the use of the skills they had learned. At a mountain school this would usually be the ascent of a major peak. At a sea school the objective might be a far-distant island demanding endurance and skillful navigation for its attainment. Solo, a period of up to three days alone in the wilderness, would usually follow. In the early days of Outward Bound solo was essentially a wilderness survival experience, with emphasis on survival skills: constructing shelters from natural materials, foraging for edible plants, and trapping small animals for food. The culmination of the traditional Outward Bound program was the final expedition. Participants would be divided into small groups, usually four to a group. For three days they would follow a demanding route through wilderness terrain, unaccompanied by their instructor. They would be on their own. For safety, each day they would sign in at a prearranged checkpoint that would be visited daily by their instructor. Final expedition was the culmination of the traditional twenty-six-day Outward Bound course.

From this traditional twenty-six-day program Outward Bound has evolved into a rich diversity of offerings. Our expedition in the Gila Wilderness is a ten-day mobile experience. Rather than working in a series of trips from a fixed base, we had been dropped in the middle of nowhere and would be away from civilization for the full ten days. The Outward Bound mobile program is based on the traditional model of those expeditions that over the years have trekked to distant places to search for Himalayan summits, to explore jungles in far-off places, or to travel the frozen expanses of Arctic and Antarctic regions. A small group is banded together by the need to exist and make progress toward a goal in a wilderness setting.

In addition to covering our chosen terrain safely and achieving certain physically challenging objectives, we also hoped to learn a little more about ourselves. Yesterday's experience had definitely been a step in this direction. I suspect that each member of our group has a little clearer sense of his or her personal strengths and weaknesses based on that experience. And as evidenced by Pam and Ron's interaction during the discussion group, we have also been given a vivid opportunity to examine our behavior in relation to each other. Are we a loose collection of cranky, independent loners? Can we work cohesively as an effective team when needed? Can we give warmth and emotional support to a needy member of the group at times of stress? The Outward Bound experience seems designed to focus carefully on and emphasize these questions, but it does not provide canned answers. The meaning and value of each experience, as emphasized by Jimbo's carefully maintained detachment and nonauthoritarian group leadership, are clearly up to each one of us.

As we hike jauntily through the high chaparral, shaded by the pines, in good spirits after our relaxed morning, these thoughts wander through my mind, and I begin to consider the factors that effect the value and the potency of an Outward Bound experience for a particular individual. In a sense the Outward Bound experience is a given, a fixed entity. A set of unusual and challenging circumstances is arranged for each participant to move through. Inevitably there is a wide range of individual responses to this fixed set of circumstances. It is a well-known fact among Outward Bound staff that within a single program or within a single group the experience can affect one person so deeply that it profoundly alters his or her view of self and reality, changing a person's life for months and sometimes years after the experience. Not infrequently one meets Outward Bound graduates who many years later state with great assurance that the experience left such an indelible impression that it permanently altered the nature of their lives. Yet within the same group one could likely find a companion to this person who had undergone precisely the same experiences but who would equally confidently assert that he or she had been completely untouched by the experience and that life went on exactly as before. Between these two extremes there characteristically exists a varied range of responses at the end of any given program. For some the experience is powerful while it happens, but the return to the routine of daily life seems rapidly to neutralize its long-term effects. Occasionally, for a small number of participants, the experience is a painful one, generating negative reactions. Other participants leave completely unable to articulate their feelings. Still others report either neutral or negative responses initially, only to change their view months or years later, when time and maturity have lent perspective. As I watch our bobbing caterpillar of green packs undulating through the trees ahead, I wonder what the range of responses will be among our little group.

Ahead the group has arrived in an open clearing. I can see packs being lowered. A fallen tree provides a convenient sofa. A water bottle is being passed around as I arrive.

"Come on, Joe, do it for us."

"Naw."

"Oh, come on."

"Yeh, come on Joe, just once."

"Not now," answers Joe, looking mildly embarrassed. "This isn't the right time."

"Sure it is," someone chips in. "We need a giggle to keep us going."

"Well," says Joe, obviously weakening, "I might."

Joe has kept the group amused earlier with his imitations of monsters. *Tyrannosaurus rex* and the Gila monster are his specialties.

"Come on, Joe," Sara laughs, "just a quickie. How's about *Tyrannosaurus rex?*"

"Oh, you want a quickie," laughs Joe to Sara with comic innuendo, "in that case—"

"Not that kind of quickie," answers Sara, blushing as the group laughs and grins at her discomfort. "You know what I mean."

"OK," agrees Joe. "But just once, and it will be a quickie."

He goes through a little performance of composing himself, flexing his arms, taking a couple of deep breaths. Then his arms jut forward straight from the shoulders, but with the forearms pointing downward, elbows bent, fingers spread to represent claws. Eyes flare. Teeth protrude. His neck elongates, and his head pokes forward. For a moment we witness a perfect *Tyrannosaurus rex.*

The group cracks up.

"Great, Joe," compliments Ron, his four-day stubble split by a big grin. "Now do the Gila monster."

But despite more urging Joe's performance is over, and it is time to move on. In high spirits, laughing still, chattering, we shoulder our packs and head off through the chaparral, now treading toward the east, in the direction of Turkey Park.

The remaining five days of our Outward Bound experience are full ones. That evening, rather than camping together as a group, Jimbo spreads us out

Joe's imitation of *Tyrannosaurus rex.*

at intervals along the bank of a small stream, out of sight of one another. Lacking the time in our shortened course to experience the full three-day solo, we have to be satisfied with one night and part of the following day alone, a minisolo.

Desert solo.

Another full day's hike brings us to a ravine bounded with steep rock cliffs up to a hundred feet high. There are steep walls, corners, chimneylike slots, and shallow grooves leading upward.

For a day and a half we exercise our minds and bodies, and safeguarded by climbing ropes, we all climb at least one of the routes.

Each member of the group also rappels. Jimbo has arranged two climbing ropes dangling over a fearsome-looking bulging section of cliff. The top overhangs the bottom by a clear ten feet. Each of us clips into the ropes, safeguarded by a separate safety rope, nervously inches back over the edge, and spectacularly slides down to the ground a hundred feet below.

The final morning comes all too soon. We are up at dawn. Again the morning is cool, the sky clear.

Starting at 6 A.M., Jimbo has marked out a five-mile marathon run, the final activity of the program. After ten days of intense physical activity it is a joy to feel our bodies working efficiently. Thinking back to our arduous progress up Granny Mountain six days ago, it is obvious that our lungs and limbs are in much better shape. Everyone completes the run in good spirits.

The remainder of the morning is spent packing and cleaning equipment. It is a time of contentment and of some sadness. We have spent ten days together. The time has gone well; moments of intense challenge have been interspersed with leisurely movements through the desert. And there have been the quiet moments, those frequent times when we found ourselves alone, looking around, touching the desert, feeling a certain kinship with its mystery. The Gila has shared itself with us. It is a giving place. It proffers its gifts freely to those who take the time to walk its canyons, explore its hidden places.

Joe is taking it easy. His chores are done, and he is sitting, back propped against a shade tree. He seems at ease with himself. He watches the activity, his face in repose. I join him, and we share a few quiet moments. Joe composes his thoughts and summarizes his experience. "It was worthwhile. Yes, definitely. It was more rigorous than I had expected. For me there were times when the physical demands—the hiking, the heavy packs, the need to get to a certain point in a given time—inhibited our group getting closer to each other. We weren't emotionally very close, I don't think. I would have liked more verbal sharing, more time to sit round as a group and learn more about each other, our hopes, our backgrounds, our goals for the future."

I ask Joe how he feels about the outdoor skills he has acquired during the ten days, if he feels better equipped to deal with the wilderness. "Yes, somewhat. But that wasn't what I mainly came for. I came to be challenged. I'm not an outdoor person. I doubt if I will ever come back to the desert, though I might. I wanted to learn a little bit more about me, about how I deal with stress. I think I have a little better sense now of my capacities and my limitations. If there had been more formal emphasis on wilderness skills, we would have lost out on the opportunity to learn about ourselves and the need to work as a team. I think Jimbo balanced his involvement just about right. He taught us enough so that we could find our way around in safety and enough so that we could always take the next step with some kind of confidence. And he was always there when we needed him. That takes a special skill. To be able to hold back like that and let us find things out for ourselves, make our own mistakes. If he had taken over, organized us, and had us follow him up Granny Mountain that day, we'd have got there quicker and with a lot less pain, but it would have been so much less of a worthwhile experience.

"This sounds trite, I suppose," Joe continued after a lengthy pause, "but I learned a new respect for water. It brought home to me how much I take for

One of the most beautiful of the canyon areas of Zion.

Climbing a desert spire in Zion.

Jeanette taking off on the high rappel.

granted, you know, how dependent I am on all the comforts. In that sense it has been a reawakening. My most tangible benefit, though, has been a negative one," he adds with a grin. "Considering that I hardly kept anything in my stomach for the first six days, I must have lost at least ten pounds. I felt positively light in the marathon. I've taken my pants belt in at least four notches." And indeed Joe does look thinner. Ten days ago he was pale and had a trace of puppy fat. Now, relaxed against the tree, burnt brown by the sun, he fits in with his surroundings. At least temporarily Joe has become a creature of the desert, at home, comfortable, adapted to his surroundings. I wonder how long it will last and how he will respond to urban Boston on his return.

The back of the Outward Bound truck is a bustle of activity. Packs are being loaded. Jimbo straddles the top, directing, trying to organize the situation.

I corner Dan Peavy, our dentist from San Antonio, and quiz him about his experience. He has not shaved for ten days. Like Joe, his weather-beaten appearance confirms that he, too, is temporarily a creature of the desert. "You know," he begins, "it took me a long time to get myself to do this. I'm thirty-six years of age, lots of professional responsibilities, a wife, and two kids in diapers. I kept asking myself, What if I get injured? What would happen then?"

"And how do you feel about that now?" I ask. "Do you feel that it has been a risky time for you?"

"No, not really. At least no more risky than other things I've done. Whenever there was any danger, whenever we confronted a potentially risky activity, Jimbo would be right there, telling us what to do and how to do it safely. I think there was just enough sense of risk to give us the feeling that we were hanging it out, but this was always backed up by the sure sense that everything was under control and that the safety precautions had been well worked out and were being attended to."

Dan went on to talk about his work. "I work under a lot of pressure. Dentists have the highest incidence of heart problems of any occupational group. I get only four weeks vacation a year, usually a week at a time. It took a lot to devote one of them to Outward Bound. And now here I am, and it's over. I haven't looked at myself in a mirror for over a week. I haven't looked at a watch or clock for the same period, and I've gotten real proficient at telling the time by the height of the sun. I haven't worried about the state of the stock exchange, and I haven't read a newspaper. And I haven't missed any of it. It's been a totally compelling experience for me. It's occupied my energy and concentration more fully than anything I've ever done."

I ask Dan what his high point was during the ten days. "That's hard," he responds, and pauses. "I guess it has to be the high rappel. I've always been scared of height a little, and I knew it was part of the experience. I was proud of myself when I was able to lean back, tautening the ropes, and go over the edge without hesitating. I had butterflies—and I loved 'em. When I got down, I wanted to go back up and do it over, but there wasn't time."

"Did things ever get too much for you? Did you ever consider quitting?"

"Not seriously. There was a moment during the rock-climbing. I'd picked a climb that I thought, from watching one of the others on it, I was going to have a hard time with. I got up there, about forty feet off the ground, and couldn't get any higher. I tried to move down and couldn't do that either. I was being held from above by the climbing rope, and with my head I knew that I was OK, that I was safe. But I still panicked. At that moment I just wanted out from the situation. I wanted to be anywhere but where I was. Jimbo was there, and he shouted some advice: 'Keep cool. Try and figure things out.' And I did. I worked out the moves and eventually made it to the top. But for a moment there—phew!"

I ask Dan if he has any reservations about the experience, any negative reactions. After a lengthy pause he replies, with a shake of his head, "Not really, not anything of any consequence. Generally the experience exceeded my expectations. God, the Gila is such a lovely place. It feels like a real privilege to have been here under these circumstances. There were times when I got irritated, pissed off, but this would be either with myself or with someone else, with

Marathon.

what was happening, not with the program, not particularly with Outward Bound. Well—I guess the trail food could have been better. But that's a relatively minor complaint."

Leaving Dan, I next seek out Ron Gray, who is seated cross-legged in a patch of shade, scrubbing a dirty cooking kit with steel wool. His moustache is surrounded by a ten-day beard. He looks cheerful, jaunty. I overhear him whistling to himself as I approach.

"Well, friend," I start, "so—back to machine tools, now, eh?"

Ron's teeth flash a big smile. "Right. That's where I'm headed, back to the old routine."

"What made you decide to come to Outward Bound in the first place?"

"Hm—I knew very little about Outward Bound. I hadn't met anyone who had been through the program. I read an article in the New York *Times* written by a lawyer who had been through an executive seminar at the North Carolina Outward Bound School. I need a little more discipline. I don't work as hard now at my business as I used to. I still make the major decisions, but things are pretty well established. So this seemed a good way to get my blood going again."

"Has that happened for you?"

"Generally, yes, though I had expected more physical stress, and more harassment."

"Harassment?"

"Yes. You know, hazing, like you get in the military. Somehow I had picked up the idea that this was part of the Outward Bound experience."

"Are you disappointed? Would you have wanted more of that?"

"I'm a little disappointed personally that the course wasn't more arduous physically. I keep myself in good shape. I wasn't extended enough. It was hard for me to adjust to the demands of lowering my physical expectations and putting energy into supporting weaker members of the group. But obviously this is one of the most important aspects of Outward Bound."

Ron sits chewing the ends of his moustache for a little while. He looks lost in his own thoughts. His eyes blink three times in rapid succession, and he looks straight at me.

"You know, I've got to work at that some more. I've gotta figure out why it's so damn important to me, at my age, to have someone else push me physically and why physical prowess is such a high priority."

I resist the temptation to pursue this further with Ron. He seems to have the question clearly in focus and undoubtedly will pursue his own answer in his own good time. But as I depart, leaving Ron to his thoughts and scrubbing, I recall some words I have read by Gail Sheehy, who has analyzed the process of adult maturation in her well-known book, *Passages: Predictable Crises of Adult Life*. She points out that the simple act of turning forty is a "marker event" in and of itself in American society. Successful businessmen who have come close to realizing their dream "often have a more rugged transition to make than those who miss the mark. These recognized successes have the problem of following their own act, an act that rarely brings the sweeping fulfillment they anticipated. If they are to avoid stagnation, they must generate a new set of aspirations and listen to the other voices in themselves that have been neglected up to now." In this context Ron's words came back to me: "I don't work as hard . . . as I used to. . . . Things are pretty well established. . . . This seemed a good way to get my blood going again." It is easy for me to imagine Ron back in Chicago, in his business suit, caring for the needs of his machine tool company and not feeling completely fulfilled. I respect him for choosing Outward Bound as one way of re-energizing his life, but at the same time I wonder if the experience will be any more than an interlude, if it will have any lasting effect, or if it will disappear at approximately the same speed as his suntan and stubble.

It is a frequently stated concept in Outward Bound that the activities themselves are secondary: "Outward Bound teaches *through* the wilderness." The emphasis is to use the experience in such a way that it acts as a mirror, magnifying and exposing both strengths and weaknesses. The goal is to give the individual the opportunity to form a clearer perception of him or her self. With this in mind, I find myself going back to my earlier question: Just what is the relationship between the outcome of the Outward Bound experience for any particular individual and the particular set of experiences presented by the program?

There is a tendency on the part of Outward Bound devotees to judge the effectiveness of any particular program in terms of long-term effects. There is a body of follow-up data on Outward Bound (to which I will refer in more detail later) which indicates that the effect of the program is indeed lasting. Using this criteria, is it fair to conclude that Ron's Outward Bound experience was of little value? I do not think so. At Ron's stage in life, with a generally satisfying behavior pattern well established (albeit with the nagging undertone that *something* is missing), it seems more reasonable to conclude that he will need to seek out a *succession* of new challenges. Outward Bound has provided Ron with a stimulating alternative to his daily routine, but he will certainly need to find other challenging experiences in the future to combat the tendency to stagnate in his settled routine in Chicago.

Considering Ron's case in relation to my attempt to analyze the effectiveness of Outward Bound leads me to conclude that a vital factor in the process is the state of the person—that is, the individual's psychological readiness for change—when he or she comes to Outward Bound. Age and life history are two important factors in the Outward Bound equation influencing the outcome. In Ron's case his age and established pattern of physical and occupational success seem related to a *not* very marked effect of Outward Bound at the end of his program.

Pondering these ideas, I next seek out Jeanette. One of those people whose skin turns pink rather than brown, she still has not acclimatized to the sun. She wears her broad-brimmed hat, keeps her sleeves pulled down, and works in the shade of a dense cottonwood tree. She is surrounded by a tangle of climbing ropes and is attempting to make order of the mess. I ask her how she is feeling.

"Alive and well today."

"Happy?"

"Yes"—after a moment's pause—"yes, happy."

"How does it feel to have it behind you, Jeanette?"

."Hm—mixed. I suspect it's been a once-in-a-lifetime experience for me. I still feel surprised that I was able to get through everything. But it feels great. I feel alive—top of my head to tip of my toes."

I know that Jeanette had arrived at Outward Bound in poor physical condition. I ask her about this and the effect it had on her experience.

"I didn't expect it to be so rigorous, that's for sure. I've never camped out before. I didn't do anything before the course to get in shape. But it wouldn't have proved anything if it had been easier."

To me, this last remark seems particularly significant. Jeanette has had the most arduous time of anyone in the group, and based on observation and conversation, it appears that the experience has had a more profound impact on her than on other members of the group.

I remember some of Jeanette's earlier statements: "I am twenty-seven years of age, the mother of a two-and-a-half-year-old daughter, and in the process of putting myself back together after a divorce." Jeanette had also said that she found her role as a woman confusing. "I had really never paid much attention to the incentive behind women's liberation because *I didn't see myself as a woman,* but more a housewife who had to work outside of the home" (my italics).

I contrast Ron's background and Outward Bound experience with Jeanette's. Relatively speaking, Ron has found the course a breeze. Jeanette has found it arduous, and the experience appears to have affected her quite profoundly.

As I watch Jeanette organizing the climbing ropes here in the Gila, I realize that our experience is almost over. The others are completing their final tasks. Ron has finished scrubbing the cooking gear and is over by the van helping load equipment. Dan is sitting cross-legged, talking with Sara, their work done. Joe is putting the finishing touches to his personal gear.

It is not long before the blue Outward Bound van drives us away from the Gila. Again we bounce our way over fifty miles of rutted dirt roads, retracing our tracks of ten days ago. Jimbo is driving. We don't talk much, our little group. As the van twists its way along, we glimpse canyons and hillsides of the Gila. Ten days ago it was an unknown place to us. Now we have shared some of its secret places. We know a little more about the Gila, and through its tutelage, we seem to know a little more about ourselves.

Chapter Two

THE NORTH CAROLINA
OUTWARD BOUND SCHOOL

In North Carolina one is constantly aware of the humidity. After the aridity of the desert I find myself acutely conscious of moisture.

It is only two days since our course in the Gila finished. Good-byes to Jimbo and the tribe were made in a rush in the Phoenix airport. We presented a grubby spectacle in that sterile environment. We had washed, in cold water from a stream, but the mantle of the Gila clung to us stubbornly. We were desert rats—and just a little proud of it. We savored the stares of other passengers, enjoyed their reactions. We *were* desert rats; we had had experiences they couldn't even guess at. We stared back assertively, feeling we'd earned the right to be grubby. It was they who looked odd in their stiff suits, print dresses, and hair styles.

The topography of Appalachia matches that of the Gila: gently rolling. It is the ground cover (a function of moisture) that differs; here there are dense trees and abundant undergrowth. The highest hills in Appalachia are six thousand feet high, occasionally seamed by steep gorges. Rocky waterways transect the landscape, adding drama to the softness. Everywhere there is lush vegetation; the trees and undergrowth are junglelike. I suspect that many secrets are cloaked by this verdant covering.

It seems that I am going to experience a more traditional version of Outward Bound in North Carolina than I did in the Gila. The terrain of North Carolina does not lend itself to a mobile course. Again I am joining a ten-day adult program. The Outward Bound School here is well established: a collection of log houses, a lodge (the dining room), and a number of permanent house trailers sheltering the administrative offices. It will act as our base for the next ten days.

The school sits on a hillside at the end of a dirt road, drawn apart from the civilization of nearby Asheville. Above the school sits a large rock. It is regarded locally as a mountain, and the school lies within its shadow. It is a rocky finger pointing skyward, precipitous on all sides; it is Table Mountain.

Now I am seated on a grassy knoll amid forty other men and women. The sun is shining brilliantly. There is a sprawling sense of languor in the group. The moist warmth is conducive to dozing. We are being addressed by a tall, handsome, soft-spoken man. We have to be quiet to hear what he is saying.

"The Outward Bound course is neither for recreation nor for learning survival techniques," he says.

His name is Dan Meyers, and he is the director of the North Carolina Outward Bound School. He has a warm smile and a caring attitude. One trusts him instinctively. There is a sense of purpose about him and a considerable reserve of strength in his casualness. He talks about the origins of Outward Bound. About its beginnings in wartime Britain.

"Outward Bound has developed considerably since those days," he says. "Originally the program was for adolescent boys. Today forty per cent of our participants are women, and forty per cent of our participants are over twenty-five years of age."

At the end of his brief summary Dan pauses. He lifts one foot onto the edge of the grassy bank in front of him and leans his weight forward toward us.

"I can't tell you what your Outward Bound experience is going to mean to you," he says. "That's up to you. But someone once said to me that they wouldn't

Left to right: Curly, Herman, Drew, Emily, Ellen, Jay, Art, and Jim.

trade the experience for a million dollars"—he grins—"or do it again for two million."

We laugh. It is the end of the introduction. Dan steps aside, and one of his staff members reads names from a list. Soon thereafter I am following a group of ten others along a dirt road that leads into the trees.

We have two instructors, a man and a woman. The man, Drew Hammond, is thickset, burly, broad-shouldered, and with a bushy red beard. He, like Jimbo, wears a Mack Truck driver's hat. This must be the vogue among Outward Bound instructors this summer.

He does not say much. "OK, folks. Er—just follow me." He heads off down the road at an easy saunter.

His compadre is a gangly woman, somewhere about twenty-four years of age. She wears a hat similar in shape and style to those worn by boy scouts. But this hat has been places; it looks as though it has been soaked and dried a hundred times. It is stained and floppy, and a collection of small bird feathers is tucked in its band. She obviously cares a great deal for this hat. I suspect that there is some kind of relationship between the configuration of the hat and her personality. Her name is Emily Lutkin, and she speaks with a pronounced Appalachian backwoods twang.

We are led into a clearing beside the road. Drew points to a horizontal log a foot or so in diameter, approximately eight feet off the ground, and about twelve feet long tied between two trees.

"The object is to get the group over the log to the other side," he says. "Once a person has passed over and is on the ground, that person cannot help anyone else over, though the person can support people as they come down to make sure they don't hurt themselves."

Drew and Emily step back.

The first decision is to change into sneakers. An animated discussion on strategy follows.

A human pyramid is formed. Two agile men surmount the pile and sit facing each other on the beam, legs wrapped around it cowboy style. With them pulling from above and others pushing from below, each member of the group ungracefully passes over the log. Kicking and thrashing is the preferred style, accompanied by loud cheers and exhortations from the others. Finally only one person remains, the oldest member of the group, in his late forties, I'd guess. His name is Jim. Standing under the beam, contemplating the problem, he looks frail and nervous. The two up on the log reach down and grasp his upstretched arms. He struggles gamefully but does not have the arm strength to pull himself up. He drops to the ground.

It is clear that his heart is not in it. Other members of the group make suggestions in a babble of voices. Jim shakes his head, stands there looking up at the beam despondently.

"Come on, Jim. Give it another try," encourages one of the men atop the beam. "We'll try to give you as much help as we can."

Again they reach down toward him, grasp his arms, and heave.

As they pull, Jim screams. It is a loud, piercing scream, startling in its intensity. He is either acting out or for some inexplicable reason is in great pain. Perplexed, his helpers lower him down.

Jim explains that he strained his arm a few days ago and that it is hurting him. But he tries again. Eventually, after two more tries, punctuated by grunts and loud cries, Jim is unceremoniously hauled over the top of the log, and the group is together on the other side.

It has been difficult to determine the degree to which Jim's arm has really been hurting and the extent to which he has been using it as an excuse for his difficulty.

The experience of crossing the log has very quickly started our group working together. Drew and Emily have watched the proceedings quietly. Now that the task is complete, they draw us together in a circle.

Drew is a forthright character. To call him belligerent would be an overstatement, but there is a directness in his manner, a certain gruff abruptness.

Now there are introductions. Drew says he does not want to spend time discussing the log; that will come later. For now he would like us to go round the circle, each give our name and also one adjective that describes us.

There are nine members in this group, including me, eight men and one woman. I note this imbalance and suspect that it is going to make for an awkward time for the woman.

"Jim Finucayne," volunteers one. He is thirty-six years old and wears a full beard and rimless glasses. There is a no-nonsense quality about him. He speaks and acts with rather formal precision. He tells us that he is a consulting engineer. Choosing an adjective to describe himself, he says, "forgetful."

Next follows one of the youngest-looking members of the group, also bearded. "Jay Strunk," he says with a warm smile. "I'm the assistant director of an affective education center in Wilmington. I'm twenty-five, and to describe myself in one word, well—thinking."

"Ellen Michalets. I'm twenty-eight. I'm a nurse in Milwaukee. I'm—outgoing." She seems tense. She delivers this information in a breathless rush. Her voice has a hard edge, a certain rasping quality. In addition to being the only woman in the group, she is also one of the smallest. I guess her height to be five feet four inches.

There is one black member in the group, a thickset man of about thirty-five. He speaks next. "Herman—Herman Freeman—er—heavy." We later learn that Herman is a quality control worker in a factory in nearby Asheville. For now he appears calm, though withdrawn. One senses that he is paying close attention to all that transpires.

The next to introduce himself does so in a cheerful, outgoing way. "I'm Art Duel." He is thirty-eight, from Connecticut, a partner in a small law firm. He is handsome, looks younger than he is, and seems very confident. There is warmth in his smile and voice, but I sense a macho side to his character. I sense that he is competitively aggressive and, partly based on seeing him in action on the log, that physical prowess is a high priority for him. Choosing his descriptive adjective, he says, "enthusiastic."

Jim, the one who had difficulty getting over the log, is next. He is hesitant and speaks in a low voice. The log incident has shaken him. He is terse. "Jim Brennan. I'm in real estate—interested."

Another Jim follows. "I'm a banker from here in North Carolina." He is tall and relaxed and has a thick mop of hair. "Just think of me as Curly," he says with a grin.

The last to introduce himself is Mike Kahler, a dentist from Kansas. He wears a moustache, is thirty-three years of age, and is tall and on the thin side. He describes himself as "happy."

Drew rounds off with "contented"; and Emily, with "active."

Introductions done, gear is collected, and we move up to the school buildings. A blue Dodge panel van is parked outside the lodge. Drew climbs on top of it and stands at the edge of the roof, with his back toward us. We watch him intently. "OK," he announces. "I'm going to put my hands in my pockets and fall backwards. I want you to catch me." He is ten feet above the ground! Our group moves in beneath him, not very organized, with startled expressions. "Ready?" Drew inquires. Without looking round, body stiff, he falls slowly backward. Nine pairs of hands receive him, break his fall, and gently lower him to the ground. He hops up with a big grin. "Great. We call it the trust fall. Who's next?"

Who's next?

The group is disconcerted. Nervous glances are exchanged, but after Drew's example we are on the spot. Our lawyer, Art Duel, is the first to respond. With a grim expression on his face, he climbs to the top of the van. Reaching the edge, he stands poised, hands in his pocket, eyes closed, for some moments. That night he was to write in his journal: "It was higher than I thought. The mere thought of falling backwards with my hands in my pockets was disconcerting. I shut my eyes and fell . . . it was *very* scary. A very exciting sensation. The adrenaline was really flowing." He, too, is caught safely and gently lowered to the ground.

For the next two hours we exchange our suitcases for Outward Bound backpacks, sleeping bags, and the other impedimentia that constitutes a forty-five-pound load. Drew and Emily watch over us like mother hens but say little. With no word from Drew about our destination, evening finds us jammed into a blue Outward Bound van, heading who knows where. We drive for three and a half hours.

It is dark when we reach our destination, a cabin amid thick trees at the end of a narrow, winding dirt road. The cabin has no electricity and no running water. On Drew's instruction we have left our watches at the Outward Bound base camp. I guess that it is close to ten o'clock. Someone asks Drew the time, and there are questions about the activities of the upcoming days.

"Forget about time," Drew responds. "At Outward Bound we want you to live one day at a time. Don't think about the future or worry about the past. Live intensely for the moment."

These instructions do little to reduce the anxiety that is present in the group. Outward Bound has a reputation for putting participants in taxing situations. Because they are unused to living in the present so totally, the uncertainty about the next few days clearly has some members of the group unnerved.

Drew moves out onto the cabin's porch, where there are an old sofa and two battered chairs. He sits and lights a candle and asks everyone to join him. We gather around, and for a moment there is silence. We are conscious of the surrounding night, the darkness, the vague forms of trees surrounding the cabin, the sound of a stream rushing close by, the crickets.

Drew changes positions on the sofa. The creaking breaks the silence. He takes a deep breath and says, "Well, let's take a few moments to share some expectations. I'd like to hear how you heard about Outward Bound and what you expect to get out of the experience."

Ellen begins. "I want the challenge of it, new experience. I'm not in very good physical shape." She does not comment on the fact that she is the only woman in the group, and no one else refers to it. Perhaps it is not important.

Jim, the real estate broker who had such difficulty getting over the log, follows. "I've always been a physical weakling. I've got six kids, and I want to show them that I'm capable, prove that I'm not a weakling. I want my kids to respect me. I want to get the word *can't* out of my vocabulary. I've also had a drinking problem." No one responds to Jim's statement. It seems that the group does not quite know how to deal with him. The situation at the log was disconcerting. His admission indicates that he has a lot riding on his Outward Bound experience. I anticipate that he is going to need a good deal of support to make it through successfully.

Herman is straight to the point. "I read about Outward Bound in a men's magazine, *Adam*." He says this with a grin and gets a laugh. "Mainly I came because I want to stop smoking and get myself healthy." He seems comfortable as the only black person in an all-white group, though he is still watchful from behind his silence.

Art Duel talks about his life as a lawyer in Connecticut. "I'm almost forty. My practice is well established. It's country club and cocktails a lot of the time." We later learn that Art owns his own plane and that flying is his passion. It is easy to imagine him comfortably settled in Connecticut, leading an active, fulfilling life. But why Outward Bound? "For a number of years I have acted as surrogate father to a boy," he continues. "His parents gave him an Outward Bound course at Hurricane Island as a present. Ever since then I've been interested in the program. Physical achievement has always come easy to me, but these days I tend to get into a rut of business and socializing. I'm at a point in my life where I spend a lot of time thinking about priorities, about what's important to me. What do I really care about? I spent a lot of time getting in shape for Outward Bound. I was regularly doing two hundred and fifty push-ups a day and running five miles."

This information produces a noticeable reaction in the group.

"Oh gawd," exclaims Ellen in a stage whisper. "I didn't do anything to get in shape."

It is apparent from the panting and struggling that transpired at the log crossing that there are other members of the group who also are not in top physical condition.

Like the group in the Gila, this group is mixed. As I listen to each one tell of expectations, of their reasons for coming to Outward Bound, I am again struck by the diversity that characterizes this program.

At the end of the meeting Drew firms up a rumor that has been circulating in the group about tomorrow's activities: We are to float the Chattooga for two days in rubber rafts—the same river on which *Deliverance* was filmed!

Next morning we are up early. A five-mile run in the cool North Carolina dawn is the first activity of the day. We pad along a dirt road through thick woods. It is misty. The morning is hushed; our footfalls sound loud. I am very conscious of the sound of heavy breathing, mine and that of Art and Jim Finucayne, who are running alongside.

Jim is surprising. He is a little on the pudgy side; his body is stout; and his chest and belly, though firm, protrude some; but he moves well. His legs are skinny, and he keeps pace with Art and myself without apparent effort. His breathing is easy. I am impressed.

Drew, despite his bulk and broad shoulders, lopes along powerfully. He works his arms and upper body as he runs, pushing himself along forcefully. He looks in good shape.

The dirt road intersects with a dirt crossroad, weaves its way through an open meadow, and crosses a log bridge over a stream. We run parallel to the stream for two hundred yards. Art, Jim, and I are ahead. Drew, a little way behind, calls to us to stop as we draw up at a small clearing. The air is cold, but our bodies are warm. We grin at each other, savoring the experience. We have loosened up and have thrown off the stiffness generated by the night spent in sleeping bags on the cabin floor. We are steaming in the cold air. Our breath condenses in puffs of airborne vapor as we pant away the exertion. Drew arrives. Kicking off his sneakers, shedding his shirt, he heads toward the stream, clad only in shorts. Oh no! I groan. Jim and Art watch in disbelief. There is a small waterfall at this section of the stream falling three feet into a pool. Without hesitation, Drew plunges into the pool, flopping about with the playful grace of an extroverted hippopotamus, dunking himself under the waterfall, having a great time. I hear Art groan audibly. He looks at Jim, an expression of agonized consternation on his face. "He can't be serious," responds Jim in a breathless undertone. All three of us study this frolicking madman, expressions of pity and concern on our faces. Perhaps he has flipped, taken leave of his senses? Maybe we should administer first aid? But, each one of us fully realizes, Drew is in command of his faculties and unfortunately is also in command of our immediate futures. Damn. It is so difficult to argue with example. If only he had stood on the bank and *told* us to go in. We could likely have wiggled our way out of the situation with a little shrewd rationalization. But there he is, flopping about like a wet puppy and seemingly enjoying the experience.

"Here goes nothing," intones Art in funereal tones. Seconds later his shirt and shoes join Drew's on the grass, and with a "Whoop!" he is in. Less gamefully, Jim and I follow. The water is *cold*. But—and I find myself making the admission begrudgingly—there is a certain crazy exuberance in the whole silly situation. We are splashing, whooping, and shrieking like crazies. Steam rises from our bodies. Jim stands there, waist-deep in the rushing water, rivulets splashing down from his beard, looking mildly embarrassed at the inanity of the situation, but his face is split from ear to ear in a big grin. Unbelievable. Grown men! Acting like kids in a sandlot.

The others have arrived. They observe us with expressions varying from stupefaction to complete disbelief. Ellen's face registers a mixed set of emotions; horror predominates.

We evacuate the pool, and the others take our places. Ellen enters gingerly (the most painful way), up to her knees, ever so slowly, up to her thighs, her breath drawn in tight; and with eyes wide as saucers, eventually she is in up to her waist. Emily is watching her from the bank. Satisfied with her effort, Ellen starts to head for dry land.

"Whoa," says Emily. "Come on, Ellen, dunk yourself under."

Ellen is unresponsive. She looks at Emily defiantly. Others add voices of encouragement, and slowly, painfully, Ellen sinks down until the water laps around her neck.

"Great," Emily applauds. "Now dunk your head and come on out."

Ellen digs in. "Not on your life," she gasps. "I had my hair done just before leaving. No way I'm going to ruin it."

Despite persuasive efforts from Emily, Drew, and the rest of the group, Ellen is adamant. She emerges, head dry, a stubborn expression on her face. Drew and Emily exchange knowing grins but do not push the situation farther. I suspect, from the nature of the look they interchanged, that Ellen's clinging to vestiges of civilization is a doomed endeavor; I suspect that the natural progression of the Outward Bound program in the next few days will automatically separate all of us from familiar habits. Ellen looks pouty but firm in her conviction—for now. The group stands for a moment, bodies steaming, relishing the aftermath of the dip. It is surprising how warm we feel; our bodies tingle. There is a sense of camaraderie, of being ready for whatever other challenges the day has to offer.

By late morning we are drifting lazily down the upper reaches of the Chattooga River in inflatable rafts approximately nine feet long by five feet wide. There are three or four of us to a boat. Our camping equipment and food are being transported by road in the Outward Bound van to our evening destination; the rafts, consequently, are light, frisky. It is a clear, warm, friendly day, ideal for messing about in boats.

At first the rafts seem unwieldy, clumsy beasts with minds and wills of their own. They go where *they* want to go, not where we want them to go. I am in a raft with Drew and Jay Strunk, the affective education director from Wilmington. In the short time we have been together, Jay has endeared himself to the group. He is warm, open, outgoing, an easy person to talk to. So far he has not said a lot, but his smile is frequently there, and he is clearly enjoying himself. Drew is in the rear of the raft, in the captain's position. Jay is forward on the left, and I am in the position on the right.

We struggle to bend the raft's will to ours. As usual Drew is noncommittal. The side members of the raft are inflated tubes, some eighteen inches in diameter. One can perch on them sidesaddle, one buttock seated and both legs inside the raft or, alternatively, sit astride, cowboy style, the tube pinched between the knees with one leg trailing in the water. The astride position puts one in a more advantageous paddling posture. With the tube gripped tightly between my knees, shoulders square to the raft's line of travel, I am able to dig the paddle deeply and firmly, exerting maximum force. The disadvantage of this position is that the outside foot is constantly wet, and more important, if the raft passes close to or hits one of the many exposed rocks in the river, there is the danger of scraping the leg or possibly hurting it seriously. The rafts, backed up by tons of rushing water, can develop considerable momentum, and I find myself alternating—leg hanging over the edge on clear stretches, inside when we approach rocks.

As we experiment with our unmaneuverable vehicle, it becomes apparent that we have to learn to read the river. The river flows along, heading consistently downstream, but its progress is characterized by a complex pattern of fluid dynamics. If we are to be more than a random piece of flotsam at the mercy of the current, we have to learn to harness the power of the river, to make it work for us. Compared with a canoe, the raft is sluggish. We cannot respond as quickly as we would like to fluctuations in the river's progress. We have to anticipate, to look ahead, to read the configuration of the river, analyze its tongues and eddies, avoid sleepers (rocks submerged just below the surface waiting to hang up the raft), and position ourselves early so that the river takes us where we want to go. If we are inefficient, we will have to paddle harder than we need in order to compensate. If we read the river accurately, it will provide most of our motive power, enabling us to conserve our energy and paddle mainly for navigation.

Drew breaks down, now that we have floundered on trial and error for a while, and gives us a few tips. We are moving along a calm section of the river. "Bob, you paddle forward on your side of the raft," he commands.

I obey, digging the paddle deeply and powerfully.

"Jay, you back-paddle on your side."

Jay is confused.

"Back-paddle?"

"Yeah, rather than dipping the paddle in ahead of you and pulling it through the water, put it in behind you and push it forward."

Jay complies. With him back-paddling on the left and me paddling forward on the right, the raft rotates briskly counterclockwise. We spin merrily around, full 360s.

"OK," calls out Drew. "Now reverse it; pull the opposite way."

I dig my paddle in behind and commence a vigorous back-paddle. Jay throws his weight into paddling forward. The raft obediently rotates clockwise.

"Fine," compliments Drew, "but that's an extreme maneuver." He explains that turning the raft this way causes us to lose momentum completely. Also— and this is hard for us to understand—it does not really help us to change our position in the river. We have been rotating on the spot, so to speak, and have not displaced the raft to the right or left in relation to the current, the two banks, or obstacles. In order to steer the raft effectively, we must first turn it crossways to the flow of the current. Then we all paddle forward— hard. Having traversed the current, we then turn the raft again to parallel the current, bow pointing downstream.

"OK," says Drew, "let's try it. Right turn," he commands.

Jay paddles forward, I back-paddle, and the raft turns to a position crosswise to the river.

"Paddle forward."

We both obey, and the raft moves across the river toward the right bank.

"Now, left turn," exhorts Drew.

Obediently I paddle forward, Jay back-paddles, and the raft swings around again until its bow points downstream once more.

"Great stuff," says Drew, "not bad at all. You're starting to get the hang of it."

Jay gives me a big grin, and we pause for a while, paddles resting across our knees, watching the banks slip by. The gorge through which the Chattooga winds its way is North Carolina's wettest region; as much as a hundred inches of rain falls here annually. Steep hillsides slant up from the edge of the river, leading up many hundreds of feet to high ridges. The vegetation is dense, impene- trable. I would hate to contemplate having to fight a way up through it if, for any reason, we have an emergency with the raft. Tall trees stand shoulder to shoulder, jostling for sunlight, and the forest canopy is an unbroken mat. Around these thick trunks cluster dense undergrowth, creeping plants, vines, and deadfall. The dampness of this region makes it home for some one hundred fifty kinds of mosses and twenty kinds of ferns. Rock outcrops break forth sporadically. It is an environment to appreciate from the respectful distance of our raft.

Drew continues to educate us in the subtleties of navigation. "The turn we just practiced is fine for short jogs across the river," he says, "but the problem with it is that the speed of the current could take us downstream before we have moved far enough across." Jay and I consider this bit of sagacity. Drew waits, and it dawns on me that he has posed a problem, one that we have to solve. I have had some experience rafting previously and know the answer. I let Jay dwell on the question. He is baffled.

Drew decides to answer his question experientially.

1. The Gila River.

2. Zion National Park.

3. Knot practice at North Carolina.

4. The Chattooga River.

"OK. Bob, you back-paddle. Jay, forward."

We respond. The raft rotates to the right, clockwise. This time Drew continues the rotation until the bow of the raft is pointed back the way we have come, upstream, at forty-five degrees to the current.

"Now," calls Drew, a note of urgency in his voice, "both paddle forward. Hard!"

We sink our paddles, chopping the water with short, vigorous strokes. Drew urges us to greater efforts. I glance over my shoulder and see he is sprawled lazily in the stern, paddle dangling loosely, observing our efforts with a grin. I mumble rebellion as my forearms and shoulders protest under the strain.

"Harder, harder, harder," intones Drew mercilessly. "Keep paddling, but check out what's happening to the raft," he says.

We are poised, maintaining a position abreast of a large tree on the bank and slowly traversing the river toward it. Our position, bow of the raft angled upstream against the current, is called a *ferry*, Drew explains. Most of our power is utilized in counteracting the tendency of the current to carry us downstream. Our angled position moves us across the river, toward the bank to which the bow points. A simple exercise in vectors and fluid dynamics, but very strenuous.

Jay groans, "I think we got it, Drew. I think we got it figured out," a slightly pleading note underlying his statement.

Drew relents. "OK. Slack off."

We rotate the raft so its bow again points downstream and relax.

For the next hour we practice a variety of other maneuvers with the raft. We learn about tongues and eddies. When the river hurtles through a constriction, a narrowing, it speeds up, moving fastest in the center of the narrows. This fluid V formation is called the *tongue*. We need to position the raft smack in the middle of the tongue and ride it down through the narrow section. To each side of the tongue the river water moves more slowly; as the river rats say, it "eddies." Behind major obstacles—large rocks or promontories jutting out from the bank—the eddies can be so pronounced that the water sits there, swirling slowly, hardly moving. Eddies can occur in the middle of frothing rapids. A highly developed skill of the river runner is to know where the eddies are, spin the raft out of the fast water into them, and pause to check out the next section, to rest, or to wait for the next raft to negotiate the fast section.

We frisk our way downstream. Fast sections of foaming rapids are interspersed with placid stretches where we can relax and enjoy the surroundings. The rapids are small. We have to stay alert, but once the route has been chosen, the current swishes us through. One of the group, Art Duel, later compared rafting to skiing: the same obligation to choose the best line through obstacles, running gates, busting through mogul fields (analogous to the rocks and obstacles of the river), moving fast from one potential crisis situation to another, stopping to scout difficulties ahead, and the excitement of fast motion as the difficulties are negotiated.

As the day progresses, we tackle larger rapids formidable enough to have individual names. The first is Dick's Creek Falls Rapid. On the right bank of the river a sixty-foot waterfall tumbles over a cliff and enters the main watercourse. Erosion and the jumble of massive boulders that Dick's Creek has deposited have created a rapid with a six-foot sheer drop. Drew screams at us to paddle hard to generate momentum to keep the bow pointing downstream as we crash through and over the drop with a stomach-wrenching lurch. (Should the raft inadvertently turn sideways in a rapid, the chances of it flipping and depositing us in the water are increased.) Other rapids follow: Second Ledge, Eye of the Needle, and the Narrows. Next comes Roller Coaster, a straight run through large standing waves. We beach the rafts prior to running this rapid, and Drew gathers us together.

"This next one's called Roller Coaster," he begins, "but we also call it Swimmer's Rapid."

We do not immediately take his point. Swimmer's Rapid? Cute name. But—so? We are grouped together on a miniature sandy beach, a tiny enclave of sand past which the river pounds furiously and behind which rises the jungle. Ellen is sprawled on the sand, wearing a bikini, not paying much attention to Drew's remarks. The day has been wearying; the cumulative effects of fresh air, sun, and physical exertion on untrained bodies have taken their toll. Others lounge, too. Drew has less than a fully attentive audience.

"OK," he asks, "who's going to go first?"

Rafting the Chattooga River.

An orange butterfly glides by. There is no breeze. It is pleasantly warm here on the sand. But *what* did Drew just say? "Who's going to go first?" Who's going to go first for what?

Drew is enjoying himself. He has not missed the languor of the group, and a mischievous expression decorates his face.

"Whaddya mean?" asks Ellen. "Whaddya mean, who's going first? Who's going first for what?"

"Swimmer's Rapid," replies Drew. "That's what they call it. That's what we're gonna do."

Swim!

Swim the rapid!

Oh—no.

The whole group wakes up with a start. He's serious. Heads turn, expressing disbelief, to inspect the water barreling by with a thunderous, crashing, heaven-shaking, deafening, turbulent, *frightening* roar. Strange, it didn't seem that bad a moment ago. The rapid has been altered out of all proportion. Through the alchemy of a single sentence it has transmuted from a friendly, fun-filled ride, to a roaring monster—with teeth. A few moments ago we visualized the rapid with a nine-foot raft as a point of reference. Now it is measured against the frailty of our bodies. Looking round, I see that I am not the only one to have suffered a debilitating perceptual disorientation.

Someone giggles nervously.

"Aw come on, Drew. Serious?" Ellen again. Her attention vacillates rapidly

Jim Finucayne negotiating Swimmer's Rapid as practice in case a raft overturns.

between the river and Drew's face. She searches for reality. "Drew's joking. Gotta be." She laughs, a weak, tremulous expression of concern.

Like criminals pronounced guilty but not yet sentenced, our crew fixedly observes Drew's expression, hoping for leniency. But it is not to be.

Drew gets serious. He explains that it is part of the Outward Bound safety drill to practice for the possibility of being flipped out of a raft. We are all wearing life jackets, he points out. There is nothing to worry about, so long as we do it right. Doing it right consists of swimming along on one's back, feet pointing downstream to fend off rocks and obstacles. Casually (the studied casualness of the pro) Drew walks to a promontory overlooking the start of the rapid. He tells us to walk down the bank a ways to a midpoint in the rapid, to observe the event better.

In addition to Drew two other river guides are with us on the trip, John Bunting (a former Olympic kayaker) and Bruce Herr, one each for the other two rafts. I notice that John has positioned himself at the bottom of the rapid and is poised with a coiled rope in his hand. He waves to Drew. All ready.

Drew checks the clasp on his life jacket—snug—and jumps into the headwaters of the rapid. Mother! Big water. He disappears from sight in the froth, only to emerge moments later, a big grin evident. As he had described, he is floating along on his back, feet pointing downstream, having a good old time. He disappears and reappears. The water boils around him; it plays with him, its massive force understated.

John tosses the rope with a skillful flick, just in Drew's path. Drew catches hold, and as the current takes him below John's post, he swings in as if on the end of a pendulum, finds himself in an eddy, and paddles to the shore.

Looking like a soaked St. Bernard, Drew squishes up to us. The moment of truth. OK, here we go. Jim plops in first. His bearded face emerges spluttering and coughing, but he manages. Later some members of the group have the temerity to imply they even *enjoyed* it—kind of. Not bad, you know, invigorating. Once you got in there—why, it was great. But for now it is a unanimously quivering set of individuals who one by one commit themselves to the maelstrom. And each and every one survives. We give thanks to the powers that determine our existence, take to the rafts again, and head on down.

One more named rapid, Keyhole, and a mile of easy water lead to an old logging road entering the river gorge on the left. We beach the rafts. The Outward Bound van is waiting.

We are weary, and the hour is late. Rain flys are pitched under the trees, sleeping bags are shaken out, and after a campfire meal, we sleep.

Morning, another fine day. We jog three miles to loosen muscles stiff from yesterday. The level of the river is the main topic of breakfast conversation. The river is categorized in sections. Yesterday we had run most of section III. The level had been up around 2.5 feet, the highest allowable level for that section. We had enjoyed a maximum run with the river at its highest for safe passage. But ahead lies section IV, the most difficult stretch of the river. If the level is still at 2.5, we will not be allowed to run; 2.3 is the maximum allowable amount of water for section IV. The high water is the aftermath of heavy rains a few days ago. Drew is hoping that the river will have dropped last night, following the dry conditions of the last few days. We stand around the campfire, eating pancakes, drinking tea, coffee, and hot chocolate, anticipating the day.

Jim, the real estate agent who had such difficulty surmounting the log on the first day, enters the conversation. He announces to the group, "I've been assessing my involvement in this program, and I've decided that the best thing I can do is leave."

This takes us by surprise. I think we have all been aware that he has been experiencing difficulty, but yesterday was a relatively straightforward day. The rafting experience, though it got the adrenaline going, was not physically demanding; and if the safety precautions are followed, the risk to life and limb is more illusory than real.

Jim goes through a list of woes. "I've been having headaches, feeling nauseous. My back has been bothering me, and my arm still hurts from the injury. And I'm a married man. I have responsibilities. I have my job and my wife and kids to think of. I mean—those things are important to me."

"But we all have responsibilities," responds Art.

Jim maintains a stubborn expression. He does not answer.

Herman addresses him. "Look, man, this program's important to you. You told us. Quit now and you'll go through the rest of your life regretting it."

"Look, I'm being realistic," says Jim. "I know there are some things I can't do."

Jim Finucayne says, "Look at it this way. You're having the kind of experience that OB is supposed to give. You are being stretched. You can probably do far more than you think you can."

"I've never backpacked before. The small amount we've done so far has been really painful," says Jim.

"You said that all your life you've been a physical weakling," Herman continues. "I thought to myself, when you said that, that you were probably using it as an excuse." Herman's voice is strong and accusative. He looks straight at Jim during this statement, making his opinion felt. "Damn," he goes on, "my back has been hurting and my legs, too."

Jim, the engineer, says, "If you reach your limit, then you are getting more out of the experience."

Art adds, "Try cooling it today, and see how you feel tomorrow. Outward Bound is both an individual and a group challenge. You do as much as you can. We'll all give you a hand."

Jim wavers. "Well—what's the drill for the day? What's gonna happen?"

Drew: "Rafting. A full day of rafting."

Art: "The fact that you jumped in yesterday and swam the rapid is more important than being able to run or carry a pack."

"I've got a back problem that put me out of work," says Herman, "but I'm gonna row. I'm gonna row until I can't row any more."

Art continues, "We all have limitations. I have a nerve problem and shoulder bursitis. If one of us can't do it, none of us can. We want you to stay, and we will do everything possible to alleviate your physical problems."

By now the group has congregated around the fire, and all are observing the interaction.

Mike adds his opinion. "We're a group. We'll all feel so much worse if we don't finish as a group."

Jay adds, "Yeah, we'll feel we've had a failure if you don't finish."

"We all felt so exhilarated when you got over the log," continues Art, "that we *all* did it."

The stubborn look is back on Jim's face. "Let me lay it on the line," he says. "I have three kids in a tuition school. If I miss work, I won't be able to meet my bills."

"I believe that if I live too much in the future," says Jay, "I'm dead."

"I agree with that," responds Jim, "but I have responsibilities."

"But if you are living just for them," responds Jay, "you can't live for yourself."

"I know that," says Jim.

"Well," says Jay, "then stay with us."

"We really want you to stay," adds Jim the engineer.

Art says, "We want you, and we'll do anything to help you stay."

But Jim is adamant, and there is really nothing else to be said. The group is supportive of him, but we have not been together long enough to form strong attachments. If Jim had been further into the program, possibly his commitment would be stronger. As it is, the group sees his continued participation as a challenge to be overcome, a response to the Outward Bound expectation of group participation, rather than a warm personal response to him. They want to want him, it seems, but the motivation stems more from responsibility, obligation, than from genuine friendliness.

"There is nothing more to say," concludes Jim. "I've made up my mind, and that's it."

Each year a small number—less than 2 per cent of total enrollment—of Outward Bound participants drop out before the culmination of their experience. The reasons are many. Failure of nerve in face of the challenges posed by Outward Bound is one. Homesickness, separation from loved ones and comforts, is another. Confused expectations about the nature of the Outward Bound experience is not uncommon. Outward Bound publicity materials tend to be more rhetorical and impressionistic than detailed and factual. Fortunately most participants flesh out this information by talking with someone who has already been through the program. This is the most reliable way for a person accurately to assess the nature of the experience and the degree to which it might meet his or her needs. But if a person responds just to the brief information given in Outward Bound publicity materials, it is possible that he or she will form an inaccurate picture of the experience. Outward Bound is a challenging experience, and it is deliberately structured this way. There are rigors and discomforts to be faced. Participants are extended physically and emotionally. There are also periods of calm, of repose, of relaxation, times to get in touch with the beauty of wilderness surroundings and to enjoy close companionship with a supportive peer group. But for a small number of participants each year the challenge, rigors, and demands of the experience are just too much. Despite support from their group and their instructor they, like Jim, drop out.

Jim has made up his mind. His Outward Bound experience is over. Today he will remain in the van with Emily while we negotiate section IV.

The river gauge reads 2.3, the maximum flow allowable for a run! Drew presents this information enthusiastically, his eyes sparkling. We inflate the rafts, pack the equipment, and move out onto the river. As yesterday, Jay and I are with Drew. Curly, Art Duel, and Herman raft with river guide Bruce Herr. In John Bunting's raft are Jim Finucayne, Mike Kahler, and Ellen. Emily stays with Jim Brennan and drives the van around to meet us.

We cruise gentle waters first. Bubbling ripples jostle us for a while, nudging us into wakefulness. The early morning sun dances at a low angle on the river, flashing diamonds of light, playing hide-and-seek with us between the shoreline trees. There is instinctive colusion in our group to preserve the silence. The water laps softly against the side of the raft. We hear the birds of the morning singing and skittering through the trees. Jay is sitting sidesaddle, his paddle held loosely across his knees. He watches the river and the shoreline intently as they slip by. He smiles the smile of one at peace.

Ahead we hear a roar, the noise of moving water. We come alert. The roar increases and wharoons about the canyon echo chamber. The lead raft swings to the right bank, finds an eddy, and beaches on sand. We follow and walk downstream as a group to observe the source of the noise.

The river fights its way through three large rocks, each the size of a medium-sized room, doglegs to the right (looking downstream), and pours over a five-foot drop in a powerful sluice. We have a river runner's map with us. This rapid, Bull Sluice, is graded five on the river runner's one-to-six scale of difficulty (six being the most difficult). The adjectives that describe class-five rapids give food for thought: "Very difficult. Violent currents. Big drops. Riverbed obstructed. Inspection absolutely necessary." This is the purpose in beaching the rafts and walking down: to inspect the rapid and chart a route through. The map has a diagram of Bull Sluice and a short description, plus suggested tactics. "The best way to run this rapid," it reads, "is along the shoreline carrying your canoe." Well, judging by the gleam in Drew's eyes and the way his finger is pointing out a path through the torrent, we can ignore that. (The description is written for canoeists. We have an advantage and additional safety factor in rafts because they are bigger and more stable.) The description continues in a morbid frame: "Several deaths testify to its danger." (Phew! A real throat-dryer). "If you feel you must run it, don't try without a helmet, life jacket, and rabbit's foot." Well, group? Adrenaline flowing along nicely?

Not only do we get to run this rapid, but we get to see each raft perform. Bruce's raft is to go first.

Art, Herman, and Curly congregate with Bruce and plan their route. We

Crashing through the big drop at Bull Sluice.

cannot hear their conversation above the roar of the water, but we see Bruce pointing at the river and sketching a diagram of the rapid in the sand. The three look impressed by the challenge. They climb into the raft and swing out into the quiet water above the torrent. Bruce is in back of the raft, the captain. Herman is at back right, Curly front left, and Art Duel front right. They head the raft toward an opening between the first two large rocks, traversing the breadth of the river. As they enter the gap, the river speeds up. They are now moving rapidly, committed. They round another large rock to their right, and we see them paddling frantically to keep the raft in tight, close to the rock, to put them in the best line for the run down to the sluice. The current tends to throw them to the outside of the curve. If this happens, they will end up too far left and run the risk of hanging up on the big rock that guards the left of the sluice. That could disorient the raft, flip it around, and send them through the sluice sideward, or backward. They are paddling at full strength, and already the violent waters are breaking over the gunwales. Art is partially standing in the bow, digging his paddle hard, surrounded by spray and flying water. They are around the rock. The raft is well positioned, bow facing straight downstream. The raft is hurtling and crashing through the waves, directly in line with the main flow of the sluice. Where the main body of water jets over

Bull Sluice.

the edge, it is momentarily smooth; then the river flows like thick oil over the edge, fragmenting in a spewing, boiling, wild foam as it hits the bottom of the drop. The raft is poised, horizontal, for a split second in this smoothness. We see the back end kick up wildly as the bow drops, and the boat nosedives into the foam. The occupants are thrown about at the impact. Art has lost his paddle and is sprawled in the bow, clutching the side of the raft. Herman and Curly are in disarray but still have their paddles. Bruce is still in position, braced in the stern, legs straight, feet wedged under the side tubes, his paddle extended behind the raft, ruddering to keep the boat straight. The raft is engulfed. It disappears out of sight beneath the foam and spray. At the foot of the drop is a hydraulic (a flow of water turned back on itself that has been known to hold boats and people in its fluid grip). Jim Finucayne, next to me, gasps, "Oh Lord," his pent-up breath coming out with a rush. But—they're OK! The raft noses its way out. Herman and Curly have resumed paddling. They have taken on a good deal of water during the fray, and the raft wallows sluggishly under the extra weight, but they have made it, and a spontaneous cheer—"Whoopee. Yeah, Art. Yeah, Herman. Yeah, Curly."—bursts forth from the watchers.

They pull into an eddy a little way downstream, bale out the raft, and walk up to rejoin us.

"You guys—" Art grins. "Whoa, are you in for one hell of a ride."

We believe him. He and the others are exhilarated by the experience.

"Never, never done nothing like that before," beams Herman, his teeth flashing big and white, water still running down his face.

"Go for it, you guys," encourages Art. "Just give it everything. Right down the middle."

John Bunting's raft goes next. Again a perfect run.

We follow. The other two rafts had four paddlers. We have three. I breathe a silent prayer that we have enough power to keep the raft on the best course. My recollections of the next moments are fragmentary. Everything happens fast. One moment we are gliding smoothly toward the gap between the two rocks. Before I have time to realize what is happening, the world explodes. The raft is bucking like a wild horse. Water pours in from every side. I have no sense of direction. Up and down are interchangeable. Downstream has disappeared as a recognizable direction, and I blindly obey Drew's screamed instructions from the rear.

"Paddle, you mothers! Paddle! Paddle! Paddle!"

I am knocked into the bottom of the raft, but I keep hold of my paddle and struggle back into position.

For a microsecond that seems to last for hours, I feel us poised on the smooth water at the edge of the drop. The raft seems to halt. The foam has gone, and I can see ahead. Then, with a vicious lurch, we are over, and all is chaos again, complete chaos. We are buried in water; it engulfs us. I am lost in an eternity of turbulence. There is water in my eyes, in my ears, in my nose, and down my throat. I keep an iron grip on the paddle. It is the only solid object in my immediate sensory environment.

Drew's voice filters through the pandemonium: "Paddle! Paddle! Paddle! Paddle! Paddle!"

He isn't kidding. I prod my paddle vainly into the foaming stuff, seeking for a solid purchase.

We are out of it. Like a cork popping from a bottle, the raft has kicked out from the holding power of the sluice's suction. We slide downstream, startled, wide-eyed.

The sun is shining. The river is peaceful. A kingfisher dive-bombs a smooth-surfaced pool. The calm is a sudden and unexpected contrast to the tumult of the past few moments.

We cruise downstream in convoy with the other rafts. The moments of tension and hyperactivity of Bull Sluice are behind us, but there is more to come. Bull Sluice has given us a taste for the adventure of the river and the confidence to proceed. We have not yet mastered the intricacies of the raft or the river, but with Drew at the helm we are ready for just about anything.

It is easy to underestimate this river. A little farther downstream we negotiate a relatively minor rapid. Jay is paddling gently, lily-dipping. No great effort is called for; as long as we keep the bow pointed downstream, the river does all the work for us. Without warning, the side of the raft hits a sleeper. We slue round. Jay, caught off balance, falls neatly, without fuss, over the side and into the waves. It is not a serious situation. Drew and I maneuver the raft close to him and haul him back in, spluttering water. It is, though, a little lesson to us not to lower our guard. As much fun as the river is, it demands respect.

Screaming Left Falls, Rock Jumble, Woodall Shoals, Seven Foot Falls, Stekoa Rapids, Deliverance Rock (where some shots for the movie were taken), Calm Before the Storm, Corkscrew, Jawbone, Crack in the Rock, Sock-em-Dog, Shoulder Bone—the remainder of the day gives us all the excitement we could want as we take rapid after rapid. We gain in skill, and as we head down the tongue of each one, the adrenaline flows.

The afternoon is not completely without incident. Seven Foot Falls is a noted raft eater. We beach the rafts and inspect this eighty-yard stretch of boiling water strewn with massive rocks in a pinched section of the river. At the end are two very large boulders, fifteen feet apart, through which most of the river pours. Inspection complete, strategy worked out, John Bunting's raft is first. Ellen, Jim, and Mike look suitably serious as their raft edges into the fast water. They do well, aiming the raft with skillful precision through the waves and through the gap between the last two rocks. The raft slams over the seven-foot drop, starts to spin, hits a rock on the left side, and turns upside down!

"Ropes!" screams Drew next to me. "Get the ropes out!"

Ropes are tossed to the swimmers. The water below the falls is calm, and it is an easy task to fish them out.

We go next. After observing the preceding disaster, I have no false pride. I'm scared. But we think we have learned from their experience. Drew talks tactics.

"See," he says, "it's important to move the raft to the right the very moment we hit the top of the falls. That way we avoid crashing into the rocks at the bottom."

"Right, captain," grins Jay. "Whatever you say."

We pull off a clean run. Drew bellows, "Draw right," the moment we hit the top of the falls. Jay and I obey like clockwork. With a stomach-wrenching crash we go over, water tumbles over us, we submerge, it seems; and then we are in calm water, in one piece and still afloat. Not bad. I turn to congratulate Drew, but he is no longer with us! At the moment we went over the edge, the raft had bucked wildly. Drew did not have his feet firmly wedged under the side tubes and had been catapulted into the air. The watchers on the bank later told us that he had flown right over the raft and landed in the water in front of it. And indeed there he is ahead of us, lying back in his life jacket, treading water, waiting to be picked up.

The third raft goes through. They stay upright, but this time it is Herman who goes flying out.

We leave Seven Foot Falls with a feeling of respect.

Evening sees us paddling our rafts across two miles of calm water. The Chattooga widens after Shoulder Bone, the last major rapid, becoming more like a narrow lake than a river; and having lost the force of the current, we have to paddle. It is an appropriate way to end the day. After the excitements of the rapids the paddling is a calming, meditative exercise.

Emily is waiting for us with the van. The rafts are deflated and packed away. We say good-bye to John and Bruce and once again are heading along narrow roads through the Carolina hills, back toward the Outward Bound School. Drew and Emily are noncommittal about our destination. We have learned not to push them about what is going to happen next.

The next morning, packs on our backs, maps and compasses at the ready, we are hiking a narrow trail up a steep hillside. The group is in a good mood, relaxed and jocular. Ellen is taking some ribbing.

"Hey, Ellen, how come you're still wearing a bra?" inquires Curly with a grin.

Ellen is nonplussed. The question is asked in an easy, bantering manner, but she has difficulty fielding it.

"None of your business," she replies primly.

Jim Finucayne picks up the topic and says with mock seriousness, "How come, Ellen. I took mine off a long time ago."

"I noticed," replies Ellen, trying to go along with the banter. But she bites her lip, not really liking the jesting.

This is not the first time that Ellen has been the focus of jokes. I do not envy her her position as the only woman participant. It seems that some of the group are using her as a relief valve, a way of dissipating some of the tension they are feeling, the beginnings of a classic situation of scapegoating.

We hike for most of the day and by midafternoon have reached the top of Shortoff Mountain, a long, saddleback, wooded ridge. We drop our packs in a clearing by a spring and lunch appreciatively on cheese, salami, nuts, and apples.

Drew calls us together, and we move into a circle, sitting cross-legged or lying belly down on the grass. First we review the river experience. It has been a high point for everyone. The thrills and perfect running conditions turned all of us on. Also we are beginning to feel like a group. Working together through those intensely demanding moments has pulled us together. The experiences of the rapids have enabled us to review and consolidate our initial impressions of each other, form a sense of strengths and weaknesses, and most important, begin to trust one another.

Art talks of the pressures of his law practice. "A lot of my life is like a leaf floating along a stream," he says. "I have very few opportunities to eddy out for a while. For me, Outward Bound is an opportunity to eddy out." He goes on to compare his life to the rushing river we have just left, emphasizing that he is forced along by the current in his day-to-day existence. "I have a role to fill, with many expectations and social obligations," he continues. "For example, in Connecticut I couldn't even let my hair get any longer than it is now or curly. I have to use a hot comb every morning to straighten it out. In a way I have everything I want in life, but I have to pay a price. I'm nearly forty years old, and I wanna know if it's worth it. I don't dislike what I'm doing, but I don't love it. The material rewards give me the freedom to do the things I want to do."

Art's remarks take us into a general discussion of the Outward Bound experience. Herman is cynical. "I just don't see anything great about this," he says. "I'm having a good time, enjoying myself, but so far haven't seen anything great changing my personality or anything."

"Is that what you are expecting from Outward Bound?" asks Emily.

"Well—well sure. That's what Outward Bound says; that's what the brochures and stuff say."

Art responds to him. "Well we've only been here a couple of days. It's too soon to assess what's happening to us. All I can say is that so far I feel I've been getting a lot out of the experience."

"Why do we co-operate so well with each other here at Outward Bound," asks Herman, "when in society we look at everyone else as a rat, until they disprove it?"

"How do you mean?" asks Drew.

"All life is winning," states Herman in a voice loaded with conviction. "Get ahead by climbing up over somebody else's shoulders. Isn't that what it's all about?"

Mike replies,"No, no. It's the other way around."

"Not for me it isn't," Herman shoots back. "You speak for yourself."

"It depends on how you've been brought up," says Art.

"I think Herman's a lot closer to the truth than many of us like to believe," adds Jim Finucayne. "That's a harsh way to put it, but it's probably realistic if you take out a few of the loaded words."

Art looks rueful. "I hate to admit it, but there are times in my business when I sure find myself acting that way."

"Do you like that?" Emily asks.

"No. No I don't. But it's just the way things are," says Art.

Herman is emphatic. "I'm gonna climb over anyone to get where I wanna go. If I don't, they're just gonna climb right on over me."

Herman's comments have provoked thoughtful expressions on the faces of most of the group. Implicitly he has questioned the nature of the Outward Bound experience. Are we really getting down to fundamentals here? Is Outward Bound just a nice time in the wilderness, a vacation, or is it an experience giving us some *real* opportunities for new insights into ourselves and into our social functioning? Herman has pointed out that already he is co-operating in this group more than is normal for him. Does this make Outward Bound an artificial and irrelevant experience, a temporary mode, or a potential way to move toward other alternatives?

The topic goes back and forth for a while. Some members of the group attempt to talk Herman out of his position, criticizing him for perceiving life as a rat race and behaving accordingly. It is a thought-provoking interaction and leaves us feeling that though it is certainly too early to come up with answers, the questions being raised are fundamental. In the short time we have been here, the experience is enabling us to focus on basic questions and values.

It has been surprising—or has it?—to note the common view expressed between Art and Herman. Two diverse individuals—the white, successful lawyer from upper-crust Connecticut and the black factory worker from Asheville— both perceive life as a rat race, both acknowledge a willingness to climb over others to get what they want. Perhaps realistically there is some of this in each of us.

It is now three o'clock in the afternoon. Drew winds up the discussion and moves us to the next activity on the agenda.

"Solo," he says. "We're going to do an overnight solo from now until noon tomorrow. You've had a lot of activity these past days. Solo should be a nice change of pace."

He and Emily talk about the purpose of solo.

"Mainly," Drew says, "it is a period for you to be alone with your thoughts. In the early days of Outward Bound solo was presented as a survival exercise. You'd forage for food, eat berries, kill small animals, and build elaborate shelters from branches. Today we emphasize solo as a meditative experience."

He reads us a quotation to get us in the mood for solo:

Always in big woods when you leave familiar ground and step off alone into a new place there will be, along with the feelings of curiosity and excitement, a little nagging of dread. It is the ancient fear of the Unknown, and it is your first bond with the wilderness you are going into. What you are doing is exploring. You are undertaking the first experience, not of the place, but of yourself in that place. It is an experience of our essential loneliness; for nobody can discover the world for anybody else. It is only after we have discovered it for ourselves that it becomes a common ground and a common bond, and we cease to be alone.

We are silent for a moment at the end of the reading. Drew is stretched out on the ground, his shoulders propped against a fallen tree, his cap shading his eyes.

"Where's that from?" asks Mike.

"Wendell Berry," answers Drew. "From *The One-Inch Journey.*"

"I'd encourage you to spend some time on solo thinking about your life plans," says Emily. "I've found that it's a good time to get things in perspective, to focus on priorities. But don't force it," she warns. "Go with the experience, with whatever is happening to you. If you just find yourself daydreaming, that's cool. If just digging on the surroundings is your thing, then get into that."

"We're gonna ask you to take a pencil and your journal with you," continues Drew. "Try and write a little. It'll help you to focus and give you something to relate back to when all of this is over."

We had been issued journals on the first day and encouraged to write up our experiences as we progressed through them.

"What else can we take with us?" inquires Jay.

"Just the basics," replies Drew. "The less you take with you, the less there will be to interfere with the experience of being with yourself. Take a sleeping bag and groundcloth, the clothes you are wearing, flashlight, whistle, a full canteen of water, and your poncho in case it rains."

"How about food?" someone asks.

"This is not a rule," says Drew, "but we'd like you to fast."

"Why?" asks Herman.

"One, you don't need it," says Drew. "Two, it helps the whole solo idea. We're trying to get you to temporarily divorce yourself from most of the crutches we all use and to give you a clear path to experience yourself."

"But," says Emily, "we're serious in saying that these are suggestions for enhancing the experience. If you seriously have different ideas, if you feel that going without food or other items is really going to get in the way, then take 'em. But think about it seriously first. The experience does have some far-out possibilities, but it's one hundred per cent up to you what you make of it."

"How about a book to read?" asks Mike.

"Again that's up to you," says Drew. "But I'd strongly, strongly recommend that you don't take something to read. That's escapism. I can't think of a more effective way of blocking yourself off from the potential of the solo experience."

Solo is one of the major Outward Bound experiences. As in the Gila, we are to experience only an overnight solo, twenty-four hours, rather than the three-day solo of the full-length Outward Bound program.

The group moves about, sorting the items they will take with them. Drew maintains his relaxed position, watching the proceedings. Twenty minutes later everyone is ready. Drew calls us together and runs through the main items that we should have for safety purposes, and the group is ready to go.

There is a curious look in Drew's eye, a little gleam, but his face is deadpan.

"Got everything you need, Ellen?" he asks.

"Sure have," responds Ellen in a squeaky little voice.

Suddenly, taking everyone by surprise, Drew dives at her, and they struggle. Ellen has her belongings wrapped up in a bundle, clutched to her chest, and Drew is endeavoring to pull something out of it.

Ellen is no match for Drew. She struggles, red in the face, but Drew succeeds. With a big grin he holds up—a candy bar.

Ellen looks mortified. She does not know what to do. Embarrassed, she defends herself. "Well," she says. "Well. So what?" Her voice is pitched high, strident.

Drew had told us we were free to take food if we wanted. But we had *not* been issued candy bars with the Outward Bound food. It dawns on us that Ellen must have brought the candy bar with her and kept it hidden in her pack during the last three days.

"It's mine," Ellen continues. "I'm not doing anything wrong." But her face betrays insecurity, and her voice lacks conviction.

"Look, Ellen," Drew says, "a candy bar doesn't mean a thing—in itself. But I was watching you packing. You were *sneaking* the candy bar, and that's what got me mad. You looked around to make sure nobody was watching, and then you hid it in your stuff. I saw you."

Ellen has been caught red-handed. It is not a big thing, but our little group has been away from civilization long enough that treats such as beer, cigarettes, and candy bars are recurrent topics of conversation as we experience withdrawal symptoms, deprived of our cultural addictions. The main reaction to the situation is laughter, and some good-natured ribbing. Ellen continues to blush. Poetic justice demands that the candy bar be shared round. We each take a nibble and file off, following Drew and Emily to our solo sites.

Drew leads half of the group one way, and Emily heads in the opposite direction with the others.

We follow Drew through the trees for three hundred yards and emerge on the edge of an escarpment. From the time of leaving our camp this morning we have hiked through thick trees, feeling enclosed. The forest canopy has shaded us, restricting our vision to a few yards in any direction. Emerging onto the top of the escarpment, we are deluged with a sudden rush of spaciousness. It is a disorienting moment. A cool breeze blows in our faces, a contrast to the muggy cloisters of the trees. It is like emerging at the top of a cliff overlooking the ocean. Beneath our feet a steep, rocky precipice drops down many hundreds of feet to curve away in a broad, open valley. Opposite the valley floor rises up again, some miles away, to form a similar steep wall. To either side the valley sweeps gracefully to the horizon. We can see a stream wending its way through the valley's depths, a line of demarcation that separates one side of the valley from the other. It is one of those spellbinding moments that comment would only dilute. No one speaks.

Quietly Drew moves forward, and we follow. He leads along a little trail that winds around the cliff top. Each one is given a spot some hundred yards from each other, out of sight and hearing.

Art Duel on solo above the Linville Gorge.

As much as, or more than, any other experience in the Outward Bound repertoire, solo consistently generates diverse reactions. For some it is the most powerful experience of the course. For others it is a bore; nothing happens. Characteristically Outward Bound staff emphasize to participants that it is *their* experience to make of as they will. It is a common complaint among these same staff that the Outward Bound organization tends to glorify the solo experience, bathing it in pseudomystical rhetoric and in the process building many up for an inevitable letdown. I felt grateful for Drew and Emily's low-key introduction.

Accepting the undeniable fact that some Outward Bound participants have nothing in particular to report at the end of their solo experience, I have chosen Art Duel's solo account, written in his journal during those twenty-four hours, to exemplify a solo that turned out positive and fulfilling, indicative of the potential of the experience. He wrote:

I am now lying on a large rock surrounded by cliffs and shrub pine, listening to the roar of a river some three miles below and watching a hawk make circles in the sky above. There is a slight breeze; birds are singing, and bees are busy sucking nectar from little white flowers at the base of my rock. Directly in front of me I can see ten to twenty miles of clear blue sky filled with mountains; Table Rock, the Chimneys, Hawksbill Mountain, Laurel Knob, Jonas Ridge, Ginger Cake, and Humpback. The Pisgah National Forest sits in front of me for a panoramic two hundred degrees. I am doing what I have wanted to do all my life—to find some peace, to have a chance to relax, think, watch, muse, observe, reflect, to consider what is important and what is not, to let my mind drift aimlessly from subject to subject as I shift from one scene of beauty to another. I don't care what time it is or what I shall be doing tomorrow. For the moment I am pleasantly fatigued, a little sticky from a good sweat climbing up Shortoff Mountain, a glow of warmth from a touch too much sun, and pensive, thoughtful, and absolutely content.

So often when one looks forward too much, the imagined event is anticlimactic, off-key, and a little flat. To the contrary, what I see before me and where I am are really too beautiful for words. However, like in a shower, one sings because no one can hear, even though one has a lousy voice, I find myself bursting with thoughts. My first moments of peace since I really can't remember when.

As I was exploring my territory (so to speak)—and I guess I shall always consider this spot my land—I saw a beautiful wild rhododendron bush with huge purple flowers. I thought, how nice to pick one or two to bring back to my rock where they could keep me company (as if I needed more beauty before me). But as I moved to snap off a twig of loveliness, I stopped and pondered. Should I end this flower's life so abruptly? Should I deny others the right to see this lovely flower? Would I not be considerate of its feelings and its existence? Later, however, I felt that perhaps it would have been pleased to be with me, to give me great pleasure and satisfaction. Then I paused, reflected, and remembered my grandma. As long as the memory of her hand could be felt in mine, as long as I loved and could feel her love, she would live, her spirit would continue to counsel me when I needed wisdom. So, too, that flower lives and will always live in my memory. So, too, was that flower near me all day as I sat on my perch watching the sun gradually move into the western horizon.

For years I have wanted to have some sort of refuge tucked away in the woods where I could be alone, perhaps only enhanced by my dog Temuchgin. As I was floating down the Chattooga a couple of days ago in between rapids and was looking at the isolation and beauty that enveloped us, I could only feel good and right. At that point I made the comment to my guide that maybe the only thing better than this would be to do the same thing with someone one loves.

Several thoughts cross my mind as I sit here: Maybe, since we are so much a part of nature as the rocks, trees, and ants that are all around us, maybe the only way we can clearly communicate with ourselves is to take away the so-called civilized devices. How can one know oneself, one's own needs, and one's own values if we are in the midst of cars, buildings, TV, debts, country clubs, social obligations, and the like? Here I am awed by beauty, by the clear air, and by the womblike effect of contentment. Nature is constantly in harmony with itself; it has progressed by the constant laws of the universe. What is right will survive, and what is wrong will fail—a basic tenet.

Outward Bound does not try to provide a school solution for one's needs; it does afford one the opportunity to see how one can live or die. We learn by experience. We learn what is right for us and maybe what is wrong for us. In reading a map, if we take the wrong trail, our instructor goes along with us. For only by traveling downhill for a while do we then realize a mistake has been made. We pay for it by having to climb up the hill again, but a few sore muscles, a little bit of sweat, are a small consideration to learn this lesson.

Outward Bound is a microcosm. We are in a new world. We are all strangers.

We are, in a sense, reborn, given a new chance to live. We are shown a world of nature, purity, symmetry, and harmony.

It seems contrary to nature to violate or abuse what is really ourselves. To throw a beer can or a cigarette butt to the ground in a beautiful setting is really to leave mud on one's face. It shows a lack of pride in oneself.

I have thought before that we are really caught on leaves as they float down a stream. It is true we stepped onto the leaves at one time in our lives, perhaps not really knowing the full impact of our action; but be that as it may, we continue on that floating leaf, carried on by the currents of life and the pressures, without really being able to eddy out, to arrest our motion so that we can not only see and feel but also listen, also think.

Outward Bound is a form of haven, a way station, a sanctuary from the world we know. If we think of how we live and how we would like to live, and if we choose something different or return changed to what we know, then Outward Bound has been successful. Outward Bound does give us the chance to know ourselves a little better. We have the opportunity to do something. Will we? That remains to be seen. Will we continue to react, or will we act? Maybe a few more solos will provide the answer. At least a spark has been ignited, and for a few days we have been given a chance to live.

At noon the next day Drew and Emily collect the group from their solo sites. Back at the meeting place we sit in a circle once more and briefly talk about the experience.

Herman seems surprised at one of his reactions, and his voice quivers as he says, "You know, we haven't been together long, but I missed you folks. I had to walk up and down the trail a few times to get my mind off it." Having said this, he sits, eyes downcast, seemingly a little embarrassed by his admission. It catches everyone off guard. No one responds directly, but the statement has interjected a warm note into the meeting. The silence is appreciative. Jay gives Herman a big smile. Herman's face lights up in response.

"I'm disappointed that it wasn't three days," says Art. "It was a unique experience for me, one that I was really up for and had been looking forward to."

For the next few moments Art reads passages from his solo journal. He reads in a strong, firm voice.

There is an awkward little silence at the end of his reading. Again the silence, judging from the expressions on people's faces, is appreciative. Our group is not particularly emotive; feelings are not readily verbalized.

Mike Kahler eventually says, "That was really something, Art. That was real powerful."

Jim Finucayne, abandoning any attempt at a sincere expression of his feelings, for it seems that he, too, has been moved by the reading, attempts to joke. "Well, well. The real stuff, eh. Communing with nature. Watch out, Thoreau." His tone of voice is inappropriate to the occasion, and unintentionally he sounds cynical. It is very apparent to him that his attempt at humor has not succeeded, and he looks confused.

In the natural progression of events (after all, we are in each other's company twenty-four hours each day and have been together for almost five days), we seem to be struggling for a natural expression of our feelings toward one another. We are a cohesive group, high-spirited, and we have been co-operating well these past few days. But so far there has been little *direct* expression of these good feelings. There has been a good deal of joking and bantering, the kind of leg-pulling that can only work when it is underpinned by positive regard. But as I think we instinctively know, if we continue to relate *only* on this level, the joking will inevitably sour. If we are to make progress as a group, we will necessarily have to move to a point of serious interchange. Herman's remarks and Art's reading have been steps in that direction.

"It was partly a frustrating experience for me," says Jay, moving to fill the hole in the discussion. "I really wanted to think about myself. I had it all planned out. But my mind kept going in different directions. I got into this weird territorial imperative thing. My feelings were mainly about owning my space, a little garden, Gethsemane, Jesus's garden. It had a holy feel to it, the flowers and trees taking surreal shapes."

"Thinking about nature got me going, too," continues Herman, "but different. I thought about how everything contributed a little bit to the life of everything else—lichen living on the rocks. But what I wanna know is what's gonna happen when we go back? We're close to nature now and have these feelings stirring, but hell, we'll get back home, an' we'll be driving along, an' we'll throw that beer can out of the window again, just like we always used to."

Ellen's experience has been less stimulating. She comes across as an automatic kind of person with a hard shell. She seems to move through the experiences unthinkingly, doing what she is told with a certain grim determination, joylessly. "I live alone and do a lot of thinking anyway," she says. "Solo wasn't much to me. I didn't feel like thinking on solo, so I didn't."

"What did you do?" asks Drew.

"Just sat, mainly. Sat and looked around and then got in my sleeping bag and went to sleep."

Drew does not press Ellen. He appears satisfied for now with the responses he has elicited from the group and suggests that it is time to move on.

We spend the rest of the day hiking through the trees, fumbling our way through a network of trails, some of which, confusingly, are marked on the map and some of which are not. That evening we arrive back at the Outward Bound School. We camp on the school grounds, on top of a massive rock. It is an unusual perch. The rock is some fifty feet high and drops away sheer on three sides. The fourth side abuts the hillside, and by scrambling up steep slopes, we can step onto the horizontal top. It is perhaps fifty feet by fifty feet, enough room to spread a dozen sleeping bags. Against the hillside there is a layer of soil that trees have invaded. Those not susceptible to vertigo, the clutching tentacles of sheer drops, nestle their bags in the tree roots. The rock is called Dangle Rock. We have only spent a few hours at the school previously, but it feels like coming home.

The next two days are spent rock-climbing. Midmorning finds us festooned in the paraphernalia of the technical climber, contemplating a smooth slab of gray rock close to our camp. The slab is approximately fifty feet high and leans back at an angle of sixty degrees. Nearby are a number of boulders, up to fifteen feet high.

Drew talks to us about rock-climbing and mountaineering, their history and philosophy. He explains that in the early days of climbing, mountains were ascended by the easiest ways and that to get to the top was the main objective. As climbers gained experience, they became more expert and sought out more difficult objectives: steep faces and vertical rocks. Over the years climbing technique has developed, as has climbing equipment, to the point where the steepest rocks can be climbed in safety.

"Before we get on to the ropes and gear," he says, "we're just going to boulder for a while on these low rocks. Bouldering," he explains, "is an aspect of rock-climbing that lets you practice for the real thing without getting very high off the ground. Even top rock-climbers," he tells us, "boulder to keep in shape and train for the longer climbs. You can push yourself to your limit on small holds on a boulder in perfect safety, build up arm and finger strength, and develop confidence and balance."

Safety has been stressed throughout the preceding days. Today is no exception. We wear hard hats, even for bouldering, and take turns positioning ourselves below whoever is climbing to spot in case of an awkward fall.

For half an hour we scramble up and down the boulders. There are easy ways and very hard ways.

"Balance is the key," says Drew. "Get your weight centered over your feet. Be conscious of where your center of gravity is. Most of the time you should be able to use your feet and leg muscles for upward movement. Save your arms for when you really need 'em. They're relatively much weaker than your legs and tire easily. Try not to pull up with your arms unless you really have

Bouldering, practice climbing on rocks only a few feet high, with spotters for safety.

to. And relax. Don't clutch. Stand in balance and take it easy. You can waste a tremendous amount of energy if you get gripped up."

We endeavor to follow these simple directions. I watch Art tackling a steep bulge. The top of the rock is only four feet above him, but it requires a complex sequence of moves to reach it. There are two good footholds, one at knee level and one a little higher. They both slope down and present an insecure perch. Above the rock is smooth, lacking positive holds for the hands. Twice Art steps up onto the footholds, perches, searches with skittering fingertips for something to hold onto, finds nothing, and jumps down.

Drew is watching. "You gotta trust those feet, Art. You gotta get your weight over 'em, get in balance, and trust 'em to stick. If you keep on trying to grab something with your hands like that, you'll peel everytime."

We are wearing hiking boots with lugged rubber soles. Though clumsy on small footholds, they give good friction on dry rock. We have to learn to trust them.

Art tries again. This time he looks more confident. Straining a little, he manages to step up in balance onto the footholds. He keeps his hands at chest height, as Drew has explained, touching the rock, pushing against it to help him balance, but not scrabbling with his fingers for something to cling to.

"Now what?" he asks after balancing in the same position for a moment or two.

"Check it out," suggests Drew. "What do you have to work with?"

"Not much, buddy," states Art firmly, "not much at all."

"There's nothing much for your hands," agrees Drew. "So, it's gonna have to be the feet that do it."

"Hey, my leg's starting to shake," gasps Art. "Dammit, quit!"

Art has a genuine case of sewing machine leg. The unaccustomed isometric strain of maintaining his balance has generated a classic case of rock-climber's quiver.

Now he has an audience. Curly, Ellen, and Jim have congregated to watch his progress.

Art's eyes are wide. It seems as though he has forgotten that he is only fifteen inches above the ground. He is straining to stay on the rock as though his life depends on it. He glances up. The top is tantalizingly close. He needs to make one more move up. He spots another hold some twelve inches higher than his right foot. To get onto it, he is going to have to balance all his weight over his left foot and step up. He shifts his weight to the left, alters his hand position, and frees his right foot. It moves up, finds the hold, and his hands reach for the top. Abandoning all pretense of grace, he grabs the edge with both hands, grunts, muscles up, and as much to his surprise as to his onlookers', finds himself on top.

"Good," compliments Drew. "Try not to grab, though. Try and move only one hand or one foot at a time. Try and keep the other three points in contact with the rock. This'll keep you stable and also give you the best chance of recovery if you slip."

"Show us, Drew," says Ellen. "Let's see how it should be done."

Drew walks to the rock and gracefully steps up onto the first two footholds. He looks very solid. His hands are touching the rock lightly, and he is nicely in balance. With fluid control he steps up onto the higher foothold and reaches a hand for the top of the rock. At this point Art had abandoned technique and relied on muscle. Drew stays with style. He reaches up with his other hand, and both hands grasp the edge. Without strain his feet continue to search out tiny points of friction, and he walks them upward. By stepping his left foot up next to his left hand, his knee bent at an acute angle, he gains the top and stands up.

"Smooth, Drew," congratulates Emily.

"That top move is called a mantelshelf," says Drew when he rejoins us. "It's just like you were trying to climb up onto the mantelshelf at home. Very useful for moving up onto ledges or topping out on a climb."

We move back to the base of the rock slab. Drew picks up one of the climbing ropes. "This is it," he says. "This is the whole show. This is what your life depends on." The rope is a little more than half an inch in diameter, made of nylon, one hundred fifty feet long. "It's stretchy," explains Drew, uncoiling it into a pile at his feet. "That's what makes it safe for climbing. These ropes test to over four thousand pounds. The strength plus the elasticity that absorbs the impact of a fall gradually, rather than subjecting the rope to a single shock load, make them very, very safe," he says. He passes one end of the rope around for inspection. "Make sure you don't ever stand on the climbing rope," he admonishes. "There is no surer way to damage it. It will force grit in between the fibers, and you also risk cutting it against a sharp stone."

"OK," he says when the inspection is concluded, "how's the rope used?" After a moment's silence he answers his own question. "For practice sessions we top-rope all the climbs. We walk around to the top of the rock, anchor the rope, and drop it down. You tie on the other end, and as you climb, the person at the top will take the rope in, keeping you snug, to stop you in case you slip off."

We learn that the person at the top of the rock is called the *belayer* and the process of taking in the rope is called *belaying*. We will all have the chance to belay each other.

"The first step in the process," says Drew, "is to tie into the end of the rope." For this we use a bowline knot. We spend the next few minutes learning and practicing this knot. It snugs the end of the climbing rope around our waists, feels secure.

"Next," says Drew, "we tie ourselves onto the cliff—I'll explain how later." For now he ties himself off to a nearby tree. He then asks Jim to tie on to the other end of the rope and stand a few feet away. Jim complies. Drew takes the rope that comes from Jim's waist and lifts it over his shoulders into a position running around his waist and through each of his hands. "Jim, would you walk toward me as I take in the rope," he asks. As Jim walks slowly toward him, Drew slides the rope around his waist, moving one hand at a time, keeping the rope snug between them. It looks simple and effective. Jim moves back, and they repeat the process. This time Drew asks Jim to try and take him off guard. "At some point before you reach me," he instructs, "throw all of your weight back onto the rope, and try and pull me off balance." We watch intently. Jim moves up toward Drew and without warning throws his weight viciously backward. The rope pulls taut between them. Drew is pulled forward a few inches, but he is securely anchored to the tree. Once the slack in the system has been absorbed, he takes Jim's weight on the rope around his waist with little sign of strain.

We are duly impressed.

"Gottcha." Drew grins. "That's basically how the system works," he says.

For the next few minutes we pair off, still on flat ground, each tied into the end of a climbing rope, and practice. The rope around the waist acts much like a ship's rope around a capstan; it provides most of the friction, and the hands are not strained. Drew insists that we move the rope through our hands systematically, following a routine which ensures that there is minimum slack in the system. As a double safety check, only one hand moves at a time. It is a simple sequence, but the timing and coordination are precise. At first we fumble, but we learn quickly. Ropes are taken in and out, practice falls are enacted, and soon we feel proficient. Drew points out to us that the rope comes from the climber, around the belayer's waist, and then into the brake hand. This is the most important hand. Its effectiveness is based on its following the rope's friction around the waist. If we attempted to stop a fall with the other hand, there would be no friction between it and the climber.

Drew next goes over the standard calls that are used between belayer and climber to ensure effective communication and minimize confusion.

"When the belayer is anchored to the cliff with the rope around his waist, all ready to go, he shouts down, 'On belay,' " says Drew. "When you are ready to start, shout back, 'Climbing,' but only start when the belayer confirms with 'Climb.' "

We toss the calls back and forth. The area echoes.

"On belay!"

"Climbing!"

"Climb!"

Practice climbing.

There are others, Drew says, but we'll learn them as we go along. We have enough to think of for now.

For the next two hours we take turns belaying each other and climbing the slab. It is easier than some of the boulder problems but higher. We have to deal with height and ensuing nerves. The main point of the morning is to master rope techniques.

Drew and Emily pepper the activity with a stream of helpful advice, coaching drawn from experience. "Don't hug the rock. Get your weight out and over your feet. Take it easy; climb slow and steady. Don't rush. Don't climb faster than the belayer can take in. There's a pinch grip just by your nose."

"A pinch grip?"

"Yes. Grab it between your thumb and fingers. It'll hold you in balance."

We learn about laybacks, underclings, pressure holds, and smears; handjams and stemming; edging and friction climbing. By lunch we have absorbed a mouthful of esoterica. Verbally we are experts. The real climbing is to come.

Afternoon finds us at the base of a sixty-foot vertical cliff two miles from the school. It overlooks the same valley on the rim of which we had soloed, the Linville Gorge. The valley dropping away below increases the sense of height. The cliff, known as the Chimneys, daunts us at first sight. Its steepness presents an obvious challenge. This is going to be like climbing the boulders, but for sixty feet straight up. A narrow trail leads to the top of the cliff. Drew rigs the anchors and organizes the belayers.

Drew stays at the top to supervise the belayers. Emily stays below to check knots. The climbs are demanding. The verticality makes them strenuous. Arms and fingers quickly tire if good technique is not employed.

Two climbs are organized. Herman belays Art up, and Ellen belays Jim. Jim later confesses that he was worried about being belayed "by a 110-pound lady," but he does not show his anxiety.

One of the tricks in rock-climbing is to stay on route. The expert tends to do this automatically, following the line of least resistance, but to the beginner one section of rock looks much like another. It is easy to be seduced into difficulties. This happens to Herman. He climbs up a few feet, looking confident. Unnoticed by either Art or Drew, he begins to move leftward up the rock face, following holds that seem more inviting than those Art had used. He is not far off the correct line, a matter of a few feet, but the holds begin to run out, grow smaller, become widely spaced.

"Hey, man, where do I go now?" Herman is beginning to appreciate his predicament. Art and Drew lean forward, peering over the edge. Herman is only fifteen feet below them—in extremis. His eyes are like saucers.

"Hey, man," he repeats, "I'm in trouble."

He is in an extended position, spread-eagled on small holds, vainly trying to stretch up to a high handhold. Each time he reaches up, his feet threaten to slip off. He is completely safe—Art has the rope secure—but in these situations the void below can have a stronger effect on one's emotions than the rational

Herman tackles the crux moves.

security of the rope's presence. Your head tells you that you are safe, but your guts say scared. And as in love, rationality succumbs to emotion.

"*M-o-t-h-e-r,*" gasps Herman. "Sheet!" A long pause. "Watch me, watch me, watch me!"

We listen. Art is all systems go. Herman has communicated his distress effectively. Art braces.

"*Phewff, phewff, phewff.*" Herman exhales like a whale clearing its blowhole. His breath comes out in staccato bursts. He is not enjoying himself. He seems on the verge of panic.

Drew, in a gentle voice, calls down, "Cool it. Easy. Don't thrash. Move back down to your last comfortable position, and try and figure it out."

Herman croaks, "Where, where?" He is incapable of moving down. His strength is ebbing fast. With adrenaline-propelled determination his fingernails scratch at the rock. They find tenuous purchase on a small hold. Herman levitates. Somehow, substituting hope for holds and faith for technique (to this day I suspect that he called upon supernatural powers), he moves himself up the smooth section. Gasping, he clutches for the top and hauls himself over, to end up in a panting heap at Art and Drew's feet. They observe his arrival with consternation. He has given a plausible imitation of a seal bellying its way onto a rocky shore.

"Man," he gasps. "Oh man, man, man."

Drew grins. "You did it!"

"Great," congratulates Art. "Great stuff."

Herman sits up, shaking his head. His face has an ashen cast. His shoulders are slumped, and his hands quiver at the ends of jelly arms.

Art and Drew wait patiently for him to recover his composure. He stands up. Art grabs his hand and pumps it up and down in a congratulatory shake. Herman gives a weak smile. "That was close," he says. Another shake of the head. "Too close."

Next door, Mike Kahler has tied on below the second climb. In his eagerness (he had displayed considerable natural ability on the practice rocks), he climbs up faster than his belayer can take in the rope. He is only a few feet up when he slips. His hands give way, and he is off. With a crunch he lands awkwardly on the rocky ground. Someone calls Drew down, and he and Emily check Mike out.

Mike has damaged his ankle. It is painful, he says. We are about a quarter of a mile from the roadhead where an Outward Bound vehicle waits to take us back.

"How painful is it?" asks Drew.

"Doesn't feel broken," replies Mike. "Probably just a sprain."

We are all gathered round by this time, looking on with concern. "Why don't you loosen up his boot," someone suggests, "make him more comfortable."

"Nope," responds Drew. "That would only allow it to swell. Right now the boot is acting as a natural splint. If it starts to swell inside and gets too painful, then we might have to loosen it a little. Till then we'll leave it laced up."

Mike is reasonably comfortable. Drew uses the incident as a practical first aid session to supplement the theory we have been learning during the past few days. He looks up at the group and asks, "Well what should we do with him?"

Jim Finucayne replies, "We should keep his weight off his ankle at all costs. Even though we think it is only a sprain, we should treat it as a break."

Drew nods in agreement. "Good," he says. "And what else."

"Treat him for shock," someone suggests.

"How?" asks Drew.

"Keep him warm, mainly," says Ellen. "We don't need to do much else. It obviously isn't serious. If it was, we'd need to reassure him, make him feel cared for, make him comfortable, pad his body. In some cases give him a hot drink."

"How about getting him out from here?" asks Drew.

"A stretcher would be best," says Curly.

"It's gonna take a while to get to the school and fetch one," says Drew. "How about it, Mike?" he asks. "With one of us on either side of you giving support, think you can hop a quarter of a mile to the truck, keeping your injured foot off the ground?"

"Try it," says Mike gamely. "Might need to stop and rest."

Drew on one side, Jim on the other, Mike's arms draped over their shoulders, the three hop-shuffle their way back down the trail. Mike's evacuation is accomplished with minimum fuss and bother. In a short space of time he is at the truck and on his way back to school.

An X ray reveals that Mike has cracked a small bone in his foot. He leaves the next day.

Acceptable risk is a central feature of the Outward Bound program. During the first few days participants are trained physically and psychologically in the basics of wilderness skill and travel. As the course progresses, they are systematically given more responsibility. The instructor plays a crucial role. In some activities the instructor will withdraw completely, leaving the group to work its way through a complex problem; Jimbo's withdrawal on the Granny Mountain ascent and Drew and Emily's nonparticipation in the log-crossing exercise are examples. During more technical activities—rock-climbing, rappelling, negotiating major rapids—the instructor will move in and exercise direct control. There is still life-or-death responsibility on participants in these situations. The belayer on a rock-climb or rappel holds his or her partner's life literally on the rope that runs through his or her hands. Negotiating a major rapids, everyone has the responsibility to co-ordinate through potentially dangerous situations. Every precaution is taken, and a detailed set of safety guidelines are set down by Outward Bound for each instructor to follow, but the risk is still real—controlled but real. This characteristic is central to the unique nature of the Outward Bound program. In Mike's case he had been instructed in safe rock-climbing technique prior to arriving at the Chimneys. Later he readily acknowledged,

"It was my own fault. I climbed up too fast. I didn't think I was going to fall."

Paradoxically it has repeatedly been shown that the Outward Bound situations that *look* the most dangerous are actually the safest. Technical rock-climbing on vertical cliffs looks frightening, but the potential dangers are well recognized. The activity takes place only under the close supervision of an instructor. Rope-handling and safety techniques are practiced on easy terrain before the participant ever gets near the real thing. Mike's accident had been the exception to the general rule. The human element had defeated the system. He had been told what to do, but for a few seconds concentration lapsed.

Accident statistics over the years reveal the most dangerous parts of the Outward Bound program are the innocuous ones. Descending easy terrain in the late afternoon after a long, demanding day climbing a mountain is a classic accident-prone situation. The summit has been reached. The body is fatigued. Attention relaxes. Gravity adds speed to the descent. A loose rock underfoot. A stumble. And the result is a sprained limb. The more adventuresome activities are highly regulated and therefore relatively safe.

The Outward Bound attitude toward safety and risk is nicely summarized on the opening page of the *North Carolina Outward Bound School Safety Policy*, which regulates all program activities:

> In Outward Bound it may be said that students are encouraged to take part in activities in which the risk of an accident may be greater than in their normal way of life. In consequence, there rests on those in charge of the training a special responsibility to ensure that adequate and continuous precautions are taken to prevent accidents. This responsibility, however, goes further than a merely negative approach based on restricting activities within safe limits. The principle is not to avoid activities involving danger, but to prepare participants by technical training and physical fitness to deal with the risk competently. The aim is to teach that the more adventurous an undertaking, the more care and prudence are needed to succeed.

Climbing the Chimneys has been adventurous for the group, but it has been only preparation for the big event. During the past two days, as we hiked toward the Outward Bound School and then camped and climbed in its vicinity, Table Rock was the beacon that beckoned to us. Tomorrow we will attempt to climb it.

Morning finds us hiking up steep wooded hillsides toward Table Rock's base. As we draw closer, its gray hulk causes us to crane our necks as our eyes search for routes to its summit. Its precipitous walls seem smooth and impregnable. The height from the base to the top is some six hundred feet. It rears up to a sharp summit, the Matterhorn of North Carolina.

There is an air of anticipation in the group. Art is bubbly as usual. Jim Finucayne seems nervous but not unduly so. Herman typically is noncommittal. Ellen's face is expressionless, but her eyes grow a little larger each time she looks up at the rock. It is early, nine-thirty, but the air is humid and already warm. We sweat as we struggle through the thick trees.

At the foot of the rock our perspective alters. We are too close now to be able to see the summit. We are confronted by two hundred feet of vertical gray rock before the walls lean back out of sight. There are grassy ledges here and there, and cracks and fissures promise opportunities for upward progress.

We divide into groups. Jay and Art are to climb with another instructor, a rock-climbing specialist from the Outward Bound School who has joined us for the day to supplement Drew and Emily. Ellen and Curly will climb with Drew; Jim Finucayne and Herman, with Emily.

Today we will not top-rope the climb. The instructors will lead up first, reach a ledge, anchor, and belay each of us up in turn. In approximately hundred-foot sections we will work our way to the top.

Lead climbing is serious business. Drew gives instructions to Ellen and Curly.

"Basically it's the same principle as yesterday. Tie onto the ends of the rope with a bowline."

Ellen and Curly obey, and Drew checks the knots.

"OK," he says, "I'm gonna lead up the first pitch." He instructs Curly to take the rope around his waist, exactly as in belaying practice yesterday. Curly does so, and Drew commences climbing. He moves smoothly upward on holds so small we can barely see them. A mistake now and he would fall twenty feet to cream himself on rocky ground.

"Watch exactly where I go," he calls down, pausing in balance for a moment. "Make sure you go exactly the same way."

We remember Herman's predicament yesterday and study Drew's every move.

Five feet higher he draws level with an expansion bolt, a metal spike with a ring in the end that has previously been fitted into a hole drilled in the rock.

Drew unclips a carabiner from a collection of these devices that hangs from a webbing sling looped diagonally over his shoulder. The carabiner is an essential rock-climbing tool. It is a D-shaped ring of aluminum, measuring about three inches by two inches. It has a hinged gate and resembles a snap link. Drew deftly clips it into the expansion bolt. He reaches down, grasps the climbing rope, and clips it into the carabiner. Now the climbing rope runs from around Curly's waist through the carabiner to Drew's waist. Should Drew fall, Curly will take his weight on the rope and Drew's fall will be arrested before he falls very far, before he hits the ground. Using this safety measure, a fair degree of protection is afforded the rock-climbing leader. Drew will anchor his rope through other carabiners as he moves higher. He moves up.

Forty feet higher Drew reaches a ledge, after traversing some twenty feet horizontally to the right. We see him anchoring to the ledge.

"On belay!" he calls.

"Oh, oh," groans Curly. "My turn." He checks his bowline, making sure it is still snug, kicks his boots against the rock to dislodge mud, looks up at Drew sixty feet above, and replies, "Climbing!"

"Climb!"

With a final check of the chin strap on his hard hat, Curly steps up. He reaches the carabiner, unclips the rope, and moves on. He is wasting no time. At the start of the traverse he pauses. The rope stretching between him and

Drew now runs at an angle off to the right. If he falls, he will swing—pendulum, as the climbers say.

"Watch me, Drew," he calls, and begins to move right.

"Falling!" His cry shatters the silence. Ellen watches transfixed; she is next. Gracefully, after the initial surge of panic, Curly swings some fifteen feet to the right, suspended on the rope. Drew's belay is firm, and within seconds Curly is climbing again. He powers his way up to Drew's ledge, climbing rapidly. We see him slump onto the ledge, and we empathize with his misfortune. But he is not traumatized. He is soon in control of the situation, anchored, and ready to belay Ellen up.

"On belay, Ellen," he calls down.

Ellen putters momentarily, making a little to-do about adjusting her rope and checking her hard hat. But the awful moment cannot be put off.

"Climbing!" she calls eventually, a note of grim determination in her voice.

"Climb," comes down the response.

The first few moves give her trouble. She is not climbing well, clutching too tight with her hands. With difficulty she reaches the beginning of the traverse. She looks shaky, makes a tremulous start on the traverse, and without warning, quietly falls off. Curly, perhaps belaying not quite so adroitly as Drew, perhaps taken unawares, has some slack in the rope. Ellen pendulums farther than Curly did when he fell and thuds into a rocky projection.

We hear her whimpering to herself.

Drew peers over the edge.

"Ellen. Ellen. Are you all right?"

Ellen is no defeatist. She gathers her composure. Her voice is strong.

"Up rope," she yells. "Climbing. I am back on traverse. I am taking off my jacket. Ready?"

And she does! She takes off her jacket while somehow balancing on a couple of small footholds! Literally and figuratively she rolls up her sleeves. I can imagine her gritting her teeth, clenching her jaw in determination. She climbs aggressively and moments later joins Drew and Curly.

"Mucho lady," remarks Herman to Art admiringly. They have been observing the events from a ledge on their climb next door.

After this the rest of the climbing passes uneventfully. The three ropes move higher and higher. The height is both unnerving and exhilarating, a seductive combination. "Climbing is hour after hour of sheer terror interspersed by moments of boredom—the waits on the belay ledges," comments Art later, exaggerating his fears for the amusement of the group.

The day is a success. Everyone reaches the top. The basic skills learned on the training climbs have been put to use in a realistic and challenging situation. I suspect that Sir Edmund Hillary's feeling of satisfaction on reaching the top of Everest could not have exceeded the triumphant feelings expressed by our group. Victory is relative to one's experience, ability, and the challenge faced.

Next morning we run a traditional Outward Bound marathon, some nine miles through the trees.

5. Navigating aboard the *Dawn Treader*.

6. Hurricane Island.

7. Hurricane Island.

8. Solo at Hurricane Island.

As we moved about the Outward Bound School grounds during the past few days, we had noticed a collection of ropes, ladders, cables, and nets stretched between branches high in a grove of trees. Early morning of the next day finds us standing beneath this assemblage, wondering what is to happen. It is the Outward Bound School ropes course. The first structure to attract our attention is a broad cargo net made of thick hemp rope, stretched horizontally fifteen feet above the ground. Above it a network of rope ladders and cable bridges crisscross.

"Before we get into the ropes course," commands Drew, "move over to the practice area."

We obediently follow him to two trees, between which is stretched a horizontal rope six feet from the ground. We have each been issued with hard hat, two carabiners, and a twelve-foot length of climbing rope. Drew shows us how to tie into the middle of the rope. A carabiner is tied into each of the protruding ends—"lobster claws" Drew calls them.

He reaches up and clips one of his carabiners into the horizontal rope. "This is your safety on the ropes course," he says. He walks along between the trees, and the carabiner slides along the rope above him. He slumps, and the rope takes his weight before his upper body hits the ground. "Each activity on the ropes course is protected by a safety rope," says Drew.

"Why do we have two carabiners?" asks Curly.

"So you can reach over and clip into the safety rope on the next activity before unclipping from the one you are on," replies Drew.

We each practice clipping in and out.

Drew then heads us over to a spot beneath the cargo net. A tube of netting dangles from it. Grunting, Drew reaches up and wiggles his way into the tube, which is just a little more than shoulder width in diameter. He claws his way up and emerges, puffing, on the flat bed of the net. From there he works his way around the different activities of the ropes course, demonstrating each one. We notice that the progression takes him higher and higher above the ground. The activities are arranged to provide challenges in balance and dexterity— and presumably nerve on the high ones. One is called the Birth Canal. It is a tube of tightly woven hemp netting, some forty feet long, suspended between two branches. It hangs in a curve. Drew squirms into it headfirst. It is also shoulder width. He lets go and, with an audible whoosh, slides down and through it like a torpedo through its tube. He pulls himself up and out of the exit end, grinning. Clearly it is an exhilarating sensation.

One at a time we climb up the net tunnel onto the cargo net and make our way around. Art is doing well. He has everything under control and is enjoying the different situations. He reaches a simple-looking problem, a log, twelve inches in diameter, some thirty feet long, lashed horizontally between the tops of two high trees. Art clips a carabiner into the safety rope that runs across the log above his head. The object is simply to walk across the log.

Art takes a probing step forward and steps back. He pauses, trying to decide

The cargo net, first obstacle on the ropes course.

whether to place his feet obliquely, like a ballet dancer, toes pointing out, or just walk across one foot in front of the other.

His journal reveals his thoughts at this moment: "It seemed a hundred variables crossed my mind . . . oh, what the hell. I had done this sort of thing seventeen years ago in the Army."

As he looks at the log, a puzzled expression creeps over his face.

"I had been apprehensive about some of the recent activities, but never really paralyzed, never so tense that I couldn't move."

Art is motionless, holding onto the tree branch.

"I started to think, and I guess that was my downfall."

He takes two or three tentative steps, turns, and grabs back for the tree. He holds on again and glances around.

"I glanced around. No one had really noticed that I had come back. If they had noticed, perhaps they thought I wanted to retie my sneakers or take a speck from my eye. I really don't think anyone realized that I was unbelievably afraid."

Again Art clutches the tree, surveying his nemesis. His journal continues: "I couldn't believe it myself. In the Army one is trained to show no fear, no weakness. If an officer shows no fear, then he is a tower of strength who others can rely on. . . . Once I visited my father, who was dying in the hospital. The reality of it hit me. I loved that man. He was my father, and he was dying. I immediately started to cry. My grandmother was next to me. She grabbed my arm and squeezed it very hard. 'Stop that. You are a man.' All of our lives we are taught to be men, not to show our weaknesses."

Screwing his courage to the sticking place, Art steps out again onto the log and again retreats. Now everyone is aware of his plight. The others have stopped, and eight pairs of eyes watch.

He puts his hand to his head and says to himself, "I don't believe this."

"Does one lose one's nerve at thirty-nine? I have never been afraid of a challenge. I know that I am on a safety line. It's not that I can't do it. . . . I know I will."

Drew also has been observing the situation.

"It's OK, Art," he calls up, "fear makes us humble. This is good for you."

Art calls down to Curly, who is next in line, "Sorry to hold you up."

"That's OK," says Curly. "We all need the break."

Art composes himself. He looks straight ahead, a glassy expression on his face. He tentatively extends one foot forward, and another, and another. Carefully he moves across the log, stiffly, and reaches the other side. A cheer wells up from the watching group. The tension breaks. Everyone continues.

Jim Finucayne is ahead of Art. He slips headfirst into the Birth Canal, whooshes through, and emerges on a thick branch some fifty feet above the ground, where Drew patiently waits. Drew has not demonstrated the next and final activity of the course.

Jim looks around. There are no obvious bridges, nets, or cables leading from

Art crossing the log after twenty minutes of hesitation.

Climbing the rope tunnel on the ropes course.

the branch. There is a small wooden seat bolted to the branch, some six feet out from the main trunk.

"What now, Drew?" Jim asks. "How do we get down?"

Drew has an evil gleam in his eye.

Jim notices that the seat is equipped with a car safety belt and buckle.

"OK," commands Drew. "Stay clipped in, and move out and sit down in the seat."

Looking concerned, Jim balances out and does as directed.

Drew reaches out and fastens the safety belt. Jim is now strapped snuggly into the seat. He looks down between his legs; the ground is sixty feet below.

"Come on, Drew," he says. "Don't be so secretive. What happens next?"

Drew is enjoying himself. He reaches down and pulls up a piece of string that dangles below the branch. He pulls it up hand over hand. It is affixed to the end of long wire cable. Drew continues pulling, and the end of the wire cable reaches him. It now stretches out horizontally from Drew's and Jim's position on the branch to a point some fifty feet horizontally in front of them. There, at its other end, a second cable is stretched tightly between two trees. The other end of the cable that Drew is holding is attached to the middle of the second cable by a steel eyebolt.

There are two loops of rope fixed to the end of the cable that Drew is holding. Drew passes it over to Jim. "Put one hand through each of the loops," he says. "Let the loop run round the back of your hand, across your wrist, and grasp it firmly."

By now Jim is worried. The uncertainty is raising his anxiety level. He is not quite sure what is happening, but dark suspicions are bubbling to the surface.

At this point Art's grinning face emerges at the exit from the Birth Canal. He remains there, his head and shoulders protruding, watching Jim.

In addition to the two hand loops a foot loop hangs from the end of the cable. Drew directs Jim's foot into it and clips him into a safety carabiner.

Jim is twitching. He resembles a nervous hamster, anxiously following Drew's every move, anticipating sudden and violent death.

It is now patently clear what is happening. The wire cable is a swing! One end is fixed to the cross cable fifty feet away, and Jim, sixty feet above the ground, is tied into the other end. Art watches popeyed. The awful truth has now dawned on Jim. His eyes are bulging, and he is glancing around wildly, looking for an out. There isn't one.

Drew reaches over and unclips the safety belt.

"OK, Jim," he says in a calculatingly cool voice. "Go when you're ready."

"Go when I'm ready!" screeches Jim. "You've got to be joking."

It is clear to anyone with an elementary knowledge of physics that the first fifteen or so feet after sliding off the seat are going to be a free fall, a downward plummet riding gravity until the cable takes the weight. Jim is an engineer; he has no difficulty visualizing the trajectory of his fall.

"It's safe as falling off a log," encourages Drew.

Jim Finucayne at the takeoff point of the Breathtaker.

Jim does not respond to this attempt at humor. Jim is now pale. His voice is a full squeaky octave above normal. This has to be a joke.

Drew proudly states that he helped design this barbaric instrument. If he had lived four hundred years earlier, he would have made a good living torturing innocents in the dungeons of some medieval castle.

Jim is oblivious to Drew's banter. What a way to end the course! He seems to be in a state of shock. After much urging, Jim, with infinite slowness, begins to squirm his buttocks forward, moving himself to the very edge of the seat. The glade is still. Jim's breath is coming out in rasps, the only sound.

"Go, Jim," urges Drew.

The moment of takeoff.

With a pathetic moan Jim parts company with the seat, drops like a stone for a few feet, and swings through the air in a graceful curve. The swing describes massive arcs back and forth, diminishing in its travel with each pendulum. Eventually the energy is spent, and Jim comes to rest. Emily is waiting and helps him down from the cable. He shuffles over to a tree root and slumps down, sitting, shoulders drooped forward, head resting in his hands.

Drew looks across at Art. "We call it the Breathtaker," he announces with delight.

"I believe you," grimaces Art.

As the day progresses, each person moves around the course, arrives at the seat, and experiences the Breathtaker. Jim's is the most dramatic reaction. Everyone else is appropriately nervous, but perhaps seeing someone else go first has broken a psychological barrier.

Everyone else but one. Herman has steadfastly remained on the ground and refuses to set foot on the ropes course. He says, "It's as challenging for me not to do it as it is to do it." He resolutely resists our efforts at group pressure and pays little attention to Drew's and Emily's encouragement. His attitude is such that the group respects his position.

With the ropes course Outward Bound is almost over. The afternoon is spent cleaning and handing in equipment and receiving our personal gear back. A celebration dinner follows that evening, with dancing to a local bluegrass band.

The last morning finds us grouped together in a room in the lodge, winding up with a final summary discussion of the experience. Art sets the ball rolling.

"In a way I learned *less* confidence in myself," he says. "The horizontal log told me that I have lost some of the devil-may-care confidence that I had in my younger years."

Art's tone of voice as he says this indicates that he is not unhappy about this turn of events. I think back to the first day and my impression of his macho streak. It seems that his experience at Outward Bound, highlighted by the moments on the log, rather than pumping him up with false confidence, has succeeded in giving him a realistic insight into himself and his capabilities. For my money it is far more valuable for him to learn that it is acceptable to show weakness than to boost his sense of physical prowess. It is significant to realize that in this day and age a person like Art, thirty-nine years of age, has gone through life fighting this male stereotype. Such are the pressures and ingrained habits that guide male behavior. Art seems content with his new picture of himself, reassured by the acceptance of the group.

Jim comments on his experience with the Breathtaker.

"It might have been different if someone had gone first, if Drew had demonstrated. I could write the equation in simple harmonic motion, but the thought of doing it—"

"But life's like that," says Curly. He is sprawled back against cushions, his feet propped up. "You never know what's around the corner."

"I'm kind of a closed person," says Jim. "I don't make contacts easily. I've really appreciated this aspect of the experience, getting close to you"—he looks round at the whole group, his eyes blinking behind his glasses—"feeling your support."

Art gives him a little slap on the shoulder.

"But I'm sure that when I get back home, all of this will fade, and I'll just be the same way I always was."

"It's kind of like the end of a honeymoon," says Art. "It's been a great, unique experience, but a once-in-a-lifetime thing. I feel that I *have* been affected. I don't see my life altering drastically when I get back, but I do feel strengthened and refreshed, and I definitely have learned some things about myself that I wasn't aware of before."

Jay says, "For me the main challenges were climbing Table Rock and then the ropes course. They were individual challenges—it was just me—but I needed the confidence that I had developed in the group."

"I feel bad about Table Rock." Dressed in her street clothes, white blouse, and tied-back kerchief, Ellen looks primly different from the often grubby-looking lady who has toiled the Carolina hillsides for the past ten days. "I feel as though it conquered me."

"No," responds Drew, "it was your finest hour. There was panic in your voice when you fell off, and then you got it together. You sailed up and kept in control."

"It gave the rest of us tremendous strength just seeing you," says Art.

"I doubt that I could have come back like that," says Jay. His earnest face takes on a solemn expression as he examines this possibility.

Herman speaks next. "I feel good about exercising my choice at the ropes course. It wasn't that I was scared; it was like a voice inside me objected to being pressured into doing everything. It was time to take a stand, time for me to say, 'This is me, and this is who I am, and I'm just not gonna do it, and group pressure can go to hell.' "

"You stood up for what you felt was right," affirms Drew. "That's the most important thing."

Yesterday each member of the group had received an Outward Bound pin, signifying completion of the course. Herman had refused it. "Nope," he had said. "I didn't do the ropes course." This statement emphasized his convictions, impressed us that indeed he had not avoided the ropes course for lack of nerve. For the group it was a disconcerting situation. Herman was distinctive as the only black member of the group, and his occupation as a factory worker contrasted with the professional activities of most of the others. But it was Herman who had rocked the boat on an issue of principle.

"I've never seen anyone refuse a pin before," says Drew.

There follow some moments of silence. Nine diverse people have been together through ten days of challenge and intimacy. The time is coming to separate.

Someone contrasts Herman's personal behavior on the course, his cheerful willingness, his volunteering to carry a heavier pack and being first to dig in with chores, and his pre-solo statements about life as a rat race.

"But now we have to get back to the jungle," he says. "We have to put our armor on, or we'll just get knocked down."

As the group prepares to depart, Emily concludes the meeting with a reading, a quotation from an earlier Outward Bound participant.

> I have learned the depths of strength and trust that are present in me and my fellow man. I shall try to remember that any of my neighbors or fellow workers could have belayed the climbing rope for me or given me his hand when I was slipping off a steep slope. I may forget, but I will try to remember.

Finishing the reading, Emily looks directly at Herman. Herman looks back, grins, and responds with a wink, a broad, obvious, telltale wink.

Chapter Three

THE HURRICANE ISLAND
OUTWARD BOUND SCHOOL

"Smith College—A Century of Women on Top." The woman standing next to the mainmast displays this feisty message in white letters on a red sweat shirt. Anne Peyton is our instructor for a ten-day Hurricane Island Outward Bound Course, and she bristles with competence. Her eyes are attentive to each movement of our novice crew. We are on board a thirty-foot open boat, in a harbor, and Rockland, Maine, is receding into the distance. Anne is a slimly built woman of twenty-five. Deceptively dainty, her appearance contrasts to the solidity of the boat she captains. There is a sense about her, beneath the external calm, that she can open up and curse at the top of her lungs. Polished manners, gutsy manner. Her voice at times (though given the Smith College proclamation, she may object to this comparison) is a low, *manly* growl. When she laughs, it comes up from the belly, a cross between a guffaw and a cough. She laughs a lot. She is very *here*, on this boat, very present. She moves about, legs spaced, feet set stably on the rolling woodworks, observing our efforts, making suggestions, telling us what to do.

"Oars," she commands.

Obediently we complete the stroke, stop rowing, and hold the oars poised, parallel to the ocean. They drip salt water as we wait.

"Toss oars."

Each member of the crew tosses a thirteen-foot oar—that is, pivots it upward—in rapid succession, starting aft, until all eight stand vertical, now dripping ocean residue.

"Boat oars."

Starting forward (*forward* is the nautical term for the front end of the boat), each crew member lowers the oar and stowes it, laying it along the center of the boat.

Three times longer than it is wide (thirty feet by ten feet), the Hurricane Island pulling boat makes its way under sail or by oar. It is a ponderous craft, solidly built. Six feet back from the bow stands the mainmast. Ten inches in diameter, twelve feet tall, the mainmast is a veritable tree trunk, the fulcrum

Anne Peyton, Outward Bound instructor.

of forward propulsion. The leading edge of the mainsail has a succession of runners sewn into it that slide up the mast in a metal groove. A rope running through a pulley at the top of the mast is used to haul the mainsail up, the runners sliding snugly in the groove. The lower edge of the mainsail is weighted down and kept straight and snug by a horizontal timber, the boom, attached to the base of the mainmast in a pivoting joint. The sail is somewhat, though not perfectly, square in shape. With the leading and lower edges held firm by the mainmast and boom, the top rear corner of the sail is unsecured, and the sail flaps loosely, ineffectually. To brace the sail and form it into the configuration to catch the wind, a third timber is hoisted. This tapering round length of wood, some twelve feet long, is called the main sprit, and hoisting it is one of the more challenging maneuvers on the boat. Two people working efficiently together can manage, but sometimes it takes three—two to hoist the sprit and one to lash it in place. The main sprit is positioned diagonally across the mainsail, its lower end lashed to the lower section of the mainmast and its other end extending up high, supporting the rear high corner of the sail. Held by the framework of these three timbers, the mainsail is ready to catch the wind.

A second mast, the mizzenmast, stands centrally in the stern of the boat, smaller, but rigged identically to the mainmast. The mainmast propels the boat; the mizzenmast provides additional propulsion and some steerage.

"Unship oarlocks," commands Anne. The final stage of ceasing to row is for each member of the crew to lift the metal bracket that supports the oar out of its hole and lay it flat on the gunwale boards. Left in position, the oarlocks are snags for ropes and potential traps for the crew as we move about the boat.

We have not rowed very far, perhaps a little more than half a mile, but the oars are heavy. The rowing motion throws unaccustomed strain on the lower back muscles. We stretch and relax. Anne has tied the bow of the boat to a mooring buoy.

"Phew," exhales the woman seated in front of me. "That really does it to you." She turns and gives me a grin. "How you doing?"

I look down at my hands, turn them palms up so she can see the red. "Much more of this and I'm going to have a blister."

"Me, too. My hands are soft. We're just gonna have to toughen up, get used to it." She smiles wryly.

She is very small—I'd guess only about five feet two inches tall—a little plump, and has oriental features and an infectious grin.

"I'm Suejee Quon." Again the big grin. I introduce myself and learn that Suejee is from Canada, where she teaches French to adults in Quebec.

Suejee is twenty-six. She tells me that her job is with the government. She works with small groups; she usually has no more than ten students for only three hours each day. The rest of the day she is expected to prepare the next day's lesson. "I can't think of a better job for me," she says. "I enjoy the freedom and have many liberties to explore my own curiosities."

She is not sure why she has come to Outward Bound. For a long time she

has had a peripheral interest in the sea and in sailing. Her initial expectations of Outward Bound are wrapped up in a picture of it as a sailing school. She has not bothered to find out very much about Outward Bound. There is a note of concern in her voice as she tells me this. It is as though she is picking up some clues, perhaps from remarks dropped by others in the group, perhaps from the unceremonious way we have been dumped in the boat and pointed out to the ocean, that this is not quite the sailing school she expected.

Suejee's husband Pierre is also here, though in another group. It turns out that Pierre had more detailed knowledge and a stronger interest in the challenge of Outward Bound than Suejee. In a sense Suejee has come along for the ride. "My presence here I think of as being drifted in with his tide," she says.

Suejee is in for an awakening.

Anne asks for a show of hands. Who has sailed before? About half the group raise their hands. Anne asks more questions, assessing experience, gauging proficiency.

"Any volunteers for helms*person?*" she asks.

The way she says "helmsperson" sends a ripple of interest through the group. The word is pronounced without particular emphasis. But it is the without particular emphasis that makes it noticeable. Anne tries to pretend that she has said nothing out of the ordinary and seems not to notice the meaningful glances exchanged by some of the males in the group. Assuming that the suffix *-person* is neutral is akin to thinking that bulls do not notice red rags. Even without the "Women on Top" sweat shirt, Anne has just made a strong statement. If the male members of the group have been at all unsure about where she stands, now they know.

But this is not the time for a discussion of sex roles. A broad-shouldered, well-built male with a moustache and a halo of curly hair is appointed helms*person*. He accepts his title graciously, though there is a mildly perplexed expression in his eyes. It is clear that he is not accustomed to the casual designation of a nontraditional, unstereotypic, pointedly nonsexist title for a characteristically male-defined role. He is obviously thinking to himself, "Helms*person?*"

Another member of the group is appointed to assist our newly designated controller of the helm *person*handle the bulky tiller over the side and into its sockets.

Anne assigns three people the task of raising the mainsail. Three others are given responsibility for the mizzen. No trial and error here. Anne directs crisply. Unaccustomed fingers stumble clumsily with lines and knots, spars and sails. Running the sail up the mast is straightforward, simply a matter of hauling on the line that runs through the pulley at the top of the mast and then tying it off to a cleat. It is the sprit that causes problems. Its tapering tip must be attached to the rear top corner of the sail. The trick is to hoist it high and then lash its base securely to cleats on the mast without allowing it to slip. If the sprit is not hoisted high and tight, the sail will sag and be inefficient. Two members of the crew hoist with all their might. The third member of the team ties the support line securely to the base of the mast. Strenuous but effective.

The sails are up; both the main sprit and the mizzen sprit are in place. The boat lies bow into the wind, sails flapping loosely. Anne appoints two others to attend to the two mainsheets, the ropes tied to the end of the boom that control the mainsail. They will take in and let out the sheets to control the angle of the sail relative to the boat and the wind. Another crew member is appointed to control the mizzen sheet in the stern. This rope runs through a pulley system and governs the angle of the mizzen sail.

Suejee is appointed bow watch. Her job is to stand in the bow, before the mast, and look for obstacles—buoys, lobster pots, and other floating impedimentia to the boat's progress. If it is foggy, she will also have the fun of blowing on a little trumpetlike foghorn to announce our presence.

Helmsperson, bow watch, controller of the mizzen sheet, two controllers of the mainsheets, and a navigator (which position Anne assumes for now)—a crew of six is needed to fill the essential positions while under sail. The positions will be rotated. Meanwhile the remaining members of the crew can take it easy, sprawled on the plank seats, until their turn comes.

The boat is swaying, lolling easily on its mooring.

A breeze is blowing in from the ocean toward the mainland. Straight into our faces.

Rockland harbor is a perfect three-sided bay. Land surrounds us to the north, to the west, and to the south. To the east is the straight line of the ocean horizon. It is easy to believe that water stretches infinitely beyond that line. Other boats pass by as we sit at mooring. They are all engine-powered, mainly small, half-open cabin cruisers with low sides, lobstermen tending their pots. They do not have the spotless trim of tourist craft; they look worn, and their paint is peeling. Working boats. We are the only sailboat to be seen.

"Hey, Anne." It is the helmsperson. I later learn that his name is Bill Dennett. He is twenty-nine and the residence director at the New England Conservatory of Music.

"Does the boat have a name?"

Anne has been rummaging in one of the stowage lockers. She pauses.

"Well," she says, "not an official name, but there is a name that I kind of like."

Bill waits.

"It's after a book I read recently. I think of her as the *Dawn Treader.*"

Bill's face crinkles. It is obvious what he is thinking, but he does not comment on Anne's use of "her" in describing the boat. I suspect the piece of data is being stored for future use.

Anne does not notice his expression. She looks around the boat, checking out the name with the rest of the crew. No one objects, and there are some smiles of approval.

Bill grins. "*Dawn Treader*. Sounds good to me."

Dawn Treader it is.

So, like C. S. Lewis's fantasy craft, we prepare to launch ourselves on our voyage.

There are thirteen in our group: myself, Anne, and eleven others. Suejee is positioned in the bow. On the portside (the left side of the boat when one is facing the bow) managing the mainsheet is a slim young woman of twenty-two: Anne Warner, from New York, the assistant advertising manager for a precious metal company. Opposite her, taking care of the mainsheet on the starboard side is a chubby, round-faced fellow with a mischievous air. Curt Viebranz is twenty-three, works in a bank in Boston. It says "Bozo" on his life jacket. The merry prankster of our group. Speciality: bad, bad, groan-inducing jokes and puns.

Sitting next to Bill Dennett in the stern, controlling the mizzen sheet, is Rohit Desai, thirty-seven, a banker, now working in New York, but originally from Bombay, India.

The other six members of the group are seated or sprawled about the boat waiting for something to happen. Maureen Doran is thirty-three, a nurse involved in burn research in Massachusetts. Susan Heacock is twenty-three, a student from the University of Hawaii. These two are sitting next to each other, amidships, chatting.

Tom Langehop is slumped back, lying on the oars, his eyes half closed. He is burly, thickset, with a droopy moustache. He has told us that he has already done an Outward Bound course in Minnesota. He is twenty-three, a schoolteacher from Indiana.

Next to Tom sits a quiet woman with sandy-colored hair. She is a teacher at Gould Academy, a noted East Coast prep school. Bonnie Pooley is thirty-one, and we later learn that she has been married for fifteen years.

Behind her sits Jim Thomas. He has said very little, and that hesitantly, almost in a whisper. He does not look confident. He is twenty-eight, an insurance underwriter from Connecticut.

The last member of our group is a somewhat Slavic-looking man of thirty-one. He has a black Fu Manchu moustache and tells us that he has just finished medical school. His name is Patrick (Pat) Dennis, and he sits staring listlessly at the horizon that awaits him.

Thirteen in our group. Seven males, six females. Age range twenty-two to thirty-seven. Average age 27.3 (so reads the Hurricane Island enrollment list for the group). Bound for the sea.

At Anne's instruction Bill pushes the tiller to starboard. Simultaneously Tom and Susan push on the boom, swinging it out, also over the starboard side of the boat, to catch the wind. Suejee looses the mooring. We are under sail. Bill glances around. The mooring buoy slips by. He looks concerned. Anne directs Curt to take a wrap of the mainsheet around a starboard cleat.

"Just a single wrap," she warns. "And keep your attention on it. Never *tie* the sheet to the cleat with knots. If anything goes wrong, you have to be able to release the mainsheet immediately."

Curt absorbs this safety precaution somberly. He understands the situation: If the mainsail is tied in place, a sudden increase in wind velocity could tilt the boat dangerously, possibly overturning it in an extreme situation. But if

the sheet is maintained snug around the cleat with a single wrap, the sail is held firmly in place but can be rapidly released in an emergency.

Curt performs a deft wrap around the cleat.

"Great," acknowledges Anne. "Keep it snug, but loosen it fast if I tell you."

We are heading out to sea, toward the horizon. But the wind is blowing toward us, from the horizon. Therefore the boat has to tack (cut the wind at an angle) zigzagging back and forth. Anne had given a brief overview of the boat's operation under sail before casting off from the mooring. Those with some experience are at the controls. The rest of us watch. Coming about requires coordination. The trick is to get the boat moving fast, push the tiller across, and release the sails so that the boat turns across the wind, allowing it to get in behind the sails for the next tack.

"Coming about!"

Bill pushes the tiller to starboard. The bow begins to turn, nosing into the wind. The mainsail slacks. Curt releases the mainsheet. Rohit releases the mizzen sheet and moves across to the starboard side. But the operation has not been fast enough. We have lost way. The *Dawn Treader* sits, bow into the wind, sails flapping idly.

"Tom, Susan," calls Anne, "back up the mainsail."

They push the boom hard, manually maneuvering the sail to port. The wind pushes in behind it. Bill feels pressure on the tiller. The mizzen sail fills, too.

Anne takes a wrap of the mainsheet on her side, Rohit adjusts the mizzen, and we are away on a port tack.

The bay is a spacious stretch of water. For half an hour the *Dawn Treader* tacks back and forth. Efficient co-ordination is needed to make best use of each change in direction. The more skillfully the boat is trimmed under way, the more real distance we make against the wind. The sails have to be set at the precise angle, pulled in tight. The crew need to place themselves carefully so that their weight helps tilt the boat advantageously. The helmsperson needs to align the boat precisely to the wind for best advantage. Tied to one of the wires that support the mainmast is a tattered ribbon of cloth about a foot long. Bill keeps his eye on it, for it tells him the direction of the wind. He must keep the boat as tight into the wind as possible. At the correct angle the sails will be taut and full. If he oversteers, the sails will pinch; the wind will get in behind the sails, flapping them and causing the boat to lose forward momentum.

Figuring this boat takes a very active group think. Even when you are just lying on the planks doing nothing, you are doing something. Any moment some-one may holler for you to move to redistribute the weight. Everybody functions all the time. Even when they're *doing* nothing. Trim is the key word. Keep the boat trimmed. Co-operation will take us where we are going, though we don't know where that is. We are so busy sailing the boat, getting the sails right, tightening the sheets, eyeing the wind that destination seems irrelevant. The wind is an axis along which we weave. Perhaps we are heading for the home of the wind, beyond the horizon. No one thinks about it. We are too busy making the boat work.

The boom is a scythe. When we nose the boat into the wind to change direction, the boom comes whooshing over, intent on decapitation. If you are sitting on the plank seats and the boom comes whistling by at shoulder height, you have to duck down low for it to miss you. The helmsperson shouts "Coming about" just before he throws the tiller across. This is the signal for those with specific functions to perform their task and for the rest to duck.

It is two in the afternoon. We are no longer surrounded on three sides by land. *Dawn Treader* has moved out of Rockland harbor. To our right, to the south, we are paralleling coastline, a mile or so out from land. The wind is stronger. Dark gray waves slap the boat as they crest by. The land to our right is Owls Head, Anne says. It is a promontory, a headland. On an instruction from Anne the boat's bow pushes into the wind. We temporarily heave to. The sails sag. Anne tells Bill to keep his hand on the tiller and to keep us nose into the wind, and she gathers the crew around the chart on her knee.

Owls Head is the southeast extremity of Rockland harbor. A little east of it is an island. Anne points to it on the chart: Monroe Island. "We have to sail the channel between Monroe and the mainland," she says. "This means rounding Owls Head, keeping Monroe to port."

"Where we gonna spend the night?" inquires Curt. "And where's Hurricane?"

Curt gives comic emphasis to virtually everything he says. Even when there is nothing particularly funny about his remarks, his round, grinning face suggests that a giggle lies just below the surface. He is *very* outgoing.

"We just gonna keep swimming round with the fishes?" he continues, baiting Anne just a little.

Anne smiles. She points to the chart. The narrow stretch of water between Monroe Island and Owls Head is marked "Owls Head Bay." It is more a channel than a bay. To the south of Monroe Island is another small piece of land, Sheep Island. "We need to sail south through Owls Head Bay," she tells us, "and swing round the southern tip of Monroe Island to this little bay." She points. "Monroe shelters us to the north and east, and Sheep Island provides some measure of protection from any winds from the south."

"Hey," responds Curt, "waddya know, a night on an island."

We get under way again. Anne has told us the sailing will be trickier in the channel. The wind will no longer be constant; buffeted by the islands, it will change direction. We need to be alert.

Curt resumes his position looking after the starboard mainsheet. I move beside him. He is wearing a lightweight, gabardine, porkpie hat, the kind that a weekend golfer might wear. It looks a little out of place.

"Big water out there," he states, gesturing with his thumb at the horizon. I expect him to wink, but he doesn't. He's like that.

I ask him about his sailing experience.

He becomes more serious.

"Not much, really. A couple of afternoons in a dingy on a lake. This stuff makes me nervous." He looks out at the ocean. "It's the immensity." A pause. "I want to get to know more about it."

I ask him the inevitable question: Why Outward Bound?

He ponders for a moment.

"A challenge." His eyes twinkle. "Look at me"—he pats his belly proudly with the flat of his hand—"city living. I'm not in bad shape, could do to lose fifteen pounds, but I'm soft."

Soft. Outward Bound—an antidote for softness? "Toughness for toughness' sake?" I inquire. "Is that what you are looking for?"

"Well nope, not toughness in the military sense. Resilience. Resilience and determination. Knowing what you wanna do and doing it."

"I don't quite understand what you mean about 'not toughness in the military sense.'"

"Look, I don't know a lot about Outward Bound. Just what I've read and heard. My sister went through the Minnesota school. This girl I used to go with went to Minnesota, too. From what I've heard, it seems to me that there is a mixture of physical conditioning and emotional sensitivity, caring about other people, wanting the best for you and the best for them, too."

Curt looks uncomfortable as he says this, as though he hadn't really meant to say it, as though it just came out, as though a little bit of self he normally kept hidden had peeped from behind the clowning facade.

"You know what I mean?"

I think I do know what he means. Outward Bound has long struggled with a hair shirt stereotype. In 1963 and 1964, in the early days of Outward Bound in America just after its importation from Great Britain, the program—somewhat justifiably—had a marine bootcamp image. Come to Outward Bound; become a rugged man. But it wasn't only Outward Bound that was saying this; it was one of society's expectations. In the mid-sixties even women who functioned effectively in the big world tended to be regarded as rugged men. Performance, function, capability—heroic *male* characteristics. Schools, with their emphasis on competitive team sports, and the great American popcorn-munching, cheering-for-blood, spectator sport industry had led many down the path of physical idolatry. To strive toward perfect physical condition necessarily implied a reciprocal shriveling of both intellectual and emotional capability. "*Cogito, ergo* jock."

"I'm expecting to be sore, tired, and hungry," Curt continues. "I mean, that's all part of it. But from what I've heard about Outward Bound, it's more than just a physical challenge."

The opening page of the Hurricane Island instructor's handbook is entitled "Philosophy and Process." "Outward Bound is an educational process through which an individual gains self-confidence and increased empathy for others," it states.

I ask Curt if empathy is what he means.

"Empathy?" He shrugs. "I guess." He reflects on the word for a moment. "Empathy means being sensitive to other people. That's important. But for me it's not enough." A hesitant expression crosses his face. "I know that people see me as too demanding, sometimes dictatorial. That is a trait I have to work on curing. More than just empathy. It's the way I am with other people."

"And you think Outward Bound is going to fix that?"

"Nope." His reply comes fast. "I don't think Outward Bound's gonna fix that at all, but it might help *me* fix it."

"Coming about!" Bill Dennett shouts.

The boat heads into the wind. Curt releases the mainsheet from the cleat. The boom swishes by. Anne Warner tightens her sheet, and we are away on another tack.

Monroe Island has appeared to port while Curt and I have been talking. For the next hour the *Dawn Treader* moves south through the channel between Owls Head and Monroe. The crew has to stay alert. The wind shifts direction a lot. It is tricky sailing.

Midafternoon. Black clouds have been gathering. "Foul weather gear!" Anne calls as the first heavy drops hit.

We struggle with thick yellow oilskins. Chest-high pants, a jacket with a high collar, and the traditional fisherman's sou'wester. We are already wearing rubber knee boots. There is no cover in the boat. We are exposed to the elements, but it is not cold. It feels cozy snuggled in foul weather gear, warm and moist. The sea around us has subsided to a controlled slow swell, for the wind dropped when the rain started. The rain varies in intensity. For a while the drops fall slow and heavy. The water's surface is flat, covered with intersecting radiating ripples, as each drop leaves its mark. Periodically the tempo increases. The rain lashes down, accompanied by gusts of wind. The surface of the water explodes, and we feel the rain machine-gunning our yellow oilskins. The temperature drops a few degrees. We huddle, thankful for layers of insulating wool.

The wind is insufficient to move the boat, and Anne orders the sails down. She gives the ritual orders for rowing.

"Ship oarlocks."

"Stand by the oars."

"Toss oars."

The oars are raised in rapid succession and held erect.

"Oars."

The oars are lowered into the oarlocks and held parallel to the surface of the water, ready.

"Prepare to give way."

In unison the oar blades are brought back, ready to dip into the water for the first stroke.

"Give way."

The oars bite the water.

There are four rowers on each side of the boat. They sit facing the stern, backs to the direction of travel. The rower closest to the stern on each side sets the stroke. It is up to the three behind him or her to co-ordinate their rhythm. Not infrequently oars clash. One oar out of phase sets up a chain reaction. It bangs into the oar in front, and they both come to a crashing stop. A third oar hits, and a fourth. Everything comes to a halt. Someone curses. And off we go again.

Keep the arms straight. Pull by moving the upper body back, bending at the waist. The arms can bend a bit at the end of the stroke to impart a final flick as the blade clears the water.

In oilskins it is warm work.

Dawn Treader has reached the shelter of a small harbor on the Owls Head side. Anne gives the calls to stop rowing. The oars are shipped.

There is a monkey line for each crew member. A monkey line is a safety line, a length of thin rope with a metal clip at one end. The metal clip snaps onto a safety line that runs around the boat's gunnels. The other end of the monkey line is tied around the crew member's waist with a bowline knot finished off with a full hitch. The monkey lines are used to clip crew members to the boat under certain prescribed conditions. Generally the crew clips in when sailing at night, though not if the risk of capsizing is high. You do not want to be clipped to a thirty-foot boat if it overturns—an unlikely event we have been assured. A crew member who is seasick clips in with a monkey line. In heavy fog everyone clips in.

We are sitting in the boat with the anchor dropped and the rain coming down. Anne tells everyone to take a monkey line but not to clip in. For the next fifteen minutes, Anne will conduct a lesson in knot tying. In knot tying! We are sitting in an open boat surrounded by sea tying knots with the monkey lines. Anne is deadpan, straight-faced. This is just usual stuff. Why not? Wet hands fumble with slippery nylon. Bowline knot. Double fisherman's knot. Figure of eight. Square knot. It's not really a lesson in knot tying. It's really a lesson in here at Hurricane Island the program goes on whatever the weather. It would have been easy to succumb to the rain, to curl up in tight little fetal balls inside the oilskins and just *wait* for the weather to stop being nasty. It would have made a great deal of sense to do something more active, like rowing or sailing the boat. But sitting in the rain tying square knots has a surreal quality. I mean, nobody sits out in the ocean in an open boat in the rain tying knots in a monkey line. Nobody. It's a scene from a Fellini film.

"Make a bight in the rope, like this, a loop," says Anne.

Her yellow sou'wester is peaked down over her eyes. A little spout of water trickles down from the back of its brim, a little gutter that drains down her back.

"Tie an overhand knot in the bight, but go around one more turn before you push the end through the loop."

The boat rocks gently.

"A figure of eight." Anne holds it up for all to see.

We try.

Sitting in the rain tying knots has an interestingly disorienting quality to it. It makes land and normal existence seem a long way away. The activity is curiously appropriate. At Outward Bound one expects to be faced with the unexpected. *This* unexpected is so unexpected that if we had made lists of unexpected things we expected to happen, we probably would not have expected this.

Japanese prints sometimes show workers in water, in paddy fields, silently attending to the task of planting and gathering rice. There is some of this quality about what we are now doing. Other than the soft drumming of the rain, we are silent. Eleven yellow Japanese-print people, heads bowed over wet knots.

The rain stops. Up go the sails. For an hour the *Dawn Treader* crisscrosses the channel. Late in the afternoon anchor is dropped in the small bay on the southern end of Monroe Island. The boat is anchored about a quarter mile from shore. Curt is curious.

"Hey, Anne. What's the story? How come we're not closer in? You planning to have us swim ashore?"

Anne's scheme is for all of us to spend the first night on the boat. This piece of information is received with interest and some dismay. We have been on the boat all day. Stretching our legs on an island would have been nice.

The new situation has to be faced. Shelter has to be arranged in case it rains. A meal must be prepared. Thirteen sleeping places must be co-ordinated.

A rope is stretched between the masts. A plastic sheet is draped over it and tied to the sides of the boat, turning the boat into a tent for the night. The oars are spread into a latticework across the seats. They form the basis for lumpy beds made a little more comfortable with spare clothes and empty duffel bags. Spartan quarters. A hot meal is cooked in the stern cockpit. The boat wallows uneasily on its anchor. There is a steady tidal swell in the bay. Some of the group are seasick.

We take turns at night watch. Two people at a time (to keep each other awake) for two-hour spells.

A gray morning greets thirteen bleary people.

It takes two hours to cook breakfast, take down the tent, pack the gear, and make *Dawn Treader* ready for the sea.

Anne gathers us together in the cockpit around the chart. Our general location is a little to the south of the western part of Penobscot Bay. To the southeast lies a large open body of water. Hurricane Island, our destination, is seven miles east.

A gyroscopically mounted compass in a sturdy wooden box is set into the cockpit. Anne teaches us elementary sea navigation, which is more difficult than navigation on land. This part of the Maine coast is a pebble-dash mosaic of islands. Some are very small, half a mile across or less. Others are substantial, up to fifteen miles across. As the boat moves along, the islands look one very much like another. The larger islands look much like the mainland. As the boat zigzags back and forth, playing its merry game with the changing wind, the effect is similar to closing your eyes, spinning around a few times, and then trying to identify your direction in a featureless environment. Today the weather is clear; fog must present a whole new set of problems.

For the morning *Dawn Treader* courses back and forth across the bay. Crew positions are rotated. We begin to get the feel of the boat and to experience the different controlling functions.

A route is worked out on the chart. A compass course is set. It is the helmsperson's job to keep us on the course. But how to know how far we have gone on a long tack? The sea rolls by. It seems impossible to calculate precisely the distance we have traveled.

Anne produces some chips of driftwood that she has secreted. Bonnie Pooley is in the bow acting watch. "Pass one of these to Bonnie," says Anne, handing one of the chips forward. Tom Langenhop is at the tiller. "Somebody got a watch with a second hand?" asks Anne.

"Sure do," replies Curt.

"OK," Anne says. "Bonnie," she calls, "when you are ready, throw the wood over the side, call as it passes the bow. Tom, you shout when it passes the stern."

"Work out the speed, huh?" pronounces Curt, fast off the mark.

"Right," responds Anne. "You clock the seconds between their shouts."

"Ready, Curt?" calls Bonnie.

"All set."

She throws the chip into the water ahead of the boat, to the side.

"Now," she shouts.

Curt checks his watch.

A few seconds elapse.

"Now," calls Tom.

The length of the boat is thirty feet. We have the time in seconds for it to cover this distance. A little mental arithmetic and we have an approximation of the ship's speed.

"About four knots," announces Curt after Anne has told him how to figure. He gives a little grin of satisfaction.

Bill Dennett is next to me, temporarily idle; others are looking after the working functions. Bill's curly hair is bedraggled. The moist ocean air, the wind, and a night spent sleeping on the oars have effectively dismantled his well-groomed appearance.

"What's the residence director of the New England Conservatory of Music doing in a place like this?" I ask.

He ponders for a moment, brushes some stray locks of hair back from his forehead in a thoughtful gesture.

"I was in the Peace Corps a few years ago. That was very intense for me." He pauses. "The job I have now has some interesting aspects. I'm in contact with the student body a good deal and with a variety of stimulating faculty members. But there's a lot of routine. A lot of paper work. It tires me out, leaves me feeling drained and, to a certain extent, unfulfilled."

"You're married, aren't you?" I inquire.

"Right."

"How does your wife feel about you being here?"

"She was apprehensive at first. 'Do you really know what you are getting into?' she asked me when I first came up with the idea. I had to confess that I had only the haziest notions of what the program was about."

"What got you interested?"

"A magazine advertisement for Hurricane. It showed a small island surrounded by ocean. Solo. I really dug the idea of having an island all to myself for a few days, just to be by myself and think."

Bill tells me that he has had a long-standing interest in meditation and practices "relaxation therapy."

"I'm looking forward to it. A time just to be with me. Wonder how I'll react?"

We spend the next fifteen minutes chatting, talking about this and that. It is peaceful being aware of the boat's motion, the movements of the active crew members, without being directly involved.

"Person overboard!" Anne screams at the top of her lungs. A spurt of adrenaline makes itself felt in my relaxed body.

"Where?" somebody gasps. Everyone is up, casting around.

Drifting off to the stern is a life jacket.

It is a practice drill.

"Phew!"

"I'm timing you," calls out Anne. "That water's cold. You have to get it out quick."

By now the life jacket is almost fifty yards astern.

Our crew is fumbling, disorganized.

"Coming about," shouts Tom at the tiller.

The bow comes around.

We are off on a starboard tack but still heading away from the life jacket.

"Let the sail out more," Anne Warner suggests. She shouts the suggestion.

Tom is confused. "What do you mean?"

By now the life jacket has almost disappeared.

"If you keep tacking, you'll never get back," replies Anne urgently. "You have to let the sail out and run before the wind, back the way we came, but make sure you don't jibe."

Tom isn't sure what this means but grasps the general idea. Suejee is looking after the starboard mainsheet.

"Let it out, Suejee," Tom instructs.

Suejee does as instructed.

As Suejee slacks the sheet, the boom moves out until the mainsail extends sideways. Tom corrects the boat's direction with the tiller. *Dawn Treader* heads back in the general direction of the floating life jacket. Two false passes are made; each time the life jacket is a few frustrating feet out of reach.

On the third pass Tom's aim is better, and Maureen Doran is able to grab it.

"Heave to," instructs Anne. Tom brings the bow into the wind, and the sails slack.

"Well," she says, "it took a little over twenty minutes." Her tone of voice says that this is not good enough, and none of us are particularly pleased with our stumbling efforts.

A discussion ensues.

"The problem," says Tom, "is that once the boat is under way, it's real hard to aim it right to the spot. Then we're past so fast and have to go through the whole performance of turning again."

"What could you do about that?" asks Anne.

Puzzled frowns.

"Well," says Anne Warner thoughtfully, her previous sailing experience coming to the fore, "what we somehow need to do is come to a stop once we are in the vicinity of the life jacket, as close to it as possible."

Anne Peyton looks pleased.

"How are you going to do that?"

Anne Warner considers the problem. "What we should do," she says in an exploratory tone of voice, "is get the boat moving, just as we did; but rather than trying to grab the life jacket as we sail past, we should deliberately pass it, a few yards to the side, and then bring the bow round rapidly into the wind. If we gauge it just right, we should be able to heave to right next to it. We'll be stopped. Should be easy to get it."

The maneuver is tried.

Everything works as planned. *Dawn Treader* comes to a graceful halt with the life jacket only a few feet in front of the bow.

Pat, on bow watch, reaches out for it, but almost imperceptibly it moves out of his reach.

It is *not* the life jacket that is moving out of his reach. One fact that has been overlooked is that when the boat is heave to, bow into the wind, sails slack, there is still enough pressure from the wind to move the *Dawn Treader* very slowly backward.

The gap widens. It is impossible for Pat to reach the life jacket.

"Oars," suggests Curt. "We could have a couple of oars ready. If we come up short, a couple of pulls and we'd have it."

Anne approves. We sail away on a tack, come about, and, as we are passing the life jacket, come bow into the wind. One pull, two pulls, three pulls on the oars and Pat is able to reach over the bow and grasp the life jacket.

"Dead on target," chuckles Curt. "Wheee."

During the remainder of the day's sailing Anne periodically flips a life jacket over the side. We become very proficient at recovering it.

The night is spent camped on the shore of an island. A driftwood fire is built in a perforated oil drum carried on board the *Dawn Treader* for this purpose. Sleeping bags are spread on the sand between low bushes that come down almost to the water's edge. A decision is made not to erect the plastic tent. The night looks clear.

Morning. *Dawn Treader* points its bow toward Hurricane Island. We are all eager to finally arrive at the island about which we have heard so much. It has taken on the dimensions of a mystical destination. During the long hours spent on the boat during the past two days a sense of timelessness has prevailed, a feeling of going nowhere and of taking forever to do it. Hurricane is tangible.

We sail through narrow channels between a group of small islands. The chart shows Hurricane only three miles away. Anne suggests pulling into one of the islands to have lunch on a beach. Sounds good. We nose into a small cove. Someone prepares to drop anchor.

"Everyone, please stop what you are doing. Listen very carefully." Anne's tone of voice, direct, commanding, gains everyone's attention.

"This is a shipwreck. You have exactly five minutes to prepare." She glances at her watch. "Grab a few personal things and only the following items." She recites, "No food, a little milk powder, a few tea bags, matches, the radio, the exposure pack, the first aid kit, plastic to make a tent, only *four* sleeping bags, foul weather gear."

The group reacts in bemusement.

"Can I take this? Can I take that?"

"No."

"No."

Anne is crisp.

Get this show on the road; minutes are ticking by.

"Time's up," calls Anne. "Over the side everybody. Head for the island."

Curt goes first. The water is thigh-deep.

"Take the bowline with you, Curt," calls Anne. "Pull us in to shore a bit."

Curt does as directed, attempting to keep the gear he is carrying out of the water, as well as handle the coils of the bowline.

Others follow reluctantly. The water is cold. In the space of a few minutes we are standing on the beach, dripping. Anne is busy lowering the sails. We watch. She lashes the sails down and sets a pair of oars amidships. I think we all feel somewhat dismayed, abandoned, as she slowly, single-handedly rows the *Dawn Treader* away, out of the cove and out of sight around the corner.

We are shipwrecked, marooned on an island with minimal equipment and provisions.

The last thing Anne calls to us as she leaves is a cheery "See you at noon tomorrow."

We turn and look at our home for the next twenty-four hours.

Spectacle Island is named for geomorphologic reasons. It is hourglass-shaped or, going with the original marine geographers, spectacle-shaped. A narrow isthmus joins together two circular pods of land. The isthmus is the nosepiece; the round pods are the lenses. Anne has deposited us on the narrow neck between the two islets of land.

Suejee, standing next to me, tentatively raises and lowers each foot; a squelching noise ensues. Some of the crew had the good sense to take off their rubber boots before wading ashore. Others either did not think of it or did not have time. Suejee has wet feet.

"Reconnoiter?" suggests Curt.

"Yep. Let's check this place out," Bill concurs.

Not very organized, members of the group trickle off to explore.

Each of Spectacle's circular islets is formed by overlapping fractured granite slabs poking up from the sea. They sit low in the water, no more than thirty feet above sea level at the highest point. On top of the granite sits a cap of earth. Each islet's surface is crowned with dense, tall trees. Undergrowth crowds around the bases of their trunks. Around the perimeter of each islet the granite rises steeply for fifteen to twenty feet and stops abruptly. The earth starts immediately, and roots stick out overhanging the granite in places. Tufts of grass stick out, too. The effect is that of a slightly too large and not particularly well made toupee sitting on the head of a completely bald man.

The neck between the two islets is devoid of trees. It is an open, sandy spit of land, the lowest part of the island. One can easily imagine, in a gale, huge waves rolling right over this low neck. It acts as a bridge, a causeway between the two islets.

Someone finds a glade in the trees on the northernmost islet that has evidently been used as a campsite before. Shouts ring out. People begin to straggle toward the noise.

A half hour later the entire group and all the gear have arrived at the glade.

A problem in communal living and sharing of limited resources has been set for us. Someone makes a joke about *Lord of the Flies;* it does not go over too well. There is a slightly eerie feeling about our presence on the island.

We are quite safe, but we are on our own. The suddenness of Anne's departure has emphasized our isolation. And only four sleeping bags between twelve people—

The first task is easy. Tom Langehop and Jim Thomas work on setting up the plastic sheet as a tent. It is tied between two trees in a ridge shape. Enough room for the whole group to crawl under.

It is now late afternoon. We were supposed to have lunch on the island. Our hasty evacuation swept thoughts of food from everyone's minds.

"Milk powder and tea bags," says Curt. "We're not going to get very fat on that."

Suejee, controlled and patient, says, "We should scout the island for things to eat."

During our second day of sailing Anne had given a little talk on edible foods of the ocean. We had each been issued a copy of a small paperback book, *A Wild Way to Eat* by Euell Gibbons. No one had payed much attention to it; the food provided on the *Dawn Treader* was ample. Suejee, with considerable presence of mind, has brought her copy ashore. Among other things for us to search for are wild beach peas, muscles, small crabs, clams, and various edible plants.

Between the island's toupee of trees and the sea there is a zone of exposed granite slabs that varies in width from twenty to a hundred feet. In places the slabs are virtually flat, making walking easy; elsewhere they rise steeply, making scrambling awkward. Circumnavigating the island necessitates weaving one's way through these steep obstacles. It is low tide, and the lower slabs are cloaked in seaweed. Looking at the extent of the seaweed, I estimate that the differential between high and low tide is almost fifteen feet. Now that the tide is out, the exposed tidal zone of rocks promises good foraging.

As I clamber down toward the water, the rocks are greasy, the seaweed slippery underfoot. A cloying, dank smell permeates the moist air. The sea pushes its way into channels between the rocks, a steady, pulsating swell that creates a slick of light foam on the rocks' surface.

There are lots of muscles grouped in clumps. Mainly they lie just below the low-water line. To get them, it is necessary to find a pool, lie belly flat, and reach an arm underwater. I deduce that the muscle's preferred environment is one not exposed to air, even at low tide. There are some muscles clinging to the rocks above the low-tide level, but the richest concentrations are below the sea's surface. Lying with my nose a few inches from the water, I roll up my sleeve and stick an arm into a choice-looking pool. The water is chill. The shiny, black-shelled muscles cluster together. A firm tug is required to detach them. Ten minutes' industrious tugging produces a sizable harvest, two to three pounds in a plastic bag.

Crabs next? Gibbons' book suggests searching beneath loose rocks in the tidal zone. I walk along the slabs, looking for possibilities. Few loose rocks here, only massive slabs of granite. Fifty yards farther I come across an inlet with a small rock-strewn beach. Some sand, but mainly a jumble of small and medium-

sized granite fragments. I can turn over the smaller ones with my hands. Ten minutes' work produces two very small crabs, about the size of a half-dollar. Hors d'oeuvres? Perhaps there is a linear mathematical relationship between the size of the rock and the size (and quantity?) of crabs hiding beneath it. A rock some three feet by two feet and a foot thick sits on top of a bed of smaller rocks. From the side there appear to be lots of nooks and crannies beneath it. Ideal crab domain? I grasp the edge of the rock, fingers curled underneath a sharp edge, bend the knees, back straight, and *l-i-f-t*. So much for that. The rock sits unmoved. What is the weight of a few cubic feet of granite?

A couple of minutes spent scrambling about in the trees nearby produces a stout tree branch. I poke it under the recalcitrant rock, lever it over a smaller rock, grunt, wonder if the branch is going to splinter under the weight, and heave. The rock lifts a couple of inches, but to no practical advantage. There is no way I can keep it raised and detach a hand to search beneath. It slumps down. With cunning on the second attempt I position a small rock next to the area that lifts. Again I get the big rock up a couple of inches, then kick the smaller rock underneath with my foot. It supports the big rock. Working somewhat like a human jack, I successively crank up the big rock a couple of inches at a time and, at each raise, kick a slightly larger rock underneath. Before long it is a foot up at one end. Lying flat, I peer underneath. Aha. Small crusta-ceans peer back. There must be half a dozen snuggled away under there. Battling green crabs are the most common variety, Gibbons tells us. *Careinides maenas.*

"Fiercely pugnacious," the book reads, "you will be lucky to gather enough for a meal without making a small blood donation."

If the crabs were out in the open, it would be theoretically possible to grab them from behind, avoiding their main pincers. Under the rock they regard me balefully, backed into corners, pincers ready. They are *never* more than three inches across, says Gibbons, but I'm still not about to stick my fingers in there. I hear some scuttling going on, a brittle rattle of shell and claws against rock, as a battle formation is organized. Technological man against the primitives. Man the hunter, the toolmaker, against miniature leftovers from the Paleozoic era. A tool is needed to provide tender fingers with an advantage over hard shells. A light, tapering stick. The crabs scuttle and rattle as I poke it rudely in among them. It works. Out they come, one at a time. Once they are out from beneath the rock, it is a simple matter to pin them with the end of the stick, quickly pick them up from behind with thumb and first finger, and drop them into the plastic bag.

For the next forty-five minutes I employ the lever system and pointed stick to good advantage on a number of good-sized rocks. Fifteen small crabs result. Under a couple of the rocks I also find a small number of eels, *Anguilla rostrata*, "the slipperiest, slimiest, hardest-to-hold fish alive." These little elvers snug themselves into the sand. Trying to pick them up is like trying to grasp a miniature greased pig; they are not about to be held. Every time I try to pick one up, it wiggles furiously and slides out of my fingers. Once disturbed, they continue to thrash wildly on the ground. Each one is only a few inches long. Again cunning is needed. I position the plastic bag with its neck open. Sliding my free hand, palm up, toward the eels, I attempt to flick them into the bag. It is like playing tiddleywinks with live counters. Mostly I miss. The eels wriggle and twist in the air and, it seems, quite skillfully avoid landing in the bag. It is a fun pastime, an animated game of skill. Eventually I have half a dozen eels added to my crop of muscles and crabs, and it is time to return.

Most of the others have returned by the time I get back. Others have also collected muscles and crabs. Additionally there are wild beach peas for salad and raspberry leaves for tea. A fire is burning. A chowder is prepared with the milk powder. Washed down with tea from the tea bags and the raspberry leaves, it makes a satisfying meal.

By now it is dark. As we sit grouped around the fire, a discussion takes place on how best to share four sleeping bags among twelve people.

"Any spare clothes and all the foul weather gear should go on the ground underneath us to insulate us from the cold coming up," Tom Langehop begins. Tom's manner is pushy. He sees himself more experienced than the others on the basis of his previous Outward Bound course at Minnesota. His attitude is not making him popular. Bill Dennett in particular seems to resent him.

"We could take turns in the sleeping bags. An hour or two each," suggests Susan.

"Naw," responds Curt. "Look, the sleeping bags open up. They have a zipper all the way down the side. All we do is snuggle up together in a big heap and throw them over us." He chuckles. "Very cozy."

"We'd never get to sleep all jumbled together like that," responds Suejee. "But we could sleep in groups of two or three, with one sleeping bag thrown over each group."

This suggestion meets with general approval. The opened-out sleeping bags are not quite large enough to cover three people fully. Someone's arm or leg always seems to stick out. Everyone sleeps fully clothed, with foul weather gear and any spare clothes for a mattress. A reasonably warm and cozy night is spent in the plastic tent. The accommodations are intimate.

Seafood for breakfast is not appealing. Most people seem satisfied with a cup of hot tea.

The morning is spent wandering about the island. Some of the group spend time writing in their journals. Sitting at the ocean's edge, staring out to sea is a favorite pastime. Some nap.

At noon the *Dawn Treader* reappears. Anne greets us cheerily, welcomes us back on board. She has brought lunch of fresh-baked bread, cheese, salad, and oatmeal cookies. It is well received.

Shortly *Dawn Treader*'s bow is turned southeast, and we are headed toward Hurricane Island.

Hurricane has a gray, bleak look as we approach. The island is about a mile long and half a mile wide, the chart shows. *Dawn Treader* rounds its northern tip and sails parallel to its east shore. Like most of the other islands hereabouts, Hurricane is formed from upthrust granite slabs. It is tree-covered, gently hilly.

Buildings appear. First a couple of small wooden structures atop a jetty built from timbers. A number of boats are moored in a small cove. Farther along larger buildings and a second pier. *Dawn Treader* heads in toward the first jetty. We draw alongside a floating wood walkway that connects with the jetty by a stairway with handrails. It takes an hour to unload all our gear, hose down *Dawn Treader* to clean off the saltwater residue, and row her out to a mooring.

The island is a haven of civilization compared with the conditions of the past three days. At six o'clock we eat a sit-down dinner in a large dining room. Other courses are operating from Hurricane simultaneously. There are approximately a hundred other students and Outward Bound staff at the meal. It is a noisy hustle after the intimacy and isolation of our small group.

Our group camps out in a grove of trees for the night, a grassy place surrounded by lilac bushes. Anne tells us to be ready at 5 A.M. Running shoes and swimsuits are the suggested dress.

"Five o'clock," snorts Curt. "How about my beauty sleep?"

"You sure need it," grins Anne. "But just think how good the dawn air will be for your complexion."

Curt does not look convinced.

Everyone in the group feels a deep fatigue. One night sleeping on oars, another on sand, and a third crammed three to a sleeping bag have had their effect.

9. Ice ax self-arrest.

10. Climbing Capitol Peak, Colorado.

11. Climbing Capitol Peak.

12. High bivouac, Capitol Peak.

Morning meeting on Hurricane Island.

The whaleback, a noted feature of the Hurricane Island marathon.

Five o'clock. No one awake. Anne's voice is the alarm clock.

"OK. Let's go, folks."

It takes ten minutes for everyone to stumble up, throw feet into sneakers, and assemble. Curt is mumbling to himself, nothing coherent, a little soliloquy of consternation punctuated by grunts.

Anne heads off at a brisk jog, following a trail through the trees. The group pads along behind in single file.

"How far we going?" someone calls.

Anne does not answer. We follow.

The path emerges on the granite slabs that form the perimeter of the island. We end up running all the way around the island, about two miles. The path weaves its way in and out of the zone of granite slabs—the constant lapping of the ocean to the right, the trees and bushes of the hinterland to the left.

At the end of the circuit the path emerges at the jetty where we docked yesterday. Anne runs out onto the jetty and waits. The group has straggled over the last half mile. In ones and twos everyone arrives puffing and congregates next to Anne on the jetty.

Anne waits until all are assembled. She gestures for everyone to move close and listen. The group has been half expecting what is to happen next. There had been some discussion of the possibility last night.

"We'll run the island each morning we are here," says Anne, "and finish off the run with a dip in the ocean."

Morning run and dip has long been a traditional feature of the Outward Bound program. At some schools, particularly those that run mobile programs, morning run and dip is no longer practiced, but at Hurricane it is a feature of life on the island and a variable at the instructor's discretion during expeditions in the boats.

Anne moves to the edge of the jetty. The sea is some twenty feet below. A small platform sits between two wooden uprights—the launching pad. Anne says a couple of cautionary words about keeping the body upright and jumping well out from the jetty. She jumps. Twenty feet seems a long way down. Splash! She swims to a floating pontoon and climbs out, dripping. She climbs the ladder to rejoin us. One after another we jump. It is a long way down. The more adventurous of the group are exhilarated. Some are nervous and go reluctantly. Curt is nervous but covers it with his usual banter.

"All right, boys and girls. Watch out, you fishes." He playfully pinches his nostrils between thumb and forefinger and with a doomed expression steps off.

It is Suejee's turn. She steps onto the platform. She does not seem to lack confidence, looking no more nervous than some of the others. She stands, looking down at the water. A soft, hazy sun rises above the distant horizon. It is warm, and the ocean surface is millpond flat. Only the impact of plummeting bodies disturbs its tranquillity. Suejee stands quite motionless at the edge. The others in the group sense her hesitation and observe in silence. Suejee moves her right leg back a few inches, pushes off from the ball of her foot, and at the same time makes a small forward motion with her shoulders. But nothing happens.

Morning dip at Hurricane Island.

She has given a little forward shrug, a gesture of intent, but her body has not moved.

"Oh," she gives a little gasp.

Again there is the shrug—shoulders jerking forward a few inches, the push with the rear leg—but an invisible wall of resistance seems to have been erected.

Anne says softly, "Go, Suejee."

Suejee pushes her arms straight down, tight against her sides, fists clenched. She strains. But something holds her back.

She turns and walks a few paces back from the edge.

Anne watches.

Suejee takes a little run at it, reaches the edge of the platform, and stops dead.

"Damn," she bursts out. "I want to do it. I really do."

She steps back from the edge, head bowed, eyes averted. There is a sympathetic swell of support from the rest of the group, mainly facial expressions. No one is sure what to do to help.

Suejee's eyes remain downcast. She is silent, but it looks as though she is carrying on a conversation with herself.

She moves back again, takes her little run to the edge, and again stops dead. This time she raises her clenched fists to shoulder level and shakes them in a gesture of frustration. She stamps a petulant foot.

That night Suejee wrote in her journal, "I was torn between crying, running away, or standing my ground and telling everyone, I won't do it and that's it. Occasionally a thought slipped through that great wall, 'Maybe I *can* do it,' but those moments were quickly swept away. I don't even remember how many times I left everyone with bated breath because I would clench my teeth, take a deep breath, and start the countdown for the first step toward the edge of the dock. As often as I did that, I would as often step back just before the edge. Even with my eyes closed I always knew when to stop—just before the edge."

Curt has been observing Suejee's trauma. He steps forward and in a whisper asks Anne a question. Anne considers and nods.

"Hey, Suejee," says Curt, stepping up beside her, "let's go together." He takes hold of her hand.

Suejee is not sure about this. She glances down at Curt's hand holding hers.

Nervously she acquiesces. Together they stand a couple of paces back from the edge. Two steps forward—and again Suejee freezes. Curt, with more forward momentum, sways and almost falls in. He recovers his balance and steps back.

"OK, Suejee," he says. "This time we're gonna go. Got it?"

She nods.

Again they step forward.

As their feet simultaneously hit the edge, Curt squeezes Suejee's hand encouragingly. With a little moan she carries through, and the pair are airborne. Two splashes. The pair swim to the pontoon. Suejee is excited; her eyes are alive. "I did it," she gasps. "I really did it."

Climbing the jetty after the early morning dip.

Jumping from the jetty does not become much easier for Suejee. For the next two mornings the group dutifully runs the perimeter of the island in the early morning dawn. Suejee jumps each time, but each time it takes a massive exercise of will to get through the invisible wall that exists for her at the edge of that wooden platform above the ocean.

Years ago, before Outward Bound came to the island, Hurricane was the home of a granite-quarrying operation. A hill toward the south side of the island had been quarried and now gives Outward Bound a series of steep rock faces up to a hundred feet high. *Dawn Treader* "watch" (as groups at Hurricane are called) spends the rest of the day rock-climbing and rappelling. Suejee enjoys rock-climbing; she launches herself at the steep rock faces with gusto, exhilarated. Her phobia of jumping does not affect her performance on the rock.

Bill Dennett's reaction to rock-climbing is strong. In his journal he writes, "By far this was the part of the experience that alternately—no . . . *simultaneously*—intrigued and frightened me." Bill is one of those people who is naturally terrified of heights and gets nervous standing near the edge at the top of buildings. He knows he is safeguarded by the climbing ropes but still feels tense. Standing at the edge of a hundred-foot drop, clipped into the climbing ropes, he prepares to make his first rappel. The climbing instructor notices his nervousness and gently encourages him. Bill, if we are to use his size and physical condition as criteria, looks tough, but there are tears in his eyes at this moment.

"Scared?" inquires the instructor.

High rappel at Hurricane Island.

Suejee Quon.

The moment of truth. A participant in the special course for women over thirty prepares to back over the high rappel.

"Through my tears I nodded," Bill wrote in his journal.

Gingerly he steps back and walks his way a hundred vertical feet to the ground. Bill does not adjust to climbing and rappelling as many people do after the initial nervousness has worn off. "I am still convinced that people are crazy to think that clinging to the side of a rock is in any way fun," he wrote at the end of the day.

The close living confines of the Outward Bound group can produce tensions as well as positive feelings. Bill is finding that he is experiencing negative reactions to Tom Langehop as the course progresses. Commenting on Tom's behavior during the rock-climbing, Bill writes in his journal, "Tom spent a lot of time wanting to be seen as the bravest and first on everything on the cliffs. Foolish person." It remains to be seen if Bill's feelings about Tom will emerge as a topic for discussion in the group, or if Bill will keep them to himself.

Next morning the group prepares for solo. The environment of Maine lends itself to this experience; each person will have a small island to him or herself. Though the course is only ten days, solo is to be three days and two overnights. As at the other schools, minimum provisions for safety are taken. The powerboat transports the group, dropping each person off at the island that will be home for the next sixty hours.

Bill Dennett wrote a long journal during solo. The following extracts give insights into his experience:

Where the hell did all this start? What brought me here to Outward Bound? My fingernails are black ruins. I've been wet more than I've been dry. I haven't shaved in five days.

I've never really done anything that was as meaningful. I'm tested every day—almost every hour.

Two cooking cans. One gallon of fresh water. One plastic tarp. One sleeping bag. Euell Gibbons' *A Wild Way to Eat.*

The boat dropped me off on Big White Island. . . . Beautiful place with 50–75-foot-high cliffs on the south side, with high-tide waves surging with great plumes of froth blowing all over.

The strangest thing about solo—when I speak to myself, my voice is an intrusion on my privacy.

I have to put the detachment of solo into my life on a regular basis.

Close by, on a separate island, Suejee was also exploring her new home. She wrote:

My solo island, Little Garden, was exquisite. How could I not help feeling like Robinson Crusoe when the boat let me off on this deserted island bordered with white and red wild roses. Before I had even settled my gear, I immediately set off to walk around my island, hopping from rock to rock. As I went along, I got bolder and bolder and pieces of clothing started coming off. Finally I was down to nothing. I saw fishing boats passing, and it was funny how I hid from them, but not once did it occur to me to be afraid of anything on the island.

But this island of everyone's dreams wasn't totally idyllic. The next day the sun forgot to shine. My nails were caked with blood from foraging for clams. I couldn't

Solo: an island to yourself.

get the fire to light in that tiny can, and after various futile attempts I had only a few matches left. I was totally unhappy!

Despite the unpleasantness, or maybe because of it, I learned something.

Yesterday's self-pitying went as far as sleeping away most of the day. I think more than anything else, I realized that *I* am the one to kick myself out of a self-pity state. These miserable condemnations of everything around me, including myself and the old aching muscles, just didn't go away until I got up and started doing something. Perhaps most significant of all was that I just followed my own behavior pattern of being stubborn, refusing to react, and waiting for someone to make *me* happy. Well here there wasn't anyone to do that, and I had only myself to please.

Two and a half days after it dropped us off, the powerboat reappears and picks up each member of the group. When we are gathered together again in the glade on Hurricane Island next to the lilac bushes, Anne asks for reactions to the experience.

"Was the time alone valuable?" she asks.

"I made a conscious decision not to eat anything," beams Curt in response. And indeed he looks considerably thinner than a few days previously.

"I had one really nice experience," says Bonnie. "I saw a seal catch a fish and eat it."

"I kept waiting for someone to kick my ass, to get me out of my self-pity," states Suejee, reiterating what she had written in her journal.

Curt continues. "For me it was very worthwhile. There are some ruts in my life that I wanted to change. Solo gave me space to focus on them."

Anne smiles. "What kind of ruts?" she inquires.

"Well," responds Curt. "At work. I tend to build too much of my life around work. I need to get out and do other things in my free time, particularly stuff out of doors. And, then, interpersonal relationships. I need to do some more work there." He looks down, preferring not to elaborate further on this.

Susan Heacock, usually quiet in the group, comments, "I pretended that I would be doing solo for a year, shut everything else out, and just took each day as it came. I didn't want to think about my life. I wanted to live it. For the days of solo that really happened."

"I watched a bird dive fifteen times for a fish," says Jim Thomas after a pause. Jim is another quiet member of the group, rarely speaking. "I thought, how stupid. Then I thought, but that's its way. Maybe I need to be more like that, decide on something and keep after it." Jim seems more relaxed than earlier. He continues. "I came to Outward Bound to think about specific things. I've been married for five years, and we've been thinking about starting a family. I thought a lot about how I'd raise a child."

Jim's talk of marriage stimulates Bonnie. "I had to stop myself making lists of things to do when I get back," she says. "I'm used to being the center of my universe and having things jump when I say so. On my island there was nothing that would jump when I said so. It was the first time since I was married fifteen years ago that I've been away from my husband and child."

There is a pause as people digest these comments.

Eventually Anne breaks the silence with a question.

"Did any of you find your emotions closer to the surface than usual?"

Anne Warner responds first. "I found myself crying occasionally. I cried when the boat came to pick me up. I didn't want to leave."

Curt grins. "My answer's yes, too, but in a different way. I shouted and sang a lot of the time and jumped up and down. People would have thought me strange if they had seen me."

Anne draws the discussion to a close. "I'm pleased at the way you have opened up with each other," she says.

"It's because of the tone you have set," responds Rohit.

"When I saw you with your 'Women on Top' shirt and heard you say 'person the oars,' I thought, *'Oh no,'* " adds Bill Dennett.

Anne grins, slightly self-conscious.

"But I'm really happy with the way you've guided us along," Bill adds. He leans over and puts an arm around Anne's shoulder and gives her a hug. Other members of the group comment in complimentary terms on Anne's leadership style.

There can be no doubt that among the key factors determining the quality of any particular Outward Bound group's experience are the nature, skills, and sensitivities of the instructor. My earlier thoughts on the effectiveness of the Outward Bound program return to me as I sit here in the grass. Previously I have noted that the same program experiences typically result in a wide variety of individual responses among participants, ranging from the most dramatic life-altering responses to virtually no effects. Much of the variability, I feel, results from the psychological space that a person occupies when he or she comes to Outward Bound, that person's readiness for change. Some people are primed for change on arrival, and Outward Bound can be a powerful catalyst. Others more settled in their present selves enjoy (or occasionally hate) Outward Bound as an experience but report little in the way of personal development. But the psychology of the participant cannot account for all the variability in responses; the nature of the Outward Bound program (its structure, experiences, intensity, and environment) plays an important part. I suppose someday it may be possible to calculate all these factors mathematically and write an equation that would enable a person to calculate precisely his or her responses to the program before involvement. You know the kind of thing: *Factor one:* Psychological readiness for change—six on a one-to-ten scale. *Factor two:* Intensity of the Outward Bound Course—eight. And so on. Social scientists call these kinds of factors "predicators," and a good deal of social science thinking and tinkering has been applied to Outward Bound over the years.

Social science methodology does have a place in Outward Bound. Its most important role is to raise questions and give a structure that makes it possible for those involved to take a more detailed and rational view of the phenomenon. But generally social science methods have not produced useful answers in understanding the nature of the Outward Bound program and its outcomes.

Perhaps it is unfair to dichotomize—social science methodology versus the intuitive response—but this has characteristically been the way things have gone with Outward Bound over the years. The overwhelming majority of staff and participants in Outward Bound act guided by intuition, by gut feelings, and to use the language of the mid-1970s, by the right-brain approach.

A participant in Outward Bound does not need to check boxes on a questionnaire to know how he or she has responded to the moments of intensity that have constituted the Outward Bound experience.

For a variety of reasons the Outward Bound instructor functions on an intuitive level—is *compelled* to function on an intuitive level. One of the deleterious effects of social science methodology on Outward Bound has been a tendency to influence the instructor in a direction *away* from faith in his or her intuitive responses to people and situations. The social science approach and the intuitive approach tend to dichotomize, to be seen in terms of either/or, better/worse. The instructor, basically an intuitive person, typically does not understand well the technical apparatus of the social scientist (particularly its shortcomings)— the statistics, instruments, questionnaires, quantification—and tends to be rather easily bamboozled by it all. It seems so impressive, so rational. "How can I possibly think that my mere *feelings* are in any way better in getting the job done?" But when it really gets down to it, this is how the Outward Bound instructor does function. The best Outward Bound instructors are those who have the ability to trust their own intuitive responses most faithfully and to act on the basis of those intuitions. It is a real act of personal faith for the instructor to respond to his or her own convictions in the Outward Bound situation, where both the physical and psychological welfare of participants are at stake.

Watching Anne deal with our group reinforces these conclusions. She is experienced, direct, sympathetic, empathetic, and possessed of a remarkably low tolerance for bullshit. When something comes up that challenges her—a situation to confront, a person to respond to on a point of importance—she doesn't mentally reach for the instructor's handbook. She doesn't flip through the rules and regulations and guidelines to find what somebody else says she should do to deal with the situation. What she does do—and you can literally *see* her do it—is first and foremost *compose herself.* Her eyes just ever so slightly glaze over, not the glaze of a daydreamer, but the intent expression of a person looking inward, a deliberate closing out of peripheral and distracting stimuli. It looks as though Anne's eyes are focused on a point in space some ten or so inches in front of her face when she concentrates. Perhaps that is the physical focal point, but it is clear that her attention is temporarily inward, checking out *her* internal response to what is happening, a prime characteristic of the fully functioning Outward Bound instructor. Anne is so good when she does this that not only does she function effectively but her students pick up on what is happening.

Their response, which of course is unarticulated, goes something like this: Here is a person who trusts herself. Here is a person with the self-confidence and experience to use her own perceptions and intuitions as a basis for judgments in difficult situations. *Here is a person I can trust.* If she can trust herself and function from her base of self-trust, then perhaps *I can learn to trust myself, too.*

Confidence is a catchword around Outward Bound, actually, more of a label that has been attached to Outward Bound by others over the years. "Outward Bound builds confidence." The image is that of Superman and Wonderwoman emerging phoenixlike from the remains of the ninety-eight-pound weakling who always used to get sand kicked in his face on the beach. But thinking back to Art Duel's experience at North Carolina—"In a way I learned less confidence in myself" (after his experience on the high log on the ropes course)—tells me that if Outward Bound deals in confidence (and I believe it does), the brand name of this confidence is a little different from that purveyed by the conventional wisdom. Anne's confidence is the kind that I feel is important: trusting one's own reactions and acting in harmony with them. This includes the confidence to recognize and accept weaknesses. "I was scared crossing that log" generalizes to "There are things that scare me" or, one step more general still, "These are my personal limitations." Recognition of limitations accompanied by the confidence still to act in accordance with what one feels—that's the kind of confidence I see Outward Bound dealing in. It's the confidence that comes from trusting oneself, and it's the kind of confidence that breeds reciprocal trust in others. It's the kind of confidence that makes Anne a little bit of a law unto herself, but in a way that I see as worthwhile and justified. It is pleasing to me to see her group pick up and respond to it. I'd bet that Anne's students learn some of this quality from her and remember it in the future, long after they've forgotten the difference between a bowline and a main sprit.

I put a lot of my own personal chips on the importance of the instructor in determining the efficacy of any Outward Bound experience. I feel that one of the historically significant attributes of the Outward Bound organization has been its ability consistently to attract a very unique body of men and women for these important positions. Experience is a key characteristic of the Outward Bound instructor. It underpins every judgment they make. Typically the best staff are those with broad experiences, in the wilderness and elsewhere, who are able to use their own intuitions as a basis for action.

Anne personifies this. Watchful, caring, she inspires trust. She is a self-acknowledged feminist. The message on her shirt and her use of sexually neutral descriptions for traditional sex roles are her most active statements. The group, impressed by her competence, has come to respect her position, though the initial surprise on the part of some of the males at having a female instructor has taken awhile to wear off. There was an incident on board the *Dawn Treader* during the second day at sea in which Anne took a more active role in defining the boundaries of sex roles. Maureen had been delegated to put the main sprit up. Tom, ever manly, jumped up to assist her. Anne coolly asked him not to.

"You were walking too much into a woman's space," Anne commented to Tom later.

"I wanted to do it myself and knew I could," added Maureen.

Raising the main sprit has become a little symbol of feminism. By tacit agreement, since the incident with Tom and Maureen, either women working together or men working together raise the main sprit. Anne has actively generated a

Two members of the women-over-thirty course raising the main sprit.

situation in which women in the group now confidently tackle a job that, if she had just let the situation go, would automatically have been done by men.

Outward Bound offers the choice of either coeducational or single-sex programs. Recently special programs for women over thirty have attracted a lot of attention. One of the reasons they work so well is that in an all-women's group women are compelled to fulfill tasks that males have traditionally fulfilled. In coeducational programs in the wilderness women have to work hard to find leadership opportunities and easily hand over responsibility for tasks requiring physical strength to males (an interesting situation in and of itself and possessing obvious learning potential in the hands of a skilled instructor). There is a ten-day women-over-thirty program operating at Hurricane at the same time as our program, and the participants clearly value the trade-off benefits they get compared with being in a coeducational group. For our group incidents like the one with Maureen, Tom, and the main sprit, emphasize the assumptions we all make about male and female capabilities. Subtly Anne works on our awareness of these assumptions. I cannot help but feel that these issues will become more explicit before the end of the program. For now, an equitable situation seems to have been generated, with the males consciously attempting to give the females elbow room in decision making and tasks requiring physical strength.

Tomorrow we are to depart on a final expedition. For the final two and a half days of the program we will navigate a demanding course, weaving our way along a prescribed route through the maze of surrounding small islands,

to arrive back at Rockland harbor, where we started the course. Final expedition is the culmination of the course. Everything that Anne has taught about this environment will come into play: the little tricks of navigation, estimating the speed of the boat with wood chips, keeping tight into the wind, following the compass, and reading the chart.

We seem to have been at Hurricane for a long time. Much longer than the temporal reality of eight days. Most of the men haven't shaved. Curt's grin is partly obliterated by stubble. Bill looks salty and waterworn. The women's complexions have taken on a naturally rosier hue. Hands have toughened from the long hours heaving on the oars and grappling with the obstacles of the ropes course and rock-climbing. Whatever debate there may be on the psychological benefits of the Outward Bound experience, there can be no doubt about its physical benefits.

Suejee looks glowingly healthy. White teeth peep out from a sunburned face. She smiles a lot these days. But she has not overcome her fear of jumping. The morning after her incident at the dip, the group moved up to the ropes course. One of the activities goes by the name Flea's Leap. A ladder leads to a platform twelve feet above the ground. From this perch a jump has to be made to a smaller platform, some two feet square and four feet lower. If one is standing on the ground looking at it, it seems to be a reasonably substantial landing point. But when one is perched on the take-off point, it shrinks to diminutive proportions. Suejee stands on the take-off platform, fists clenched, eyeing her destination with mistrust. She wants to jump. Oh, she wants to jump so bad. It shows. But again she is rooted. Anne and Curt stand below, encouragingly, and ready to spot in case she falls. For twenty minutes Suejee goes through her little stop-start act.

"Come on, Suejee. You can do it." Curt's voice wills her to step off.

"It's only a few feet," encourages Anne.

"Damn. Damn. Damn." Suejee is in torment. Energy wells up inside her but doesn't go anywhere. The effect is like that of a balloon being blown up beyond normal size. The air will have to be released, or the balloon will burst. Suejee will have to jump—or explode.

"Yeah, Suejee."

"Oh those quiverings of the stomach, sweating of the brow, and asking myself why I was here," Suejee wrote in her journal that evening. "So much is relative. The more I resisted, the more it became my own personal barrier. I had to do it before all those doubts could creep into my brain."

And she jumps. Instinctively she lands nimbly. As her feet touch the platform, she bends her knees, goes into a crouch, and grasps the platform with her hands. Afterward she is trembling but grinning.

Now, these challenges behind, Suejee prepares for final expedition with the others.

There was a time at Hurricane Island when students on final expedition would take the boat out unaccompanied by an instructor. Since that time Coast Guard

The Wall, a traditional Outward Bound problem-solving exercise. The objective is to get the entire group over as quickly as possible; the dilemma is how to retrieve the last person.

regulations have tightened up, and it is now mandatory that a certified instructor be aboard each boat at sea. Anne's presence will be a safety measure. She has said that she will stay completely out of the business of running the boat. It will be up to the group.

The first two days of final expedition go smoothly. The course is long, demanding more hours on the boat each day than we have done before. But we are into the routine. Functions are exchanged. People take turns at the tiller, the sheets, bow watch, and navigating. The teamwork is satisfying; there is a pleasing sense of accomplishment in our progress. Everyone does a little of everything. It is a nicely liberated situation. Women raise the main sprit as though they came from a long lineage of main sprit raisers. The tiller is competently personhandled. Everyone persons the oars, and so far there have been no persons overboard. Poseidon smiles.

On the evening of the second day *Dawn Treader* finds herself becalmed. Before the wind dropped, we had decided on Butter Island as our destination for the night. From our current position in the Fox Islands Thorofare, Butter Island lies eight sea miles to the northeast. It seemed at first, when the wind dropped, that it was probably a temporary state of affairs. We had unshipped the oars as a token gesture and in desultory fashion lily-dipped our way east, heading out of the channel. After a half hour, we suspect that the wind has gone somewhere else for the rest of the day. The ensuing debate explores various possibilities: changing the destination to somewhere nearer, cooking a meal while we wait for the wind, dropping the sea anchor. Somehow—probably from pride, partially assisted by a lack of consensus on any of the other options—we just keep on rowing and rowing and rowing. Keep the bow to the east, swinging more north as we round the point. In the absence of wind fog drifts in, percolates in slow swirls, garbing the smooth surface of this windless ocean. An eerie cacophony of sound comes to us. Seabirds. An occasional foghorn. Bow watch blows back. In the quiet the rattle of oars in oarlocks sounds loud. Each splash as the eight blades bite adds a peculiar liquid metronomical tempo to our progress. The occasional clash of wood on wood as someone attempts to syncopate the beat barely disturbs the *Dawn Treader*'s motion.

Nine miles. We end up rowing nine long miles without a break. There are eight rowing positions and thirteen of us on board. We take turns at the oars. Anne, faithful to her committment not to involve herself in the decision-making process, does earn her passage by taking her turn with an oar.

Dawn Treader glides quietly through the intermittent fog. Occasionally islands appear. We pass Bald Island and Eagle Island to starboard. Anne Warner in the navigator's seat tells us we are on course.

The fog makes us damp. Drops of moisture collect on our eyebrows and hair. Humidity must be a hundred per cent.

The rhythmic splash of the oars punctuates the silence of the evening. No one speaks. It is a purposeful, meditative silence as we move this boat through the water, the concerted result of eight sets of straining muscles.

Capsize drill.

Someone hums a tune. We row stirred by its sound. The humming changes to song:

> *Sail bonny boat*
> *Like a bird on the wing*
> *Over the sea to Skye.*
> *Sail bonny boat*
> *For he who'll be king,*
> *Gone with the sailor's cry.*
> *Egg on the port*
> *Mull on the stern*
> *Rhum on the starboard bow.*
> *Sail bonny boat*
> *Like a bird on the wing*
> *Over the sea to Skye.*

We all sing. And other songs, too: "Where Have All the Flowers Gone," "When Johnny Comes Marching Home," "Kumbaya."

In the dark we arrive in a sheltered cove at Butter Island. Everyone is worn out. In the dark our efficiency goes down. For some inexplicable reason we row three times around the cove—as though we haven't had enough rowing! There is a certain zombielike quality to the rowing now. Anne is at one of the oars. I can sense her frustration level rising. For a moment she abandons her resolve not to become involved in what is going on.

"Goddammit," she croaks in a voice hoarse and comically sotto voce, "drop the frigging anchor, somebody."

Obediently the bow noses to shore, and the anchor goes down.

A quick meal and everyone crashes, sleeping bags thrown haphazardly among bushes on the sand.

Dawn is a pink-fingered, stealthy event. We are up with it and in the boat fast. Today is the last day. Butter Island is a long way from Rockland harbor. It will be our longest sail of the program. The final challenge. Anne has money with which to purchase lobsters from fishermen on the mainland when we arrive for a final feast.

Pat is appointed captain and Tom navigator. Anne hovers as they huddle over the chart figuring bearings. Their meeting is brief. The anchor comes up. We are off. The bow points toward Rockland.

It is a little after 8 A.M. So quiet this early dawn time. The *Dawn Treader*, in its element, whispers across the water. Pat gives orders firmly but without raising his voice.

"Susan, Suejee, Anne, raise the mainsail."

"Aye, aye, captain."

"Bonnie, Rohit, take the mizzen." His orders are calm, sure.

Bonnie and Rohit move to obey.

The mainsail and the mizzen rise swiftly.

"Bill, Curt, put the rudder in."

Curt consults with Tom on the course once the rudder is in. He is serious. Today is an important day.

"We gotta correct for the tide. Let's correct twenty degrees. Two-seventy plus twenty—that's a true bearing of two-ninety. Need a speed check."

A speed check is taken.

It is a long, long day. Tom and Curt work together on navigation. The winds are unfavorable. Many tacks are needed. Fog descends. A foghorn on the mainland provides a bearing, but its position through the fog is uncertain. As the day wears on, the sense of pressure increases. It is unthinkable that we will not reach Rockland harbor today. But it is a possibility. As the possibility makes its presence felt, I notice that Pat, Tom, Curt, and sometimes, Bill have virtually fully assumed the decision-making process. The women operate the sheets but do not actively involve themselves in discussions of progress or participate in decisions on adjusting the course. There is a noticeable lassitude on the part of those other than the four men who are making the decisions. Last night's row was exhausting, and there is a general weariness from the previous two days of sailing. The women seem complacent, glad to be told what to do. The four men are energized by their leadership roles and come on strong.

It is dark when we reach the mainland. A fifteen-hour day. The lobster fishermen have long since closed up and gone home. We search through the food bags for remnants to put together an evening meal. It is decided that we will cook and sleep on the boat for this final night. We are anchored in a sheltered cove half an hour from the Outward Bound School mainland base. Tomorrow morning we will rise early, head in, clean up, and depart.

Dinner is an impromptu affair—bread, salad, and boiled potatoes. Ah, those lobsters we missed.

As dinner ends, Anne begins a final discussion of the experience. Snuggled under the plastic boat tarp, in the dark, cozy, tired from the long day, we look back on what has transpired.

Anne wastes no time getting to an issue she feels is important.

"I was watching carefully what happened today. How is it that there were no women participating in the decision-making process?"

There is a lengthy pause as the group digests this question.

Suejee responds, "Well—I had been navigator yesterday."

Bonnie says, "Me, too."

"But yesterday there were both men *and* women assigned to the main roles, and there was also a good deal of informal involvement from women in what was going on," Anne points out.

Another long pause.

Suejee comments again that the events of the day had nothing to do with sex roles and reiterates that she feels that she had contributed yesterday.

"I'm hearing some evasion of responsibility," replies Anne.

"Well," says Suejee after another pause, "there were some things that frustrated me. Tom seemed to keep messing up on navigation, and between him and Curt we seemed to do a lot of sailing this way and that."

There is a single candle burning. We are all sprawled out on the oars, in a circle, listening. The boat sways gently. We are completely adjusted to its motion. Above our heads the plastic rain fly blocks out any sense of the outside. We are isolated from our surroundings, concentrated on the focal point of the candle, a separate society, intense. Anne is into pushing the issue of sex roles. The group is on the defensive.

Anne ponders what Suejee has just said. A light breeze rocks the *Dawn Treader*, makes the plastic tent crackle.

"If you felt that way about Tom and Curt today," Anne says, "why didn't you express your feelings at the time?" Anne sits cross-legged, her back straight. Her eyes move around the group. She is focused, purposeful.

Tom interjects, "I felt these last three days were old hat, just a rehash of what we had done before, not particularly challenging. Didn't seem worth the effort of trying to involve everybody. We got here, didn't we?" His voice is irritatingly arrogant. For the first time I share Bill Dennett's earlier reaction to Tom.

Anne is patient. She responds in a controlled, even tone.

"The point is," she says, "partly because of your domineering manner, Tom, Suejee missed the opportunity to participate in the decision making and also didn't express her feelings about it."

It is difficult to see people's faces in the gloom of the single candle. From what I can discern of Tom's expression, he looks unconcerned, perhaps a little petulant. Doesn't like being confronted by a woman.

He shrugs. "So?"

Anne continues. "It seems to me that for the past ten days, when the going was easy, we were all able to play the equality game. But when the going got tough today, we reverted to stereotypes. The men took over; the women remained passive."

Anne Warner interjects. She is upset. "I feel that far too much is being made of this. I see it as a case of each individual throughout the ten days assuming a variety of roles in relation to their skill and experience and not in relation to their roles as male or female."

Suejee speaks again. "Same for me. I had captained the day before and just wanted someone else to have a chance. It just happened to be men."

Bill Dennett asks Anne Peyton a question. "Were you disappointed that the women didn't participate?"

"Yes, I was," she answers.

The discussion continues back and forth for a while. It is late. Everyone is tired. It looks as though some of the group might already be asleep, sprawled back on the thwarts. Curt, usually vocal, has not said much.

The final discussion at the end of an Outward Bound course is typically a recapitulation of the significant happenings during the experience, an expression of highlights, low points, criticisms, congratulations, suggestions. Anne has chosen to focus the last flagging energies of the group on an issue that she feels is important. The emotional tenor of the group is not warm. There is strong resistance to dealing with the subject. Anne comes across more assertive than at any previous time during the past ten days. As something of an outsider in the group, involved but detached, I admire Anne's decision to push an issue that is clearly unpopular but that very clearly stems directly from the activities of the day.

Every Outward Bound experience is qualitatively unique for the participants. Rather than having a preprogrammed laundry list of learnings that must be accomplished (with the exception of course of the basic technical skills), a good instructor will capitalize on the experience of the group, deal with the issues raised, and not be cowed in the face of group resistance when issues they would prefer to ignore arise.

Despite the hour and the inherent difficulties of facilitating a meaningful discussion in the face of the fatigue we all feel, I personally feel supportive of Anne's efforts. A real learning situation has been explored, and the events of the day have not been left hanging. Perhaps tomorrow morning when we dock at Rockland, there will be an hour available for a warm sharing of the experiences of the past ten days before we leave.

Shuffling, rustling, squirming—people bed down. Little groans punctuate the activity as tired muscles search for places of repose on the oars. The candle is blown out. The only remaining sound is the occasional creak as the *Dawn Treader* sways at her mooring.

Morning arrives quickly. In no time at all, it seems, we are up in the gray dawn, sailing again. Rockland is a bustle of activity. Now comes the readjustment of entry back into the complexities of the civilized life. The Outward Bound

base is a large warehouse structure, new, modern, jarring after the simplicity of the *Dawn Treader*.

There are the formalities. Gear is checked in, the boat is cleaned and hosed down with fresh water. Course impressions—final evaluations of the experience—are written. Personal possessions are returned: suitcases, clean clothes, money, airline tickets, car keys, all the trappings. It is a bittersweet time. We still have one foot on the *Dawn Treader* but feel the pull of our next destination. It is time to move on, but it is a time also to regret separation from the existence of the past few days. Re-entry, that's how Outward Bound folks describe the transition, stepping from one culture back into the parent one. The dissolution of a temporary society and reabsorption into the organization of the permanent one.

There is no time for a group discussion. Good-byes are said with hugs, handshakes, some tears. Curt's inevitable bad jokes, the awkward one-liners, tenuously cover deeper emotions of separation. He grins at everybody, punches people in the stomach (gently), invites all and sundry to Boston sometime.

We spend a couple of minutes together, separate from the others. Curt becomes a bit more serious. "I know that people occasionally think me too demanding, dictatorial. Sometimes I'm impatient and want to get things done too quickly." There is a concerned expression on his face. "Other times I'm overzealous about being helpful, and I may step on other people's toes." A small grin. "But—" He lets the "but" dangle. I know what he means. He doesn't have to finish the sentence. "Come to Boston sometime, huh." He drifts off to chat with the others.

Bill Dennett is prowling around, throwing his arm around people's shoulders, looking lost. We talk. "My main experience with Outward Bound," he says, "has been reaffirming my faith in myself. This reinforcement of my positive attributes is damn important given the relative isolation of my job." He sits down on the floor, crosses his legs, looks reflective.

"How about the future?" I ask.

"Outward Bound will be that quiet experience in my mind to which I can return in fantasy for strength," he replies. "When the conservatory seems to be falling apart, I can think of that navigation through the fog and then wonder how and why the bureaucratic BS is getting to me."

"What do you see as being the most important factor in the Outward Bound process?"

This is a hard one. He screws up his face.

"Well." A pause. "I guess I'd have to say that for me it's the way we were forced to deal with ambiguity under stress. I think that's the biggest single attribute; creating order from chaos is the basis for the Outward Bound experience."

The bus arrives. Last hugs, and they are gone, each to a separate direction.

Six months pass, and I receive a long letter from Suejee. It is November; Hurricane Island seems an aeon or two ago.

"Each day that goes by brings me further away from those memorable ten days off the coast of Maine," she writes.

In the body of her letter she recaps the highlights of her Outward Bound experience: the first day on the boat, reactions to Anne and the others in the group, her insecurities, raising the mainsail, sleeping on the boat, learning the skill of controlling the *Dawn Treader*, run and dip—and the dilemma of the first morning's jump, solo—Little Garden island, her self-pity and recognition of her need for self-motivation, final expedition, and the late-night discussion on the boat at the end of the final day.

"I had gone to Outward Bound without any expectations and, in essence, I had simply spent ten days in discomfort and austerity, living through an experience best described as being without creature comforts. Yet, somehow, I'd go back without one second of regret.

". . . So, I asked myself why and how Outward Bound left such a positive impression in my life."

I flash back to Suejee perched on the edge of that twenty-foot drop above the ocean, back to her on the platform of the Flea's Leap, her "Damn. Damn. Damn," the clenched fists, the intense determination to overcome the obstacles that impeded her.

"The day after my return, I started work. . . . Everyone was perceiving me with this aura of health. . . . I went straight home that day and stood on the scale. I had lost those ten pounds that I had been struggling with for years

. . . incredible! Then I took a good look at myself in the mirror. . . . The physical self that looked back was great . . . but more than a physical improvement, I remember thinking, 'Funny what a little bit of self-respect can do to a person.' "

"If I were to describe the next weeks," she writes, "I would have to say, 'glad to be alive.' I found myself in an improved state of physical fitness unlike anything I'd felt in a long, long time. I could do things that were unheard of before Outward Bound."

Probably the most painful thorn in the flesh of Outward Bound staff is that provided by the question, "But what about afterward?" Does Outward Bound have any lasting effects? It's an intense experience, sure, but does it have any long-term effects on the way a person feels about him or herself? Does it have any lasting effects on *behavior?* The more jargon-oriented staff, the educators, those who have been to graduate school and who read books by John Dewey and Jerome Bruner, talk about "transfer," changes resulting from Outward Bound that carry over and last in the person's home environment. There is a body of research data on Outward Bound: statistics, reports, follow-up studies. They indicate that for some people Outward Bound does have lasting effects. I value Suejee's letter more than the questionnaire data. It's simple, direct, personal.

She tells a little story: "For example, there's a mountain that rises up from the middle of downtown Montreal. It was always my nemesis. I would normally get off my bike at the second light before the last, steepest rise. Then I'd walk to the point where I could continue with minimal effort and glide all the way home.

". . . But one particular week . . . 'Yes, I can. Yes, I can.' . . . What a thrill. I absolutely gloated getting over that mountain in one shot."

So interesting. For most of her time at Hurricane Suejee sat on a boat. Agreed, she ran around the island a couple of times. Not enough exercise to have any dramatic effect on her physical condition, though. Just *what* had taken place to give her the oomph to pedal her bike in one go over that nemesis hill in Montreal?

In her letter Suejee continues, "The washing and rebuilding of my self-image through this Outward Bound experience was just what I had needed. . . . The me that looked out at the world was friendlier, more relaxed, and also braver and less paranoid of life. I decided that bravery was not just a word we used to describe other people, the ones in the movies. Even *I* can do things that can be considered brave."

Suejee's letter brought home an indefinable, indescribable, uncommunicable element of the Outward Bound program. Uncommunicable, that is, to those who haven't experienced it. A complex amalgam of responses that so far has deftly defied analysis, scientific probing, and the insults of the categorization of jargon.

Suejee recognized her bravery, her worth. That did it quite nicely for me. A cardinal sin in social science research is to take the data obtained from a single individual and apply those data to the population that the single individual represents. Well, for my money I'm happy to stand accountable for a considerable amount of generalization from Suejee's case because in her uniqueness she is typical.

Every Outward Bound instructor you talk to will have her or his list of Suejees, of those who weeks, months, years after the program have written to talk about what has happened to them since.

Chapter Four

THE NORTHWEST
OUTWARD BOUND SCHOOL

White Pass sits on the six-thousand-foot contour, a snow-blanketed depression on a long, broad ridge. Below, the deep valley cradling the Sauk River extends to the west. It is 6 P.M., and the sun shafts rays of gleaming light through tiered cumuli. The clouds stand in heavy, solid ranks. There is a brooding intensity that presages rain. Flashes dance on the horizon. Around White Pass the air is still, damp, evening-heavy.

To the east is White River. The monolithic side walls of its valley rise five thousand feet from river to ridge crest. Morphological immensity, massive sculptured muscles that stand out from the earth's torso like a weight lifter's abdominals. These mountains, the Cascades of north Washington, are among the most rugged uplifts on the North American continent.

Camp is in a grassy depression. A few stunted pines, meager shelter, rim its perimeter to the east. Two red tarps and a smaller blue one snuggle among the trees. A fourth tarp, a tenuous construction held aloft on ice axes and dead branches, occupies the center of the open grass. It eschews the shelter of the trees to take advantage of the penthouse view. Its occupants seem unfearful of the wind that could roar up from the Sauk River depths to transform their red roof into a high-flying kite.

White Pass was reached after a day and a half's grueling slog up the White River valley. The walk emphasized the bulk of this topography, the grossness of the landforms. To traverse the slopes of these mountains takes indefatigable persistence.

A weary, silent group reached White Pass an hour ago. Now the evening's peace is mutilated.

"Awh shit! You asshole!"

The exclamation comes from the red tent in the middle of the grass.

"Goddammit, motherfucker. I couldn't help it." The response echoes.

"Liar. That was the clumsiest, stupidest thing you coulda done if you'd tried."

"I couldn't help it. It was an accident."

The voices drop a little after the first decibel-charged exclamations but can still be heard from fifty yards away.

A steady bickering ensues. Another voice joins in. And a fourth.

"Hey. Hey!"

The fifth voice, more commanding, comes from the blue tarp in the trees. Its owner peers out. He is about twenty-four. A mop of blond hair wearing a leather eyeshade. His is the voice of authority.

"What's happening over there, you guys?"

"It's Gregg. The asshole kicked over the soup."

A pause.

"Well keep it down. Make some more."

"Hey, Dog? How's about if we take him out and bury him in the snow," one of the voices calls back.

"I don't care what you do to him. Just do it quietly."

There is laughter from the red tent.

The blond-haired head withdraws. The wearer of the leather eyeshade pushes it back an inch or so on his forehead and absently tugs at a stray blond curl. He is horizontal, propped on one elbow, the lower half of his body tucked into a sleeping bag.

"Dammit," his companion comments. "They just have to mouth off all the time."

"Damn right."

"It's a problem."

There is silence for a while, during which the two consider.

There are three of us under the blue tarp. Yellow Dog, the wearer of the eyeshade, is the instructor, his companion, Fritz Moritz, the assistant. I am along for the ride.

We are now in the second week of the course. Yellow Dog has been the reply on more than one occasion to my request for his real name. I have accepted it and stopped asking the question.

Fritz is a pleasant-faced, smiling young man in his early twenties. He is earnest and considerate. Yellow Dog and Fritz have a group of ten boys, aged between sixteen and nineteen, in their charge. It is a standard twenty-three-day Outward Bound course, and we are now at the end of the second day of the Alpine expedition, toward the end of the course.

When Outward Bound was first started in Great Britain the program was exclusively for adolescent boys. Lawrence Holt, an owner of merchant ships, noticed that young seamen cast adrift in open boats after their ships had been torpedoed succumbed more easily than their older companions. Holt theorized that the older men's enhanced survival capacity resulted from their years of experience dealing with life's hardships.

At that same time a German educator, Kurt Hahn, was the headmaster of an elite British prep school in Scotland, Gordonstoun (a private school favored by the British aristocracy, which both Prince Philip and Prince Charles were to attend). Hahn had been a teacher at the noted Salem School in Germany and had fled the country after publicly criticizing the Nazi party.

At Gordonstoun Hahn had integrated certain character-building activities into a classically academic preuniversity curriculum. One of the pillars of his character-building program was outdoor adventure. Pupils from Gordonstoun regularly undertook hiking, climbing, and camping expeditions in the nearby wild Scottish mountains.

The concept of social service as an educational vehicle was also propounded by Hahn. Gordonstoun was located by the shore of a Scottish sea-loch. The school operated the coast guard service for a twenty-mile stretch of shore. Under the supervision of their teachers, pupils trained regularly and manned the lifeboats during actual rescues.

Lawrence Holt was familiar with Hahn's work at Gordonstoun. The two men discussed the idea of a crash course in which Hahn's character-building experiences could be provided for immature young seamen. From these discussions the first Outward Bound program grew. The program, at Aberdovey in northern Wales in 1939, lasted four weeks and was the embryonic model for Outward Bound schools throughout the world in later years. Today there are Outward Bound schools throughout the world: in the United States, the Netherlands, Austria, West Germany, Norway, Great Britain, Kenya, Nigeria, Rhodesia, South Africa, Zambia, Hong Kong, Malaysia, Singapore, Australia, and New Zealand.

From the earliest days, when programs were designed exclusively for adolescent boys, Outward Bound programs have proliferated to encompass a variety of diverse populations: girls, coeducational groups, schoolteachers, industrial executives, juvenile delinquents, women over thirty, and others. Here in the North Cascades, Yellow Dog and Fritz are leading the most traditional type of Outward Bound group.

"You really have to be like a sergeant major with 'em sometimes," says Fritz.

Yellow Dog grins. "Yep. There are times when the only thing they understand is getting their asses kicked."

He reflects for a moment. "It's hard, you know. On the one hand you want for them to do it themselves, just figure it out. But at other times there are things to get done, places to get to, and it just can't take all day."

Yellow Dog and Fritz go back and forth for a while, debating the pros and cons of directive versus nondirective leadership. Classically the Outward Bound instructor will be directive at the beginning of the program, phasing him or herself out as the course progresses.

"One thing I have noticed these last couple of days," comments Fritz, "is that they seem to make better time hiking when we're not around."

Yellow Dog considers this. He absentmindedly picks at his teeth with a sharp piece of twig.

"I hadn't noticed. But you're right. They do."

"Probably," Fritz offers, "because they know they don't have us to rely on.

Yellow Dog teaching map and compass.

When we're around, they get used to having us tell 'em what to do. We're the authority. They're perverse. They enjoy keeping us waiting. When we're not there, they get it together and get on with it."

Yellow Dog nods in agreement. "You're right. They came up that last section of trail today real well. If we'd been around, we'd have wasted time cussing 'em. They'd have got into sitting around and moaning and what have you."

I ask a question. "I notice that you camp separately. Is that part of the same line of thinking?"

"Sure is," answers Yellow Dog. "If we camped with 'em, well, sure they'd be a bit quieter." He cocks an ear. Raucous voices erupt periodically from the other tarps. "But basically I think it's good for them to get their jollies out without us sitting on them all the time. They figure everything out eventually. May take awhile sometimes, but they do it."

Yellow Dog's style is earthy-rough. He is, frankly, plain grubby most of the time. He just doesn't put much energy into keeping clean. His shirt is raggedy, pants darned and patched. Most nights he sleeps in them. As he talks, he occasionally runs his fingers through his twisted mop of hair or scratches. He reminds me of a fur trapper roaming these mountains over a century ago, before soap, combs, mirrors, hot baths, the amenities of civilization, were thought of. He also has the elemental honesty that we romantically attribute to the pioneers. When Dog itches, he scratches. When he's mad, he curses. When he's thoughtful, there's a lot of concern on his face. When he's happy, he can dance with glee, whoop, slap the flat of his hand on his thigh, and infect his companions with high spirits.

"Come on, Dog," I say a little later. "How about it?"

He knows what I'm getting at but gives a sly grin.

"How about what?"

"Your name. Yellow Dog. Where's it from?"

He ponders.

"Well—"

He enjoys keeping me waiting.

Eventually—

"It's an Indian name. A few years ago I was living in the woods." He doesn't say where. I don't ask. From the way Dog acts, it seems natural to assume he has *always* lived in the woods. "There was this old Crow Indian, a wise, wise old man. He was the fruit of many reincarnations. He gave it to me, told me it was my *real* name."

Dog's eyes glaze perceptibly as he speaks. For a while he is silent, in touch with the one who christened him.

I reflect on what he has said. Fanciful? Perhaps. But there is strength of conviction in Yellow Dog's words. He *lives* the lore of his beliefs. There is no doubt in my mind that he resonates here in these mountains to the same callings that influenced the native dwellers of many years ago. I was mistaken comparing Yellow Dog to a fur trapper. To all intents and purposes here in these mountains he feels himself as Indian.

But, not to romanticize him, there is the crude and ornery side, too. With a grunting laugh he exclaims, "Sleazy Mothers. Listen to 'em."

The Sleazy Mothers. Yellow Dog's name for the patrol.

"Guess we'd better go talk to 'em if we're gonna get anything done tomorrow," Fritz says.

"Hey, Sleazy Mothers!" Yellow Dog pokes his head outside the tent and hollers. "Everybody. Get together at Tom's tarp. Pronto."

It is a raggedy group of ten who gather under the tarp. Grimy faces, ash-smeared from the campfire, matted hair, refugees from the final chapters of *Lord of the Flies*.

John Hotchkiss, tall, blond, is the natural leader of the group. He comes from Shawnee Mission, Kansas. "Normally I'm a loner," he has told me earlier. "I can be by myself, even when I'm with this crew. I just close 'em off."

Everyone is crammed under the red tarp with the penthouse view. There is good-natured jostling and ribbing going on. "OK. OK. Cool it for a while, you guys. Dog's got something to say." John's voice is assertive. Quiet descends.

"We hiked eleven hours today," says Yellow Dog. "That's not bad. Tomorrow we should be able to reach the bivvy site for Glacier Peak about four hours from here."

"A bivvy? What's that?" The speaker is an earnest-looking boy wearing a navy blue wool hat pulled down at the front so he has to peer out from under

John Hotchkiss.

it. Tom Biggs, one of the quieter, more sensible members of the group. Fit, well-organized, solid.

Yellow Dog chews his bottom lip. "It's camping where there isn't a real campsite. We're gonna be huddled in the rocks on a really exposed ridge."

"How come?" It's Gregg, the demolisher of the soup.

"Because it's the best place to start the climb from. If we're gonna make the summit and be back in good time, we have to camp as high as we can the night before."

Glacier Peak is the major mountain of this area. In fact, we have been traveling through the Glacier Peak Wilderness Area for the past few days. The map shows the summit height of Glacier Peak as 10,541 feet. It is a complex snow mountain. Each flank is formed by steep glaciers converging on the summit: Cool Glacier, Sitkum Glacier, Chocolate Glacier, Ptarmigan Glacier. The mountain is a gigantic snow castle from which occasional bands of black rock protrude.

The glaciers are living entities. They move imperceptibly down the mountain, furrowed by deep crevasses—perilous to the mountaineer.

Outward Bound's record in reaching the summit of Glacier Peak has not been good, Yellow Dog tells us. We are the second group to attempt it this summer. The first group, a month ago, failed. Last year, throughout the whole of the summer, no groups were successful.

Crossing the White Chuck Glacier.

"Why?" asks John Hotchkiss.

"Weather, mainly," replies Yellow Dog. "We can only go for the top if the weather holds good."

The weather in the Cascades is notoriously fickle. There is considerable precipitation—rain at lower elevations and snow higher. We have neither enough food nor enough time to wait more than two nights at the high bivouac. From Dog's description of the past failures it seems that the odds are stacked against us.

"Tomorrow," Dog continues, "we'll be on snow most of the way."

We had reached the snow line a couple of hours before arriving at our present campsite. Tomorrow we will leave White Pass early and cross a ridge that we can see a few hundred feet above us. Beyond the ridge the map shows a broad white expanse some two miles across: the White Chuck Glacier. We have to traverse it to reach the bivouac on the south ridge of Glacier Peak.

Dog and Fritz spend half an hour talking to the group, going over details of the coming day. We need to be well organized and away from camp early to take advantage of the hard snow, frozen by the night cold. If we are late or slow, the sun will melt the snow's surface, making progress laborious and, as snowbridges over crevasses soften, more dangerous.

Dog's shout echoes through camp half an hour before sunrise next morning.

"Let's go! Come on, Sleazy Mothers! Out of the sack! We're out of here!"

It takes two hours to breakfast and pack. Not bad. Some Outward Bound groups have been known to take up to four hours getting ready in the morning.

The traverse of the White Chuck Glacier is uneventful. The snow is firm; the going, straightforward. There are a number of gaping crevasses, but they are obvious, and we give them a wide berth.

It is an impressive place, this expanse of snow glacier, an easy place in which to feel small and insignificant. It is a sparkling blue-sky day. The low morning sun irradiates the snow. White glow, not too hot—yet.

Glacier Peak is right there in front of us. It fills the horizon two miles away. Seeing it on the map is one thing; dealing with its reality is another.

"Shit!" exclaims one of the group, Doyle, a curly blond-haired youth with a ready grin, when we first top the ridge and see it. "That's it?" he asks rhetorically.

"That's it," answers Dog. "Biggest snow pile around here a ways."

The average elevation of White Chuck Glacier is six thousand feet. The slopes of Glacier Peak directly in front of us are four thousand vertical feet high. The lads are suitably impressed. We traverse the glacier, drawing closer and closer to the mountain. The nearer we get, the bigger it seems.

We are at the bivvy site low down on the south ridge by noon. It is a windy, exposed depression. The snow has melted, and there are exposed rocks. There is no real shelter; previous parties have built rickety stone walls two to three feet high to protect tarps from the wind. The group works pitching camp, reinforcing the walls with more rocks, snugging in.

That evening Dog is optimistic. The weather has been fair all day. "If it stays like this," he states, "we have a good chance tomorrow."

"What time do you want us to leave?" asks Paul Koehler. After John Hotchkiss, Paul is probably the second natural leader of the group. He is a thoughtful-looking boy, intelligent and articulate. He seems a little out of place in the rambunctious company of the Sleazy Mothers. He comes from Rhode Island and attends Portsmouth Abbey, an East Coast prep school.

"We need to be away from here, actually moving, an hour before dawn," replies Dog.

Paul does some mental arithmetic. "Dawn is at five. To get going at four, we're going to have to get up somewhere around two-thirty to three."

Groans from the group.

"You're kidding," somebody mutters.

"Nope. That's about right," confirms Yellow Dog.

"You're gonna have to wake us up, Dog," John Hotchkiss says. "You know what we're like."

"Not this time," responds Dog. "Time you all started taking a bit more responsibility."

There are worried looks.

"What you are gonna have to do," suggests Fritz, "is set a night watch. One person at a time takes an hour each through the night. That way you're sure to be awakened."

The plan is adopted. Gear is organized for the coming climb: packs, food, first aid, emergency kit (one stove, one tarp, one sleeping bag), climbing ropes,

ice axes. By eight o'clock everything is ready. It is already cold; a chill wind whips over the ridge.

The group is subdued. Most people retire to sleeping bags early.

"Nice to have 'em quiet for a change," says Dog, joining me sitting on a pile of rocks overlooking White Chuck.

"What do you make of these clouds?" I ask.

Afternoon cumulus is common. Usually it disperses in the evening, but these clouds are hanging in. They appear to be building.

"Never can tell," replies Dog. He studies the sky. His nose twitches. "Might be all right. It's cold. That's a good sign."

The clouds are high. The summit of the mountain sits below them, another good sign. If the clouds continue to build during the night and drop, we may be facing trouble. I look around at our bleak surroundings.

"Wouldn't like to be here in a storm, never mind climbing the mountain," I say to Dog.

He nods his head in agreement. "No. If the weather shits out, we'll be out of here and down just as fast as we can."

I wake once during the night and stick my head outside the tarp. It is hard to tell in the dark, but the clouds seem lower. It feels a little warmer, but maybe it's just the effect of being cocooned in a sleeping bag.

The tarp is being shaken. I roll over. Dog grunts. "It's three o'clock," announces a voice outside. It's Paul.

Dog shakes his head, sticks his head out. "What's happening?"

Paul squats next to the tent. "I'm worried," he confesses. It is still dark outside. We can just discern the outline of his figure. "I'm not sure, but I think the clouds are down low."

"Oh, oh," comments Dog. "Have you wakened the others yet?"

"No," whispers Paul. "I thought I'd let you take a look before I did anything."

Dog grunts and grumbles his way out of his sleeping bag and lumbers out of the tarp. Still half asleep, I hear him making his way through the boulders to the edge of the ridge. In a few minutes he is back.

"Well?" I ask.

"Wouldn't ya know it. Clouds right down. Shoot. Too good to be true, yesterday."

"What's gonna happen?"

He shrugs his way back into his sleeping bag. "Don't know. I told Paul to wake me up again at dawn.

"One good thing," he adds. "The wind has dropped."

At dawn I leave the tarp with Dog and Paul. The clouds *are* low. They come swirling over the ridge intermittently. During clear patches we can see that they are below us, shrouding White Chuck.

"Strange," comments Dog laconically.

He stands peering out, trying to make sense of the phenomenon.

"What do you think, Dog?" asks Paul.

Dog cocks his head to one side.

"Doesn't look too good."

The next two hours are spent sitting around, brewing tea, assessing the situation.

Dog has not yet given the word to abandon the ascent for today. Everyone is up. The mood is listless. People mooch about, occasionally walk to the edge and peer out.

While we are sitting around the cooking stove, it is Fritz who comments, "Seems to me it might be thinning out a bit."

Dog looks up. Suddenly he gives a whoop. "Hey, you guys! Look up there."

A dozen pairs of eyes turn uphill. Above, the mountain has emerged from the clouds. Patches of bright blue show.

"Damn. An inversion," says Dog.

He's right. The valleys below us are filled with moist air; the heights are clear. Through a break in the mist we see the tops of a sea of clouds extending to the horizon. We are above them.

"What do you think?" Fritz asks. There is excitement in his voice.

"There's a chance," responds Dog. "We might just be all right."

He shouts instructions. Within ten minutes packs are hoisted, and the line is heading up the ridge. We are almost three hours later than planned, but Dog seems to think there may still be time to make the top.

"No time to waste," he admonishes. "We're really gonna have to truck."

Fortunately there are no lame ducks in the group. A brisk pace is set and maintained. Rest stops are held to a minimum.

The lower slopes of Glacier Peak.

An Outward Bound group roped together for glacier travel.

As we move up the ridge, the clouds continue to thin. Spectacular rolling plumes circulate below us, an ocean of clouds. The surface looks so solid, it is easy to imagine walking on it. Down below in the valleys it must be a gray, drab day, while we are majestically enthroned in the splendorous blue of the high mountains.

Occasionally spumes of cloud rise and obscure the view. We are in a shifting world of expansive openness alternating with the claustrophobia of enveloping mist. It adds adventure to the ascent.

Dog is at the front. The first part of the ridge is broad, low angle, easy. Ropes are not needed. Ice axes are used as walking sticks.

At eighty-five hundred feet the edge of Cool Glacier is reached. It is steep, heavily crevassed. Ropes are put on. Dog leads an intricate route in and out of the crevasses.

Toward the top the glacier steepens. A cold wind has begun to blow. A narrow couloir, a steep snow tunnel between protruding rocks, leads to the summit. The ice axes go in for security. Boots are kicked firm into the snow. The rope is kept taut.

The final steps to the summit of
Glacier Peak.

Dog tops out. We hear him whoop. "Come on, Sleazy Mothers. It's great up here."

In ten minutes everyone has joined him at the summit, a flat plateau, maybe a quarter of a mile across. It is a noisy, ebullient party. From the moment of rising this morning, throughout the ascent, there has been an atmosphere of suppressed intensity in the group. On top it blows.

Raucous shouts, laughter, people rolling in the snow, wrestling, oaths. Some members of the group cannot open their mouths without cursing.

"Ah well," grins Fritz. "Back to normal."

"Thought it was too good to last," adds Dog.

There are four other climbers on the summit. They have come up the mountain from the north. From the expressions on their faces it is clear that they are grossed out by this invasion of shouting exuberance.

Dog groans. "Hey, you guys," he calls to the group, "if those people ask, tell 'em you're from NOLS."

The National Outdoor Leadership School is a wilderness program somewhat similar to Outward Bound.

The summit of Glacier Peak. The Sleazy Mothers triumphant.

"Sometimes," he adds to Fritz, "I just don't want to admit that we're Outward Bound."

From the summit we can see to the horizon in every direction. It is noon, and the sky is still brilliant blue. There are the beginnings of afternoon cumulus as moist air rises, but we still have the sea of clouds below us. We can see other mountains protruding. Some two hundred miles away to the southeast the massive volcanic triangle of Mount Rainier stands proudly.

The descent is uneventful. The snow softens, and care is needed through Cool Glacier. Camp is reached at midafternoon.

Our group is flushed with success. The remainder of the afternoon is spent in siesta: brewing tea, sunbathing on the rocks, taking it easy after the rigors of the climb.

"What's the plan for tomorrow, Dog?" John Hotchkiss asks.

"Glacier school."

During the earlier part of the course the basics of rope work and handling the ice ax had been practiced. But this had taken place at low elevations where there were no crevasses. Tomorrow comes a taste of the real thing.

Our fortunes are holding. The morning brings another splendid day. Dog and Fritz lead down, back onto the upper reaches of White Chuck Glacier. Camp is left pitched on the ridge. We will return to spend the night. Ropes, ice axes, emergency gear, and lunch are all that is carried.

The mountaineer's ice ax is a formidable weapon. Its business end is a curved point: the pick, backed by a much shorter, flat, spoonlike projection, the adz. A wood handle thirty to thirty-six inches long tapers slightly to a metal point.

The ax has three main functions: It can be embedded in the snow in a variety of ways as an aid to balance. On easy, low-angle snow it is used as a walking stick. As the slope steepens, the metal pick can be stuck into the snow and a technique from the French Alps, *piolet ancre,* employed. Its second function is safety. By thrusting either the shaft or the pick firmly into the snow, the ax can act as a backup should the feet slip. Its third function is that of a brake. Snow is slippery material. Should a climber find him or herself whizzing down a slope at the tender mercy of gravity, the pick of the ax can be *carefully* applied to the snow's surface to reduce speed and come to a halt.

Most of the morning is spent practicing these three uses of the ice ax. Stopping a slip is the most fun. Dog finds a steep slope that runs out onto a flat area at the bottom.

"If you ever actually slip," he cautions, "you are really going to have to be on the ball with the ice ax to do anything about it."

"How come?" asks Gregg.

"Because if you slip, it'll likely happen on very steep snow. Before you know what has happened, you'll be zipping downhill really fast. You'll have to have your self-arrest technique with the ax down pat."

He demonstrates.

"First thing is to place your thumb under the adz, like so."

He turns the head of the ax around so that everyone can see the position.

Climbing steep snow with two ice axes.

"Then all four fingers curl over the top of the ax, so."

Everyone is watching intently.

"There's a tendency to stick the ax in above your head if you slip. No good. It'll just wrench out. What you need to do is hold the shaft diagonally across your chest, your other hand low down on the shaft, so you can get some weight on it."

He holds the ax in the correct position for everyone to see.

"Next you need to spread your legs wide and dig your toes into the snow to give stability and also to help slow you down."

Dog lies down, face to the snow, ax diagonally across his chest, pick in, and his legs wide.

"One of the reasons for the legs being wide apart," Fritz adds, "is that it's real easy to flip over once you get moving."

"OK," says Dog, standing up and shaking off loose snow, "spread out across the slope and try it."

For the next hour the group develops proficiency in stopping an involuntary slide. Dog is right. Once you start sliding, it doesn't take long to find yourself moving at a considerable clip.

In addition to the basic method, esoteric variations are practiced. The most

Practicing the ice ax self-arrest
headfirst.

Crevasse rescue practice on the North Cascades.

intricate of these is falling over backward and sliding downhill headfirst. A wild contortion is needed to get the feet down below the head and the face toward the snow before the ax can be planted.

The afternoon is devoted to crevasse rescue. Normally when crossing a glacier, three, sometimes four or five climbers will be roped together, traveling single file, at least fifteen feet apart. If a snowbridge gives way below any one person, and he finds himself disappearing into the yawning jaws of a crevasse, the others hold the rope tight and stop him before he goes too far. That's the theory, anyway. On the Outward Bound program there are usually enough hands available to haul the person straight out. Smaller parties have to resort to complex pulley systems improvised with climbing ropes and other equipment.

Dog finds a massive crevasse, and the afternoon is spent pulling people out of it.

Evening finds us once again back at the camp on the ridge.

Tomorrow we will depart. Dog tells the group that the destination is the upper Napeequa Valley. The map shows a ten-mile jaunt for tomorrow, ten *long* miles by the look of it. The way follows the Honeycomb High Route, an intricate passage across glaciers involving traversing steep slopes and, after dropping down a few hundred feet, crossing a high pass.

We are away at dawn. First across Suiattle Glacier, directly east and below camp. Then Honeycomb Glacier. There are many open crevasses, but they are easy to see, and the snow is firm. However, taking no chances, we travel roped together. We are moving downhill on Honeycomb. Fast going. Dog is keeping his eye on the rocks that form the right side of the glacier, the steep lower slopes of a jagged rocky upthrust, Tenpeak Mountain. It rises two thousand feet above us, its summit ridge crenellated. Dog spots a series of ledges. We leave the glacier and traverse them, contouring around the mountain. It is steep going, demanding care.

Early afternoon. After climbing upward some hundreds of feet, a weary group tops the pass at the head of the Napeequa. I am reminded of that moment when we emerged at the rim of the Linville Gorge in North Carolina. The Napeequa is an enchanted place: a green, lush, open valley in its lower reaches, flat in the center, with a lazy stream meandering through. Its walls flow upward, ever steepening, to rock peaks, snowfields, and tumbling glaciers. Dog tells us that the Napeequa is one of the most isolated valleys of the region. It is many miles in any direction to roadheads. Few people come here. We sprawl on grass, looking down, feeling privileged. Even the loudmouths appear quietly appreciative (a state undoubtedly partly promoted by their current weariness). The Napeequa will be our home for the next four days, the site for solo.

That evening, at a camp in the trees by the stream, Yellow Dog prepares the group for solo.

We have been in the mountains for more than two weeks. With each passing day Dog, Fritz, and each boy in the group have become more at ease in the wilderness, more acclimated, more attuned to the rhythm of the mountains. Yellow Dog has, in subtle ways, become even more Indian—the way he looks

Solo in the Napeequa Valley.

at the sky, the ease with which he walks the trails, the degree to which, at times, he keeps to himself. Sometimes he sits alone, looking, biding his time it seems. Part internal, part observing the surroundings, his gaze is reflective, contemplative.

There are times when Dog is impatient with the group. He cracks his tongue at them, snaps. It is as though at times they interfere with his experience of the mountains, as though there are occasions when he would like to be moving alone, silently, through these valleys, in the way of his adopted ancestors. But Dog *is* a teacher. Part of his impatience seems to say, "Learn. Grow. Develop." He seems frustrated by the group's progress, by its clinging to the artifacts of adolescence. He knows they must grow at their own pace, but he is impatient.

Sitting at the campfire, he talks about the course, about solo, about preparing for solo. He talks of the Indian heritage of aloneness, of vision quest, the trancelike state attuned to truth, of the Four Directions. In a low voice he talks of the earth, "The earth is mother."

Dusk has laid its gentle hand on the valley of the Napeequa. A plume of smoke from the campfire rises straight up. There is no wind. Dog sits cross-legged before the fire. He is calm. When he speaks, his voice is steady, compelling. The circle is attentive.

"When it starts," he says, speaking of the Indian vision quest, "the medicine man speaks to the young man. Three other old men, elders, wise men of the tribe, chant and rub earth on the youth's skin. Then for many hours he sits in a heated sweat box, surrounded by magic objects, until a vision comes—or not, as the case may be. Vision quest is not a dream; it is a state somewhere between waking and sleeping."

Earlier in the evening Yellow Dog had given instructions for a tarp to be pitched close to the stream, its edges pulled down flush to the ground. A second fire has been lit close to it. Round rocks are heating in the fire.

Dog continues. "There are many ways to get into solo. The experience is limited in time span. For some of you it will be a bore. You'll each find your own thing."

He goes over the basic ideas: what to take, safety, keeping a journal.

"My way of starting solo," he says, "is Indian style. The tarp by the river is our sweat bath."

As the evening darkens, and as Dog speaks, there is a sense of anticipation in the group. There have been no questions. Dog has asked for none. He is comfortable in his monologue.

For a while he is silent. The fire pops. Each person stares into it, alone with his thoughts.

In a low voice Dog begins to chant.

"Haiee-ya-ya-yah. Haiee-ya-ya-yah. Haiee-ya-ya-yah. Haiee-ya-ya-yah."

At first he chants alone. Before long the chant is picked up around the circle. "Haiee-ya-ya-yah. Haiee-ya-ya-yah. Haiee-ya-ya-yah. Haiee-ya-ya-yah. Haiee-ya-ya-yah."

Initially there is a self-conscious note in the chant, but as it continues, this dispels.

"Haiee-ya-ya-yah."

"Haiee-ya-ya-yah."

"Haiee-ya-ya-yah."

Someone adds the rhythmic beating of two pieces of dead wood.

There is now a driving power to the chant.

Taking everyone by surprise, Yellow Dog jumps to his feet and begins to dance. His feet come off the ground only an inch or two. His knees are bent. Three shuffling steps forward and then a timed up-and-down. Three forward, up-down. Three forward, up-down. His arms are bent at the elbows. One arm extends a little forward; one, a little behind. As he dances, he continues to chant.

"Haiee-ya-ya-yah."

The movement of his body energizes his chanting. He makes a complete circle around the fire. In the dark he is a shadowy figure, more heard than seen. He continues. I do not know who is the first to join him, but before he has fully completed his second circuit, there are twelve more shuffling figures following him. Dust rises. The fire lends an eerie glow.

"Haiee-ya-ya-yah."

"Haiee-ya-ya-yah."

"Haiee-ya-ya-yah."

Thirteen pairs of lungs chorus. As the dance continues, the volume and tempo of the chant swell.

"HAIEE-YA-YA-YAH.   HAIEE-YA-YA-YAH.   HAIEE-YA-YA-YAH. HAIEE-YA-YA-YAH-HAIEE-YA-YA-YAH-HAIEE-YA-YA-YAH-HAIEE-YA-YA-YAH-HAIEE-YA-YA-YAH."

Breaking the circle, Dog leads away from the fire, toward the stream.

"HAIEE-YA-YA-YAH."

Close to the stream there is a muddy area of ground. Still chanting, Yellow Dog strips off his clothes, wallows in the mud, daubing his face and body.

There is a momentary hesitation. Someone mutters, "Crazy bastard," but in the space of a few moments there are thirteen naked people wallowing. Ten white, middle-class, all-American boys are transformed to mud-daubed primitives, as are three adults.

"HAIEE-YA-YA-YAH."

"HAIEE-YA-YA-YAH."

The steady pulse of the chant gives it hypnotic intensity.

Dog heads for the sweat tent. Using a stick, he works some of the hot rocks from the fire into an old tin can with a wire handle and carries it inside. He has a cooking pot of cold water waiting. Only half the group can fit inside at one time. Six daubed savages crawl in. The others will tend the fire and keep a supply of hot rocks coming until their time arrives.

Inside there is a faint glow from the fire illuminating the tent, just enough to see by. The six occupants squat around the can of hot rocks—so hot they glow red. The chant continues.

"Haiee-ya-ya-yah."

"Haiee-ya-ya-yah."

Dog splashes water on the rocks, and steam erupts. The temperature rises. It is hot, moist, gloomy inside the tarp. The six squatting occupants sweat profusely.

I try to make out the faces, but there's no use. Identities have disappeared. If John Hotchkiss, the tall, blond-haired boy from Kansas, or Paul Koehler, the studious-looking one from Portsmouth Abbey are in here, they are unrecognizable. There is no conversation, just the chanting. One person continues to beat two pieces of wood together. Another accompanies the rhythm with two palm-sized round stones.

In the tight confines of the tarp the noise, the heat, and the steam combine to transport imagination. Can this possibly be twentieth-century America? Are these really the same young people who normally spend their summer evenings watching television, cruising down to the Dairy Queen, or going to a movie?

We have been in these mountains forever. Modern civilization no longer exists. The universe is the tarp, the fire, the hot rocks, the steam, the sweat, the darkness, the Napeequa, and the chant.

"Haiee-ya-ya-yah."

"Haiee-ya-ya-yah."

Each group remains inside the tarp for half an hour. A plunge in the cold stream concludes the experience. Exhausted by the day's long hike, heavy-lidded from the heat, thirteen people quietly find their bags and sleep.

In the cool stillness of the following morning Yellow Dog leads the group out to solo sites. They are spread throughout the upper Napeequa, out of sight of each other. I wonder if Yellow Dog's purification ritual will enhance the solo experience for them.

After solo comes the final expedition. In groups of four we follow a demanding three-day route, trending south, back to the area where the course started. For safety, each group checks in with an instructor once a day at a predetermined place.

Almost before we realize it, the course is over, and the Sleazy Mothers have left for home.

Reflecting on this program brings home to me how far Outward Bound has developed since its early days in Great Britain. One of the astonishing things to realize about Outward Bound during the 1970s is the tremendous appeal the program has for adults. Having just witnessed a traditional adolescent boys' program, there are several comparisons that I can draw. First, the boys' natural

resilience and relatively high physical fitness tend to make them more blasé about the experience. With adults a little stress goes a long way. The Sleazy Mothers handled the rigors of the North Cascades with cocky nonchalance. Second, there were few explicit signs from the boys during the Cascades program that they were changing or growing much as a result of the experience. At the beginning of the course they were clean and noisy; at the end, *dirty* and noisy. The accumulated layers of grime hardly seemed worth the five hundred and fifty dollars tuition.

Theorists talk of the "rites of passage" aspect of Outward Bound for adolescents. Seeing the group in action, the way they dealt with the rigors of the mountains, the glacier crossings, the ascent of Glacier Peak, one can accept this principle and not be too dismayed by the boys' inability to verbalize what was happening to them *at the time it was happening.* A great deal has to be taken on faith in terms of the impact of the course on their lives. Most of their verbalizations were of the "Man, I'm beat," or "The food's lousy," or "Wow—great climb!" ilk. Adults are able to—and need to—verbalize the meaning of the Outward Bound experience *as it progresses.* Adolescents differ in this respect.

I talked with most of the group individually at the end of the program. As was to be expected, John Hotchkiss and Paul Koehler were the most verbal. John commented, "I wanted to learn about myself, to gain a better understanding of myself in relation to nature, other people, and myself. The course lived up to my expectations. I feel I have experienced the entire spectrum of human emotions."

Paul, the most introspective member of the group, had the following to say: "It has given me more confidence in myself, and I have learned to be more

High rappel.

patient with others. I feel I am more sympathetic to others' needs. I really don't think that I have changed as a person because of Outward Bound. The things I have mentioned were always in me; it just needed something like Outward Bound to make them shine."

During the months following the program in the North Cascades, after the Sleazy Mothers were firmly established back in their normal routines, I received letters from six of the ten members. The following extracts typify the range of reactions. On the whole, they demonstrate that no matter how grubby, loud-mouthed, and seemingly resistant to change a group of adolescent Outward Bound students can be, somewhere, deep down, growth and learning are taking place.

GREGG SWAYZEE: "In general, the Outward Bound experience has opened the gateway of adulthood for me. In many respects I've changed my attitudes toward the civilized way of life . . . from just accepting everything to caring and even trying to change ways of life.

"On solo . . . for the first time in my life my well-being depended solely upon my own judgment.

"I won't condemn the civilized way of life and then take the easy way out by running away to the wilderness. Instead, I will try to right the wrongs civilization does. Outward Bound has taught me to take life as a challenge."

JAMES BIRCH: "I guess it is good that we hiked so much because I now think nothing of walking a few miles and appreciate food more. The only thing that changed here in the city is that I hate it that much more. To me Outward Bound was something that was hard and something I didn't like all the time, but at the end I was very proud of what I did."

PAUL KOEHLER: "I find that in this past semester at school I have been getting less frustrated with other people and am more able to sympathize with their particular situations. . . . Another thing it [Outward Bound] has done for me is give me self-discipline. For instance, I am more inclined to hop out of bed in the morning or go jogging in the afternoon."

Burma bridge over a fast-flowing mountain stream.

DOYLE MURRAY: "Before I went to OB, I had self-confidence but not a whole lot, and the things they made us do like repelling [*sic*] and jumping in freezing-cold water boosted my confidence considerably. I can now do things that without this confidence could never have been done. . . . I feel more responsible for my actions."

Doyle.

JOHN STANGER: "As the weeks passed by after returning, I began appreciating [Outward Bound] more and more."

TOM BIGGS: "I have found many instances where I am presented with a problem or situation where I find myself relating these situations to an experience at Outward Bound."

JOHN HOTCHKISS: "I was able to learn things about myself which I might not have seen for years, or maybe not at all. . . . I found the greatest challenge to be coming home and accepting what I had temporarily escaped."

Chapter Five

THE COLORADO
OUTWARD BOUND SCHOOL

Winter. The Colorado Rockies, fourteen-thousand-foot peaks, snow, ice. Extremes. Temperatures below zero, days so hot the sweat trickles off you. Cracked lips, sunburnt faces, thirst. The swish of a waxed ski. The uphill grind. Digging a snow hole, spending the night in it. Constructing an igloo. Making a fire, seeing it melt way down into the snow. Dark glasses against the glaring sun. Long nights. PolarGuard sleeping bags that keep you warm even when damp Spindrift. The wind that tears down from the high peaks, sculpting the snow. Sastrugi (frozen ocean), hard snow carved into sinuous ripples by the wind. Long johns to keep your legs and crotch snug. Falling down in the snow, staggering up again. Ski tips crossing. Whoops! Another face plant. The Telemark turn, graceful when done right. Chilly fingers, metal so cold you stick to it. Hot tea with sugar and milk. The roar of the cook stove, the quiet. Seeing fresh tracks of a snowshoe rabbit. Wondering if that snow slope you have to cross is stable. Avalanche. Windslab. Depth hoar. Ski the powder. Point those skis downhill. Nobody been here before, virgin white. Figure-of-eight with me. Snake those boards downhill. Can't? OK. "Figure-of-nine?" We're easy, laugh a lot. Christ, this gets your blood moving. Dusk, *l'heure bleu* (that hour just before dark—when the light hangs heavy and still and all the other colors are filtered out—that the French call the blue hour). Moonlight reflected off the snow. The frozen snow cracking under your ski. Colorado. The high mountains. Winter.

"Change into shorts all of you. Don't worry. No privacy here. You'll all be pissing in the same snow cave soon."

The bus has just arrived. Thirty-five men and women have stepped from its artificially heated comfort into the cold gray of an overcast Colorado winter morning. The character instructing them to disrobe partially is a formidable physical presence, big, one of those people who might have been described as rawboned if he'd turned up in a Zane Grey novel, which is where he may well have come from originally. He is tall, gangly, with bear paw hands, long

hair, and beard. A lot of intensity here, a lot of purpose. A voice that doesn't come out often, but that, when it does, comes with conviction. A throaty laugh. Randy Udall, Colorado Outward Bound School winter program director.

"OK," intones Udall in a voice that carries. "First off, we're gonna run." He jostles the group. Everyone speeds up. Soon we're down to shorts, sweat shirts. Some are wearing sweat pants; others, leotards.

Udall wears a half-cocked grin on his face. He looks down a lot, as though he's embarrassed, but it's just an affectation, sharp intelligence playing country bumpkin to sucker the folks along.

"We're gonna stretch a bit first, then run a few miles along the road to get loosened up," he calls.

It's not really cold; the temperature is probably hovering right at freezing. But the altitude *here* is close to ten thousand feet.

Udall admonishes, "Take it easy. This is just a jog, a warm-up. Walk if you need to."

For the next hour thirty-five people walk-jog some five miles up and down the road. Most are aged between twenty and thirty; a few are older, one or two are younger. Efficiency varies. There is some heavy breathing among those dashing out in the lead. Slower ones amble in twos and threes, talking to each other. Plenty of action, not too much talking. That seems to be the order of the day.

After the run the thirty-five are divided into three groups of nine and one of eight and introduced to their instructors. Two groups are composed of people who are beginning skiers; and two groups, of those with skiing experience. I join one of the groups of experienced skiers—eight people, four men and four women.

We have two instructors (officially an instructor and an assistant). Ron Mateuse, the instructor, is physically diminutive. He has long, straight, light-colored hair, verging on blond, and a matching beard that comes to a point. He wears wire-rimmed glasses. Mature, alive, sharp, attentive—Ron's face has all these characteristics, plus the active wisdom of youth. One of those curious young-old combinations. He's probably twenty-four. There is a certain reserve in his manner. He is precise in everything he says.

Among other things Ron has climbed the three-thousand-foot-high face of El Capitan in Yosemite Valley, California, and also the north face of the Eiger in Switzerland. Perhaps these accomplishments contribute to his serenity.

Introductory chores are attended to. Gear is issued; personal items are handed in. A major task is the fitting of skis to boots. Each person has brought his or her own mountain boots. Ron checks them over. They are all satisfactorily sturdy, but all of differing sizes and design. A lightweight, short (approximately 180 centimeters) metal ski is used for ski mountaineering in the Outward Bound program. The binding differs from that used in recreational downhill skiing because in ski mountaineering one uses the skis to *ascend* hills as well as to descend them. The name of the mountaineering binding is Raimer; it is hinged at the toe so that the heel can lift on uphill stretches. The foot sits on a narrow metal plate, clamped toe and heel, and the toe end of the plate is fixed to the ski with a hinge. When one is climbing upward, the foot is held securely laterally. As in normal walking the heel of the rear foot lifts at each step. Additionally, the toepiece hinge is also a safety device—too much lateral pressure and the foot pops out.

It takes awhile to adjust the bindings to everyone's feet. They must be just right: too tight and the safety release will not work, too loose and they will pop off spontaneously.

"Having your skis adjusted perfectly is essential if we are going to make good progress in the mountains," Ron stresses patiently. He flits around the group. A screwdriver applied here, a pair of pliers there. Ron's energy is infectious. Nothing is to be left to chance.

Skis fitted, Ron heads everybody outside to try them out. The Outward Bound School winter base camp is a collection of brand-new buildings close to Leadville, Colorado, which were designed and built specifically for the school. The buildings, dormitories, and dining room are of wood, straight-sided, suburban-modern, clustered among pine trees. There is a small frozen lake, maybe half a mile across, next to the buildings. Ron heads in that direction, and for the next hour the group skis back and forth on the level surface, getting the feel of it, checking and adjusting the bindings. One or two of the group have clearly skied a great deal before. A wavy-haired girl in her early twenties looks very proficient.

"I'm Ingrid Miller," she tells me.

I comment on her proficiency on the skis.

"My mother is Swedish," she says. "From childhood I have skied, both downhill and cross-country."

Ingrid is twenty. She is an undergraduate at Bowdoin College in Maine. Later I ask her why she has come to Outward Bound.

"My two brothers and my father all went through the program. I've always been in love with the outdoors, and everything I heard from them interested me."

"Why winter?" I ask.

"I've backpacked in summer and skied in winter but never camped out in winter. I guess the rigor of being out in winter appeals to me. It seems like a real challenge."

There it is again. The majority of Outward Bound participants of whom I have asked my "why?" question have responded in terms of challenge, adventure.

We all intuitively know that our limits are beyond what we normally impose on ourselves or beyond what civilized existence imposes on us. Outward Bound provides *one* way of temporarily stepping outside these self-imposed and societal strictures.

Ingrid is into aesthetics as well as challenge. She tells me that art, particularly drawing, plays an important part in her life. Environmental architecture is her career goal. "And being here fits into that, too," she says with a gesture to the high, snowcapped mountains that surround us.

Ron's assistant is Jock Cochran. He complements Ron. A little more outgoing, somewhat looser, Jock projects real warmth. In his mid-twenties, he is prematurely bald and wears a moustache. Concern and consideration are his manifest qualities—and a quiet sense of humor. He is moving about the group, giving tips on the correct skiing motion, also helping to adjust bindings.

On the flat, kick-glide is the way to go on these skis. Special wax is rubbed into the base of the ski to make it stick to the snow (different waxes are used for different snow consistencies; the colder the snow, the harder the wax) during the kick phase made with the rear leg. The advancing leg pushes forward, the weight is transferred to it, and an efficient forward glide results. The characteristic of the ski wax is that it will stick to the snow during the kick but will glide freely under the forward-moving ski. Waxing is both a craft and an art. Experience and instinct both play important parts in waxing correctly. The wrong wax will necessitate far more effort being expended because the skis will slip back downhill on ascents.

Jock explains: "Start with a hard wax. Blue is hardest. Green next. Then up through purple and red. You can put a soft wax on top of a hard one, but not the reverse."

Conditions on a ski expedition will vary hour to hour, sometimes minute to minute. In trees the skier will constantly be moving from sunlight to shade. The snow in the shade will be colder, asking for a harder wax; the snow in the sunlight will be warmer, perhaps needing purple or red. But it makes no sense to rewax every twenty feet. A compromise has to be figured out. As the day progresses, it will become warmer. Where blue or green may do the job nicely in the early morning, purple or red may be necessary under the afternoon sun. If it gets very hot, as it can do, klister may be needed. Klister is the softest wax, sticky stuff in a tube, used for icy, wet snow. Messy.

It is March. We are midway between winter and spring. We can expect a great range of conditions: of temperature, of snow, of weather.

Camping in winter is an activity that challenges both skill and endurance. The trick is to have everything so well organized that the cold and wet stay outside and the warmth and you stay inside.

Ron and Jock produce snow shovels and bright red ripstop nylon tent tarps.

"In winter," Ron says, "I prefer not to use the tent, just the tarp."

The group looks puzzled.

The tarp is the sheet that is draped over the top of a tent as a second skin to keep out the rain. The tents are pyramid-shaped, and the tarp has the same configuration.

"What we do," says Ron, "is dig a hole in the snow, two or three feet deep, and the same size as the base of the tarp."

He and Jock take the broad-bladed snow shovels and demonstrate by excavating a square about eight feet on each side. They have to keep their skis on while digging; otherwise they will disappear hip-deep in the snow. It makes for interesting contortions as they step around each other, shovels flying, snow erupting over their shoulders. They are fast; five minutes later they have the requisite depth.

Skiing up Lake Creek on the first training expedition.

Ingrid.

Cub corks his wax to a smooth polish.

"Now," says Ron, panting a little, "pass me the tarp, please, Pat."

Pat Steinhart is twenty-nine, from San Francisco, a special education teacher—speech and languages. Earlier, when I had asked her about her interest in Outward Bound, she had talked about wanting to learn more about herself, wanting to know more about her limits.

Ron erects the collapsible metal tent pole and sticks it in the snow in the center of the snow trench, placing a piece of dead wood underneath it to keep it from sinking farther into the snow. The pointed top of the tarp is draped over the pole, and the sides are extended out over the edges of the trench.

It takes Ron and Jock a few more minutes to pile snow onto the edges of the tarp to make a windproof seal.

The result is a pyramid structure snugly nestled over the snow trench. It is a single-room habitat with a white snow floor and a red nylon roof.

"Works great," says Ron. "Keeps out the wind and snow, and the trench makes it real secure."

The group divides into twos and threes, each with a tarp, and for the next half hour practices building the homes that will be our shelter against the elements for the coming three weeks. The thin nylon of the tarp appears flimsy, but its pyramid shape offers minimum wind resistance. Inside everything is bathed in eerie red light from the nylon.

The next two days are spent around base camp developing competency in the skills of winter survival and preparing for the first expedition. Skis and bindings are worked on, adjusted, and where necessary, repaired. First aid is covered, as are the basics of looking after oneself and keeping warm in the snow. Map reading, compass, the mysteries of avalanche prediction—of major concern in the Colorado winter. Ron and Jock go over each detail painstakingly.

By early Friday afternoon all the basics have been attended to. Expedition food is stowed. Backpacks are loaded. Skis and poles are assembled. Last-minute details checked: sun cream? first aid kit? red wax? snow seal (waterproof goo for boots to keep the snow out)? flashlight? notebook? gloves?

An Outward Bound van takes our group thirty miles from the base, and high on Independence Pass, near Aspen, the group is dropped by the side of the road.

A narrow jeep road leads off the main highway, following a steep-sided valley, we are told. Now the road hides beneath many feet of snow, but we can follow its direction by the swath cut through the trees.

Everyone bustles. Skis rattle. Packs are adjusted. Sun cream is vigorously rubbed in. Zinc oxide, applied in thick white layers, makes our faces look like those of paint-daubed aborigines. The sky is a brilliant blue. The glare, intensified when reflected off the snow, can strip the skin from the face of the unwary like paint from the walls of an old house.

Ernie is frisky. He wears a moustache and an infectious grin. He just returned from two years with the Peace Corps. Twenty-five, his last name is D'Ambrosio. He looks Latin, a Mediterranean swarthiness. Ernie is excited about the people aspect of Outward Bound. "A group in the wilderness needs to work together, depend on each other, trust others who maybe you don't know very well," he said to me earlier.

Ingrid and Pat get on well together. Ingrid has her skis on fast. She grins, skis a circle around a flat spot, ready to go. Pat is slower. Ingrid skis to her, gives advice.

The youngest member of the group is also called Pat but is male. His nickname is Cub, to differentiate him from Pat Steinhart. Cub Barnes. He is seventeen, just graduated from high school in California. Immediately after Outward Bound, he tells us, he is heading to hike the full length of the Pacific Crest Trail—2,650 miles—from southern California, up through the Sierras, finishing in the North Cascades of Washington. He is high energy, irrepressible, infectious good humor. Cub has his skis on and his pack loaded and is ready. He wants to be off, following that swath through the trees.

Beneath his eager youthfulness, Cub hides a serious side. He recently converted to the Mormon church. He describes his involvement with zeal. He plans to spend a year as a Mormon missionary at the end of his summer hike. Seeing him now, all skis and sun cream, it is difficult to imagine him as one of those dark-suited, necktied, earnest young men, knocking door to door with the Mormon word. "It's important," he says. "All Mormon men should do it, but only a few do." Cub is looking forward to solo, he says.

Teresa.

The crocodile forms: The person at the front breaks trail, pressing the soft snow down into two firm tracks. It's easier for those behind. The track firms up with the weight of each passing person.

The first hour is an erratic stop-go time. People fall over. Skiing smoothly with a fifty-pound pack is no mean feat. Skiing through the trees, it's hard to get the wax right. Try purple, or purple with a red kicker underneath the foot, or all red. If too soft a wax is used, the snow sticks to the ski. Too hard a wax and the ski won't hold on an uphill climb. Feeling one's skis slowly sliding back downhill is a sensation calculated to inspire a nun to mouthed obscenities. The tails of the skis dig in, and before you know, you're "turtled," lying on your back in the deep snow, arms and legs jerking fruitlessly, pinned by the weight of the pack. It takes a massive effort to regain your feet. The skis crisscross; snow finds its way into everywhere; you try to get your legs underneath you, plant your poles, heave and grunt. Sometimes it takes one or two other people pushing and heaving to get you upright again.

The crocodile goes on.

The trees begin to thin. Broad summer meadows are now flats of Arctic whiteness. Leafless willows, occasional wisps of shriveled twig, poke through. The wind darts down from the high country and picks up speed through these open spaces. Parkas are zipped up high to the neck. Woolen hats go on. The altitude is eleven thousand feet, almost tree line.

One of the group, Scott Nystrom, is having more problems than anyone else. He stops frequently to adjust his skis. He is tall, well built, fit-looking.

Twenty years of age, Scott has a background significantly different from other members of the group. Not long ago he was sentenced to ninety days in the county jail. He had been working as the maintenance man at an apartment building and had lost his job. Shortly thereafter he committed a burglary and pawned the stolen items. His ninety-day sentence was deferred by the judge, and Scott is currently enrolled in a two-year forestry program at El Paso Community College in Colorado Springs. He is nervous and tense much of the time. At an earlier discussion he informed the group that he was taking medication for depression. "I become emotional real easily," he explained.

During the first couple of days Scott projected an image of tough competence that his performance out in the mountains is belying. There was an exemplary incident that took place during an earlier discussion of expectations. People were sharing their concerns and talking about co-operation in the group. Scott thoughtlessly said, "We need to help each other. If someone falls down, we guys need to help."

Ingrid, sitting opposite, responded immediately. "Guys? Why *guys?*"

Approaching the summit of a thirteen-thousand-foot peak on skis.

At this point in the course, before the group had actually been out on skis, Ingrid's competence had not become apparent. Scott mistakenly was assuming that he possessed some physical superiority. Ingrid's tone of voice stopped him dead.

"Well, er"—he paused, at a loss for words—"in mountaineering guys are stronger."

"That's a chauvinistic statement," responded Ingrid. There was resentment in her voice.

Scott looked puzzled.

Jock interjected. "She's talking about you making a sexist statement. We all have to watch that. I do it, too."

"You've made others," continued Ingrid.

Scott looked petulant. He made no attempt to acknowledge that he had picked up on what Ingrid was saying.

Now, as we ski along through the snow, the fallacy of Scott's remark is readily apparent. Ingrid handles her heavy pack with no problem. She has figured out the right wax, and her skis are well adjusted. She glides along at the front of the line, looking extremely competent. Scott is toward the back. He is not happy. In addition to problems with his skis he is finding the steady uphill going very strenuous. He just is not physically as fit as his size and build indicate. He copes by cursing, mumbling to himself, and snapping at others in the group who try to offer assistance.

At a point some five miles up Lake Creek, we reach an old cabin. Tarps are pitched around the cabin for the group's first night out. The cabin is used as a communal room for cooking and meeting.

Early next morning we leave our heavy equipment at the cabin, and the group is on skis on its way to attempt to climb a twelve-hundred-foot peak close by. A saddle is reached on the ridge, but the summit is still some hundreds of feet above. Scott is complaining bitterly about the difficulty he is having. The summit bid is abandoned. The group skis down through incredible powder. An exhilarating fifteen-hundred-foot descent to the cabin.

The afternoon is spent in avalanche clinic. Ron and Jock go over the techniques for avoiding avalanches and also cover what to do if one occurs.

In winter each Outward Bound student carries a tiny Piepes transmitter that emits a high-frequency signal. Should the person be buried by an avalanche, the signal gives a fix for searchers to dig. Their use is practiced.

A snow pit is dug. By digging down through the snow to ground level, the successive layers of snow are revealed. Study of the layers gives information on snow buildup and aids in avalanche prediction. The pit reveals a layer of slush on the surface, the melting effect of the hot sun. Next comes six inches of crusty snow in a compact slab. Beneath the crust is two feet of sugar (loose, coarse-grained old snow). The combined effect is that of a plank lying on top of ball bearings, a potential slab avalanche situation. The group is going to have to be careful crossing certain exposed slopes.

After dinner, when we are gathered in the cabin, a discussion takes place.

Scott is the focus of concern. He comments that he is down on himself, bummed out by his problems skiing. He tells the group he is contemplating quitting the program.

Next morning the group skis back to the roadhead and is taken by van to another area for the Alpine expedition. Ron and Jock's plan is to ski nine miles up Pine Creek to a high valley called Missouri Basin, which is ringed by a number of 13,000- and 14,000-foot peaks. The ascent of Missouri Mountain, 14,067 feet, is planned as the high point of the Alpine expedition.

At the end of last night's discussion Scott had been encouraged to stay with the program at least a couple more days. For now he is still reluctantly with the group.

Tuesday morning and the group is up and away early. The trail up Pine Creek on the northern flank of a wooded hillside is covered in deep snow. At this early hour the snow is frozen hard; the sun has not yet reached it, and the surface is firm enough to walk on without sinking in. Skis are strapped to packs and carried. Their additional weight, plus a week's food, make the packs heavy. A slow pace is set.

In the first three miles, fifteen hundred feet of elevation are gained, a backbreaking slog. At the eleven-thousand-foot contour the trail tops out into a flat, open meadow. This broad expanse is exposed to the sun for most of the day. Much of the snow has melted. There are intermittent sections of exposed grass, alternating with snow patches up to two feet deep and a few hundred feet across. This snow is soft. The next few miles are frustrating. Skis have to be put on to cross the snow, then taken off and carried across a grassy area. It is exhausting work. Each time the skis have to be changed, packs have to be taken on and off. The snow is crusty. Even with skis the person at the front periodically breaks through the crust and sinks knee-deep.

Scott is vociferously negative. He has a sneering, whining manner when things are not going well. Now someone notices that Scott is staggering. Ron and Jock catch up with the group. Scott slumps down next to his pack in a grassy spot. Ron and Jock question him.

"How are you doing? Do you feel OK?"

Scott does not look OK. He pants and is flushed.

"Dehydrated," Ron says to Jock.

Scott is suffering from liquid depletion, the result of sweating profusely on the fifteen-hundred-foot ascent. In the dry winter air it is all too easy for the body to lose its precious fluids. It is important to drink from the water bottles regularly. Scott has not done so.

Now Scott is slumped down in the meadow. The direct exposure to the sun does not help his condition.

Ron gives instructions: "Rig a tarp to give him shade."

This is done. Scott lies in the shade of the tarp, panting. Ron encourages him to drink. At the end of an hour of this treatment, Scott appears considerably recovered.

Meanwhile, Cub and two of the others have skied on ahead to locate the cabin that is to be the resting place for the night. It is only half a mile from where Scott lies under the tarp. Cub returns, having dropped his pack at the cabin.

"Hey, Ron," he says, "I can take Scott's pack if he can make it to the cabin."

Unburdened of his pack and feeling better after his hour of rest and liquid intake, Scott is able to ski the half mile to the cabin. It is now late afternoon.

The cabin is snug. It is constructed of solid, weathered logs, and a converted fifty-gallon oil drum, which acts as a stove, sits in one corner. Dead wood for fuel is plentiful. The stove smokes a little, but no one cares. The important thing is that it is warm and cozy. Outside, the nighttime temperature falls way below freezing. The snow hardens. The moon comes up and illuminates the ring of Alpine peaks surrounding the meadow. The winter night has a piercing immediacy to it. Standing outside the cabin, one *feels* the cold and *sees* the mountain. This blend of visual and tactile sensation gives the mountain night its unique quality: still, cold, gleaming. One instinctively stands unmoving, reluctant to intrude. It is the kind of silence you can hear. A silence so perfect that only minute changes in air pressure on the eardrums bring it to consciousness.

The cabin is the halfway point to Missouri Basin. The next day the meadows are left behind. Deep snow becomes continuous. The trees thin. By late afternoon we reach an altitude of twelve thousand feet. There are still a few trees, sparse clumps.

Missouri Basin is a wide, spacious bowl. It rises in a tiered series of undulating snow terraces. Three miles across, expansive, open.

A campsite is selected in the lee of one of the uppermost clumps of trees to give shelter from the wind. The site is at the top of a steep slope where the angle lies back to form a broad ridge. Snow has collected here many feet deep. Enough, Ron says, that tomorrow we will be able to dig snow caves in which to live and spend the nights. The plan is to stay here for three or four nights, dig in, establish a base camp, and from the base, attempt to climb at least two of the surrounding peaks.

For tonight trenches are dug and tarps erected.

Scott is moody and sullen. He is here physically but not in spirit. He has withdrawn from the group. He responds in monosyllables, rarely initiates a conversation. Ron and Jock are worried about him. Jock has taken a major responsibility in encouraging him along but feels that at any moment Scott could snap and insist on leaving. Perhaps now that the most strenuous time is behind and base camp reached, Scott will be able to accommodate himself more readily to the situation.

The night in the tarps is the coldest yet. Temperature drops with altitude. At twelve thousand feet the nights are noticeably chillier.

The sun climbs over the horizon next morning and erupts into our east-facing campsite. It is going to be a scorcher.

Randy Udall has arrived. As course director he trys to visit each group for a day or two. Today he helps Ron and Jock instruct the group in the intricacies of snow cave and igloo construction.

A deep snowbank is selected on the lee side of the ridge on which we are camped, and the broad-bladed snow shovels are brought into play. We take turns, for it is exhausting work in the rarefied air, and a tunnel just big enough to allow passage of one person is dug straight into the snow. The tunnel penetrates some six feet. At its end the digger begins to enlarge a chamber. The chamber eventually measures some eight feet square by six feet high. It is connected to the outside world by the narrow entrance tunnel. At night, blocks of snow, together with backpacks, are piled in the entrance tunnel to seal the inhabitants off from the inclementness of cold and wind. In a snow cave, the temperature consistently hovers at freezing point, relatively warm when one considers that the outside night temperature in winter can drop down ten, twenty, even thirty degrees Fahrenheit below zero. The unique characteristic of a snow cave is its quiet. Outside a gale can be howling; inside the snow depth blankets out all sound. It is one of the snuggest feelings in the world to be securely ensconced inside a snow cave while the elements sound their furious antiphonies outside.

Igloo building is an art. Blocks of snow approximately a foot square by two feet long are cut from the quarry, a deep hole excavated in the snow. The blocks are jigsawed together in a circle. As the wall rises, the diameter of the circle decreases. The trick in the business is fitting the last few blocks that form the roof without the whole thing collapsing. Udall is a self-admitted igloo

Left to right: Pat Steinhart, Barbara Calkins, and Cub Barnes. (Photo by Bob Davis).

Ernie and Ingrid cozily ensconced in their snow cave.

expert. An elegant structure grows. It is large, big enough to hold half a dozen people.

Shoveling snow under the glaring sun has taken its toll. A number of people in the group have badly sunburnt faces. Barbara Calkins, sixteen and a half, the youngest woman in the group, has blisters on her cheeks from the glare. She comes from Massachusetts. "I love being outside with people of similar interests," she says.

There are two other members of the group. Teresa Greiner, twenty years of age, is currently working as a grocery check-out clerk. She has previously taken an Outward Bound summer course in Colorado. Glen Grant is a stocky sixteen-year-old from Florida who looks as though he might be a wrestler.

By noon the snow caves and igloos are completed. After lunch Emerald Peak (13,904 feet) is our objective.

The snow is soft on the surface as the group starts up. The summit is almost two thousand vertical feet above camp, but the going is relatively easy. The view from the top is stupendous. Row after row of snowcapped mountains extend on all sides to the horizon.

Udall climbs Emerald Peak with the group and then leaves early to join up with another instructor.

That evening, around a blazing fire, responses to the day are shared. We are huddled close to the fire, sitting in a circular pit dug in the snow. It is dark; the winter night surrounds us. I imagine how we might look to an observer hovering in an airplane. On all sides Missouri Basin extends in eerie darkness; the moon has not yet risen. Our existence is signified by the pinprick of light from the fire. In the mountains in winter warmth is equated with life.

Pat Steinhart speaks first. She refers to her feelings on the summit of Emerald Peak. "I don't go to church or anything, but for me it was a supremely religious moment." Pat is the mother figure of the group. At twenty-nine she is the oldest, and there is a warmth and sincerity about her. She is one of those caring, dependable people who invariably elicits feelings of trust in those with whom she comes in contact. She had a hard time physically on the slog up to Missouri Basin but did not complain.

"It put me in perspective," says Teresa. "Being on top of that mountain amid all that beauty, and having earned the right to be there, kind of put me in place." Teresa has long blonde hair. She is just a little overweight. She is enthusiastic about the course.

Ingrid, sitting next to her, is a painter. "It was a peak experience," she says. It is clear that she means this sincerely, but her natural mischievousness prompts her to say "peak" in a way that makes it a pun. "I was just blown out on the summit," she continues. "There we were at thirteen thousand feet, snow everywhere. There were some rocks sticking out of the snow right at the top. They were covered in lichens. Beautiful colors, really intricate patterns. I just couldn't believe that *any* life form could exist in that barrenness."

The dead wood in the fire crackles and pops as we talk. Socks and gloves

An igloo, home in the Colorado winter.

are propped up on sticks around it to dry. There is a break in our circle at one side, where the smoke from the fire blows out.

Scott has become progressively more isolated from the group. He remained at camp, alone, while everyone else climbed Emerald Peak. Now he hovers on the periphery of the circle, keeping himself separate, not talking.

The time to sleep arrives. Unfortunately the igloo did not survive the hot afternoon sun. Ron speculates that it was built a little too big. The roof has melted. But there is enough room in the three snow caves for everyone to spend a cozy night. Scott declines to sleep in a snow cave. He spends the night alone in one of the tarps.

Morning brings unsettled weather. The sky is gray; it is cold. The wind blows icy spindrift through the camp. Breakfast consists of oatmeal eaten with cold fingers. The Optimus stoves take a long time to heat food and water. Today is the day for the attempt on fourteen-thousand-foot Missouri Mountain. The conditions are not promising.

Jock has spent a lot of time talking to Scott. Despite the bad weather he has managed to persuade him to give Missouri Mountain a try. Scott puts on his skis and follows the group out of camp.

There are occasional brief flashes of blue sky, just enough to suggest that if we persevere, the weather may turn fine.

The way to Missouri Mountain heads north up gentle slopes. The skiing is easy, but the wind is chill. After a little over a mile the slope steepens. The rocky summit of Missouri Mountain occasionally peaks out from the clouds that envelop it.

Scott is skiing at the back of the line, with Jock skiing along separately, bringing up the rear, a hundred yards or so behind. As the slope steepens, Scott slows. He does not look happy. Jock catches up to him.

"I just don't see the point of this," Scott complains. "The weather's shitty. I'm cold. Why are we doing this?"

Jock knows that it is up to Scott to define his own meaning. "I can't answer that question for you," he answers. "All I can say is that if you stick this out, you're probably going to feel good about yourself when we get back this evening, a lot better than if you quit now."

Scott stands motionless, head down, looking at his skis. Moments pass. Jock watches him, a concerned expression on his face. Scott stamps one of his skis on the snow. He looks up at Jock, turns, and heads off again uphill, following the tracks left by the group.

The higher we climb, the more arduous the conditions become. Now we are in a thin mist that obscures visibility. Again Scott drops back. We hear him shouting, "This is fucking ridiculous. I've had enough. You're all crazy. I'm going down."

Pat Steinhart skis back to him.

"Hey, Scott," she says, firm but supportive, "look, you're being a real pain. You're not the weakest person in the group, not by a long ways. If I can handle this, then you damn well can, too."

This brings Scott up short. He looks at her. Pat is pretty steamed up.

She skis right alongside him and puts an arm around his shoulder. "We really want you to stay with us," she says. "You're important to us. If you fink out now, we're all gonna feel bad. And I know that you are gonna feel rotten."

"I just don't see the point," Scott responds.

He jabs his ski pole hard down into the snow in a gesture of pent-up anger. "All I wanna do is pack my stuff and get out of here. I just wanna leave. It's pointless."

Pat squeezes his shoulder. "Come on," she says, "we've almost got this licked"—she gestures with her ski pole to the summit now only a few hundred feet above—"we're almost there."

Scott looks up. He continues to argue. Pat continues her encouragement. Eventually, with a resigned shrug of his shoulders, a what-the-hell gesture, Scott acquiesces and skis along behind Pat to rejoin the group, who have been patiently waiting.

"Or-right," encourages Cub. He is high-spirited despite the poor conditions. "Come on, Scott," he grins. "It's all of us together or none of us."

Scott responds with a strained half grin. For the moment he is with the group, but it is clear that his commitment is tenuous.

A little higher and the slope steepens to the point where Ron decides it is time to take the skis off. They are left sticking in the snow as we climb the steep section. Ron moves to the front of the line. During the last few days he has kept himself divorced from leadership decisions, but now, faced by difficult terrain, his place is at the front.

So far we have been weaving a zigzag path up the slopes. Confronted by increased steepness, Ron decides to follow a more direct line. One steady step at a time he kicks the toe of his mountain boot into the crusty surface. He plants one foot and stands up in balance on it. He has kept his ski poles, as has everyone else in the group, and uses them for balance. He lifts one foot behind him, bent at the knee, until his heel almost touches his bottom and in a swift, controlled downward arc, kicks in. Swing, kick. Swing, kick. Methodically he moves up. We follow in line. Unfortunately the crust surface is only a few inches thick. Beneath it lies hip-deep, unconsolidated snow. The crust supports Ron's passage, and the person after him. But with each passing step, the crust collapses. Those toward the back of the line find themselves wallowing strenuously. Ron stops periodically for the line to catch up. After half an hour we are some three hundred feet above the point where we left the skis.

Ron reaches an outcropping of rocky ledges, windblown clear of snow, and waits. We congregate around him. He is noncommittal. But the way he glances around says that he is keeping a very careful eye on the weather and on the snow conditions.

A brief rest is taken—not too long, for we must keep moving if we are to stay warm.

"How's everyone's feet?" inquires Ron. "Make sure you keep wriggling your toes," he instructs. Toe wriggling keeps the blood moving and wards off the possibility of frostbite.

"Mine are a bit cold," says Glen, "but they're OK. I can still feel 'em."

Ron leads off again up the slope. We are now just below the summit ridge. The wind increases to a howl, whipping stinging snow particles into our faces. It is difficult to see. Ron pauses. He looks up at the ridge only a short distance ahead, then glances down at the distance we have covered, and observes the strained faces of the group following his every move. The situation now has a serious dimension. There is no doubt that the level of trust in the group is such that we will follow Ron wherever he leads. He deliberates. This is not a place for group decision making. Whatever Ron says goes.

Finally, "Sorry, folks." He calls down in a voice that carries above the scream of the wind. "This is as far as we go." He shakes his head regretfully and gives a last glance up at the summit so tantalizingly close.

The retreat begins. Downhill progress is rapid. Shortly we are regrouped on the rock ledges. There is disappointment, but everyone instinctively realizes that the point has been reached where the desire to succeed has to bow to prudence.

"Hey, Ron." It is Glen. "I'm worried about my feet. They feel as though they might have gone numb."

Ron moves to Glen, and the rest of the group gathers around.

Ron questions him. "Try wriggling them. Feel anything?"

"Nope," responds Glen after a pause. He is cheerful. "Don't feel much at all."

A predicament. We are still three hundred feet above the skis. We are tired and cold. A quick decision has to be made.

Ron is crisp. "Gather close round everybody. Make a windbreak."

We huddle round them as close and tight as possible.

"Right, Glen. Take your boots off."

Glen looks quizzical. Ron's instruction is unexpected. This hardly seems the place to be without boots. But he complies.

Ron slackens the belt of his pants and pulls up his shirt at the front. He sticks Glen's feet under his clothing, against the warmth of his stomach.

"Wriggle those toes," he commands.

Glen does so. Slowly—the result of the wriggling, the warmth of Ron's body, and the fact that his unconstricted feet encourage the blood to flow more freely—sensation returns.

"How are they now?" Ron asks.

"Better," Glen grins. "A lot better. I can feel 'em again."

"OK. Boots on. Let's get out of here."

In fast time Glen's boots are back on, and we are once more descending. The skis are reached and snapped on. Tips are pointed downhill, and in graceful swoops we are heading back to camp.

A winter ascent of a snow ridge.

Later, drinking tea in the snow caves, the retreat is discussed. Feelings are mixed. On the one hand everyone realizes that to have pressed on would have been folly. But climbing a fourteen-thousand-foot peak in winter had become a major goal. Disappointment is tempered with realism.

A major victory for the group is the fact that Scott had stuck with it as long as anyone else. Pat and Jock were the two most directly responsible for encouraging him, but the rest of the group had waited and had made it clear that they really wanted him to continue.

In a real sense fighting the bad weather on the slopes of Missouri Mountain has likely been the physical and psychological hump of the program. Now that it is behind, perhaps Scott will be inspired to complete the remaining days.

Next morning the group packs camp and descends the mountain. A different route from that used on the ascent is taken. It proves shorter in distance but more arduous. A trail leads down Missouri Gulch. Unconsolidated snow, deadfalls, and some very steep sections make the descent of the trail harrowing.

At the road, waiting for the Outward Bound van, Scott announces that he plans to complete the program. Ron and Jock are pleased that all their efforts and encouragement have paid off. The group also feels a sense of accomplishment. It is an Outward Bound tenet that the group moves at the speed of the slowest person. Part of the challenge is giving support and assistance to those having difficulties. Service to the broader social community and to one's more immediate

Teresa tends to a blister.

companions has always been a fundamental concept of Outward Bound, as stressed by the program's founder, Kurt Hahn. Scott has provided the group with a fine opportunity for service and compassion.

The final few days of the course are spent at lower elevation in a broad, sunny valley where there is little snow. The group spends three days on solo and three days on technical rock-climbing. The sun-warmed rock contrasts with the snow world of Missouri Basin.

On solo Cub decides to go without a sleeping bag, a tarp for shelter, or food. "I want to see if I can survive with just the minimum," he says. He takes the clothes he is wearing, a few matches, and writing materials. Typically Outward Bound instructors encourage their students to take only minimum equipment. Usually a person will choose to take either a sleeping bag or a tarp. Cub has cut it right to the bone. He and the others will be checked once each day by Ron and Jock for safety.

On his solo Cub finds two logs that have fallen forming a V. He constructs a wall of aspen branches against one side and a roof of two-inch-diameter timbers. By peeling the bark from fallen aspens, he is able to make his shelter reasonably windproof and watertight. Ron and Jock have made it clear that they do not regard solo as primarily a survival exercise. "It's a time for contemplation," Jock had said. Cub spends a lot of time on solo thinking about his commitment to the Mormon faith. "For months prior to Outward Bound it had been running

my life," he tells me after solo. "On solo I realized that that's just not where it's at. I used my three days on solo to re-evaluate my motives. I experienced a complete reversal in my feelings. I no longer consider myself a Mormon."

Solo has provided Cub with the opportunity to evaluate one of his basic beliefs. It is rare for a person on solo to experience such a clear-cut reversal. But it is a mistake to say that solo has *caused* his change of heart. Rather, it has given him a period of time in which to identify his beliefs more clearly.

The final day of the course arrives. There is to be a banquet in the evening. A live goat is purchased from a nearby farmer to be barbecued. The goat's death is achieved by a slipknot around its neck. All thirty-five students pull on the ends of the rope. The goat's death is swift and painless. It is a ceremony designed to remind each person that death is a precursor to the meat eaten at table. For a number of people the ceremony creates a deep impression. It is another way that Outward Bound gives participants direct contact with aspects of life from which they are divorced amid the conveniences of civilization. The goat's carcass roasts slowly throughout the afternoon in an open barbecue pit outside the dining room.

People are wandering here and there, sorting equipment, preparing to leave. I spend a while with Ingrid, discussing her experience. "It has been a chance for me to participate in my own evolution, rather than just being swept along," she says. "There are some intangibles that I can't measure, but for sure they are there."

I ask what has been the most important part of her experience. "The group," she says without hesitation. "I feel myself very lucky to have been part of such a warm, caring community for these three weeks."

Each Outward Bound group differs. This one has been exceptional for the warmth and co-operation present. Scott's behavior has been the exception. I ask Ingrid how she feels about Scott.

"I have some mixed feelings about Scott," she answers. "Personally I found him very difficult to be around, right from the first time we crossed swords on the male-female thing. And looking back, I see that I just tended to ignore him. I deliberately kept away from him."

"So in a way," I say, "you avoided putting energy into what was clearly a major problem facing the group?"

Ingrid pauses. "Well yes. That's true. I really wasn't seeing dealing with Scott as part of the Outward Bound challenge at the time all of the difficulties were happening. Pat was much more supportive than me. She spent a lot of time encouraging him."

"Do you think it has been a positive experience overall for Scott?" I ask.

"Well a couple of nights ago we all sat around and discussed the course. Scott talked about how worthwhile he felt the experience had been. I think we all felt glad that he had stuck with it and not split partway through. He talked about facing challenges more determinedly in the future. But then yesterday he hitchhiked most of the way on the marathon. True, he didn't have running shoes, just his mountain boots, but he could have easily borrowed shoes. To me it was just another example that he talks a lot but doesn't follow through."

I find Ernie D'Ambrosio sitting by the stove fireplace in the dining room. He looks lean and fit after his three weeks in the mountains. I ask him how he feels about Scott.

"It was a good experience for Scott."

"What makes you so sure?"

"First he was able to discuss his problems with the group. More than before he came here, he now knows that he has more capacity to succeed than he previously thought. From what I know of his background, his pattern seems deeply entrenched. He has had lots of failures in the past. He is always afraid of failing again, but his fear doesn't prevent him from failing. In fact, quite the opposite. It makes him more likely to fail. It's one of those human paradoxes."

Ernie takes a moment to reflect. "As long as he tried," he continues, "then others in the group would help him. But at those times when he said, 'I don't give a damn,' then we would respond the same way. I think Scott learned this. It's not as though Outward Bound has *solved* any of his problems. But the experience has helped him to see his problems more clearly, and this should help him sort his life out in the future."

I talk a little more with Ernie. His responses to Outward Bound are overwhelmingly positive. I try to pin him down on any reservations or negative feelings, but draw blanks. "It was just what I needed," he says. "I'm basically lazy. It was great to be pushed. The end result was worth every scrap of the effort."

An instructor demonstrating vertical ice-climbing technique with crampons and two ice axes.

I next seek out Pat Steinhart. I want to talk to her about her experience in general and about her relationship with Scott in particular.

"I'm twenty-nine," she begins, "and a woman. Believe me, I was anxious those first couple of days. I mean, Cub, Scott, Ingrid, and some of the others looked in such good shape. I remember thinking to myself, 'God, I'm just never going to be able to keep up with these people.' You know, me, the oldest person in the group, a married woman."

Pat looks serene and composed as she recounts her earlier feelings. She has lost a little weight from all the exercise, and her suntanned complexion makes her look conspicuously healthy.

She continues. "There were some real hard times for me. The day we slogged with heavy packs on the first section up to the meadows below Missouri Basin, I was sure I was going to die. I was absolutely exhausted. I just couldn't help myself. I started sobbing. Ron came up to me, put his arm around my shoulder. It was nice to be babied. That day was the worst. With that behind me I felt I could tackle just about anything."

"How do you feel about Scott, Pat?" I ask. "You seemed to spend more time and energy with him than anyone."

"I just kept thinking to myself that I was having my own problems to deal with and Scott was having his. I recognized how good I felt when people helped me out and felt that at least I could do likewise for Scott."

"Your encouragement seemed to go a long way in helping him. Did you think he'd stay?"

"He had so much negativity to express. I kept asking myself what I could do to get it focused in a positive direction. 'Give yourself one more try. Do it for yourself,' I'd say to him. Sometimes I was hard-ass with him. But mainly I felt that support and kindness can go a long way."

Scott has certainly been a central focus of concern for the group. For a number of reasons I feel glad that he has been along. Without him the group would likely have had a more harmonious time but would have missed the chance for a learning opportunity that is at the core of the Outward Bound experience—working with, understanding, and giving support to people with different backgrounds and values.

Earlier, when thinking about the process of Outward Bound, I had begun to assemble some thoughts on the program's efficacy. Scott's experience brings to mind another important consideration. In Outward Bound a primary group, numbering from eight to twelve people, is thrust together, twenty-four hours a day, with responsibility to develop effective social functioning while at the same time overcoming challenging problems that necessitate perseverance and co-operation. No mean task. "The group travels at the speed of the slowest." This Outward Bound tenet applies to psychological as well as physical dimensions of the experience. It is a *group* challenge as well as an individual one. The composition of the group is important in determining outcomes. The diversity of backgrounds and the degree to which supportive interactions are established are important factors. Each group will have its own peculiar composition, its

Approaching the fourteen-thousand-foot summit of Snowmass.

identity. Some groups will be highly verbal, comfortable in dealing with both formal and informal feedback. Other groups will be action-oriented, opposing verbalization of the experience. Cohesiveness and a sense of common purpose characterize many Outward Bound groups. Occasionally there will be fragmentation, with struggles for power and leadership dominating. Whatever the character of a particular group, there is no doubt that its composition is an important factor in the outcome for each and every individual in the group.

I have tried to put my finger on a number of factors that seem to contribute to the effectiveness of any particular Outward Bound program. In summary, they are the individual's psychological readiness for change; the deliberate use in the program of acceptable risk; the building of realistic self-confidence; the development of insights into one's self and one's social functioning, including empathy for others; the crucial role of the instructor in facilitating the progress of each individual and the degree to which the instructor acts as a powerful role model; the way in which Outward Bound provides participants with insights into functioning in male-female sex roles; and the degree to which transfer from the Outward Bound experience takes place on a person's return to her or his home community. To this list I now add the important concept of the composition of the group and its effect on the overall learning experience.

There is an inherent randomness in the composition of any particular Outward Bound group. It is an aspect of the process over which Outward Bound exercises little control. People apply for whatever reasons they may have. Physical and psychological screening is done. A physical examination by a physician who understands the rigors of Outward Bound is required. Some people are turned down because they have physical problems. Likewise, Outward Bound attempts to screen out individuals with histories of significant psychological dysfunction, those who have been institutionalized or deeply involved in therapy, for example. One of the significant characteristics of Outward Bound is that a broad cross section of men and women participate. It is possible in one group to find great social diversity. (I think of Herman and Art Duel at North Carolina in this respect.) The diversity is deliberately generated by Outward Bound (many scholarships are made available to low-income applicants) and is an important contributing factor in the program's outcomes. Here in the Colorado winter much of the group's diversity has been provided by Scott.

Scott is in the dormitory when I track him down. It is the evening of the final day of the course. Tomorrow the bus will leave in the early morning, taking everyone home. Scott is packing. I pull him away, and we find a quiet place to sit in the dorm lobby.

Scott sits hunched forward. His elbows rest on his knees. His fingers are interlaced. He repeatedly jerks them apart and retwines them. He has lost little of the tenseness that characterized his manner in the early stages of the program.

He talks for a while about himself: reviews his problems with the law, goes over his ninety-day deferred sentence again, and ruminates on the set of circumstances that led to his committing burglary. This leads him back to mention of his childhood.

"I've always had trouble," he says. "I just don't seem to have had many good strokes from people in my life." He clasps his hands tightly as he says this. "I was at a private school. It was rough. I got bullied." There is a sense as Scott tells his tale that he is partly playing for sympathy, that he wants to excuse his actions and be liked. I do not begrudge him this. The inconsistency between what he says and what he actually does has been blatant throughout the program, and he has received regular feedback on this dissonance. I refrain from pressing him. I feel like hearing what he has to say without interjecting critical comment.

"My mother—" he says. A pause. "No strokes from her either"—he looks down at his hands, frowning—"no love." Another long pause. "We'd go six months at a time without her barely saying a word to me."

Again the childlike petulance that is a frequent expression on Scott's face shows.

"Even as a kid," he continues, his fingers clenched tight, "I was on tranquilizers. Just couldn't keep my emotions in check."

I sit without comment, waiting for his tension to ease, attempting nonverbally to communicate that I'm not censuring, that I'd just like to hear what he has to say.

He moves on to talking about the college program in which he is enrolled and his part-time tree-trimming job.

"Talk about Outward Bound," I suggest, after a while.

He looks at me, frowns.

"I felt separated from the others a lot."

A lengthy pause.

"It was a lot of mental trauma. The cold got to me. I could feel myself holding in a lot. Building walls, not doors."

"You seemed very confident the first day or two," I say.

Scott thinks about this.

"That was a bummer," he says wryly. "Just looking at those women, I had it all figured that I was going to be Mr. Strong in the mountains."

"Ingrid gave you a hard time on that right off, didn't she?"

Scott grins ruefully.

"God, I really blew it. I really set myself up for a big comedown."

"How did you feel when it became apparent on the first expedition that you weren't in as good shape as you thought and that some of the women were in better shape?"

"At first I couldn't really believe it was happening. I mean, I'm a lot bigger than they are." He shakes his head. "But it was. Ingrid, Barb, even Pat. They really had their shit together. They could really do it."

For the first time in the conversation Scott relaxes a little. His fingers remain intertwined, but loosely. On this point at least he seems to have come to some kind of terms with the discrepancy between the way he projects himself and the way he really is. Self-knowledge is a primary goal of Outward Bound. In this respect, on this point at least, Scott apparently has learned *something*.

He leans back on the bench, stretches his legs out straight in front of him, takes a deep breath. For a moment we don't talk. The expression on Scott's face says he is considering what has been said.

Given Scott's past history, his dependence on tranquilizers from an early age, and his performance on the course, it could be said in retrospect that perhaps he should not have been at Outward Bound. He came very close to leaving the program halfway through. If he had done so, it would have been one more failure to add to an already impressive list of failures. The Outward Bound screening process is not infallible; occasionally people do manage to arrive who, for their *own* good, should not be here.

Scott volunteers a piece of information. "I think one of my strong points was that I was open to feedback and criticism from the group. There were times when I was feeling down, depressed, and kept myself cut off. But there were a lot of times when I talked about my problems and listened to what people had to say."

To a considerable extent this was true. I remember Ron commenting on this and it being a factor in his and Jock's decision to put a lot of energy into encouraging Scott to stay with the program. I relate this to Scott, and he nods in agreement.

Scott has a highly developed capacity for self-deception. It is clear that when he is projecting a verbal picture of himself the way he would like to be, that at that point he temporarily *really* believes it. The inevitable letdown as the fantasy clashes with reality puts him in a state of dissonance that generates anxiety, withdrawal from the group, and his subsequent depression.

To expect Outward Bound to provide a comprehensive solution to Scott's problems is expecting too much. Yet, I do not note any particularly negative impact of the program and feel reasonably assured that the learning that has taken place is a step in the right direction. Outward Bound has brought home to Scott the discrepancy between his fantasy self and his real self in a clear-cut and undeniable manner. I conclude that for Scott, Outward Bound has been worthwhile, an experience that for him has been timely and growth-oriented in a positive direction.

I ask him to summarize what has happened to him.

He says, "I learned some things about myself. I'm lazy. I'm stubborn. I see myself more clearly now. I need to open up more to other people, to try to work on not getting so depressed, to try to not build myself up to be more than I am—that's one of the things that sets me up to get depressed."

He concludes, "At least, I'm clearer now about what I need to work on than I was before I came."

13. Pierre Lakes, Colorado.

14. Climbing Snowmass, Colorado.

15. Mountain rescue practice, Colorado.

16. Paddling the North canoe.

Chapter Six

THE MINNESOTA
OUTWARD BOUND SCHOOL

"This is Union Jack. We've been off the air for two minutes. Has anything developed?"

"Read you, Union Jack. You've got a Smokey at two-ten."

"Thanks, good buddy."

The speedometer of the Scout is nudging sixty-five.

An eighteen-wheeler passes in the other lane, heading in the opposite direction. The driver waves.

The speed of the Scout drops to fifty-five. Its driver moves the handset back to his mouth. "This is Union Jack. Do you read me?"

"Black Pirate to Union Jack. I read you."

"Where are you, Black Pirate?"

"Two-oh-eight, good buddy."

"He's north of us," comments the driver of the Scout.

"What's happening your way, Black Pirate?"

"You've got a brown bear at one-nine-two taking pictures."

The driver of the Scout checks the speedometer. Still fifty-five. Taking no chances with a state patrol car doing a radar speed check at mile 192.

"Union Jack to Black Pirate."

"I read you, Union Jack."

"Hey, Black Pirate, you ever hear of Outward Bound?"

A pause. The CB crackles. "Can't say I have, good buddy," comes the response. "What's that?"

For the next couple of minutes the driver of the Scout gives a thumbnail sketch of Outward Bound over the CB. He is an Englishman in his mid-forties. He wears a short-sleeved open-neck sport shirt. The sun has burnt his arms and face deep brown, the tan of one who has spent a lot of time outdoors. Derek Pritchard is the director of the Minnesota Outward Bound School. We are driving north from Minneapolis toward Ely, the location of the Outward Bound base camp, Homeplace. It is something of a surprise to find that this dapper Englishman is a CB freak.

Derek Pritchard, director of the Minnesota Outward Bound School.

Derek Pritchard is one of those legends in his own lifetime that one occasionally meets in the Outward Bound program. He started working for Outward Bound in England way back when—some twenty years of continuous involvement. While working at the Eskdale Outward Bound School in England, he carved an indelible niche for himself in the school's memory by rolling one of the Land Rovers down the hairpin bends of one of the Lake District's steepest passes. In Africa, as the director of the Kenya Outward Bound School, he earned a listing in the *Guinness Book of World Records* for the greatest number of climbs to the eighteen-thousand-foot summit of Kilimanjaro. He also organized a special Outward Bound course for blind students during that period, and the all-blind group made it to the top of Kilimanjaro! Derek Pritchard has had a continual interest in adapting Outward Bound to the needs of handicapped people. At Minnesota he has run courses for the deaf and for the physically handicapped. A Grumman canoe with a folded wheelchair in the stern is a typical sight in one of these courses.

It is now August. We are heading for Homeplace to participate in a special Outward Bound program, a seven-day seminar run in conjunction with Outward Bound, Inc. (OBI), the national Outward Bound organization. The participants are a small group of wealthy people from throughout the country, specially invited by OBI. One of the major goals of the seminar is fund raising.

Homeplace is in the northern part of Minnesota, in the Superior National Forest and close to the Quetico Provincial Park. The Quetico-Superior area is a maze of lakes, waterways, and low-wooded islands. It is a place for canoes. Canoeing is the main physical activity at the Minnesota Outward Bound School.

I am half expecting the experience to be a hand-held guided tour for the participants.

I ask Derek what he has in mind for the seminar and mention my suspicion.

"Not bloody likely," he responds.

It is fair to say that Derek's appearance is debonair, even a little suave. A mop of wavy hair, a handsome face, a certain flamboyance of manner, and a well-groomed appearance give him a certain presence. He is thoughtful but no-nonsense. He uses "bloody" with flair.

"It's only seven days, but it's going to be an Outward Bound course. The best way"—he pauses and adds—"the *only* way to learn about Outward Bound is to do it."

I know that most of the seventeen participants are over thirty. Lawyers, business people, corporate men and women. I suspect from the expression on Derek's face, the twinkle in his eye, that they have little inkling of what lies in store for them.

The group arrives midafternoon, Sunday, August 22. Nine men and eight women. Ages range from thirty-one to fifty; no one is less than thirty.

Sunday evening is spent getting acquainted. The only activity is a swim test down at the jetty. The program starts in earnest at dawn.

The seventeen participants are divided into two groups. Derek Pritchard acts

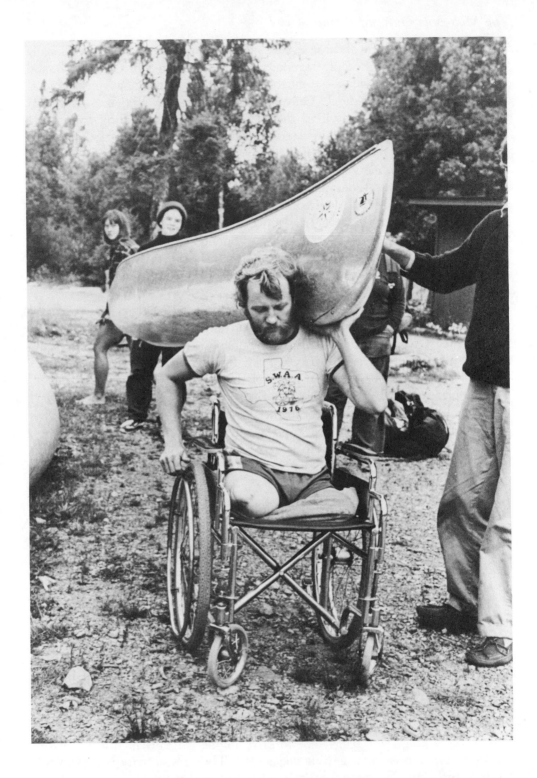

A participant in a Minnesota Outward Bound special program for the handicapped learns to portage a canoe. (Photograph courtesy of the Minnesota Outward Bound School)

as instructor for one of them. He is assisted by John Rhoades, a staff member from OBI. Rhoades is young-looking, slightly built, with blond hair and a moustache. One of the Outward Bound in-house thinkers, he wrote a Ph.D. dissertation entitled "The Problem of Individual Change in Outward Bound" while a graduate student at the University of Massachusetts. Denny Kelso is the instructor for the second group. Denny is a ruggedly built fellow with a beard, a big warm grin, and a devilish twinkle in his eyes. He plans to go to Harvard Law School. He is assisted by John Erkkila, an ex-Outward Bound instructor, a medical doctor, and now a trustee of the Minnesota Outward Bound School.

There are two other people from OBI participating in the program. Hank Taft, the president, is a well-built, energetic man in his forties. He plans to be "just a participant" in the seminar. A female member of the OBI staff, Leslie Simmons, is also along.

Dawn, Monday. It is still and peaceful in the Minnesota woods. Gently wakened by their instructors, both groups jog a couple of miles along dirt roads and paths through the trees. An early morning dip in the stream completes the waking-up process. From the responses, it is clear that dawn stream dipping is not part of the regular East Coast morning routine. The water is warm, refreshing.

Breakfast at Humpy, the dining room, consists of coffee and sticky buns made by Rena, one of the pillars of the Outward Bound community. She raises a large brood of children, presides over the kitchen, and serves food as though it is her self-appointed task to provide a solution to the world's starvation problem.

John Rhoades.

If this is the pattern, the possibility exists that participants at the Minnesota school may put weight *on.*

I align myself with Derek's group—five men and four women.

The day is spent around Homeplace. First aid simulations—mock-ups of a drowning, a rockfall, a burn, and a badly cut arm—are dealt with. The simulations are realistic, with screaming victims giving dramatic performances.

An introductory rock-climbing and rappelling session takes place at Quiet Rock. The face is only thirty feet high and not too steep, but it is an exhilarating experience for most of the group.

In the evening both groups congregate in Derek's living room, together with the instructors, for a discussion of expectations. Derek's wife, Pat Pritchard, will be participating in the seminar, and she, too, is present.

The discussion begins with questions about the upcoming week. Derek is evasive. "Expect the unexpected" seems to be the rule at Outward Bound.

Derek sets the stage a little. He explains his conviction that even on a seven-day seminar the best way to learn about Outward Bound is to do it. "In the time available, we plan to stretch you and challenge you," he says.

There is some consternation in the group, but the mood is generally one of cheerful anticipation.

Derek suggests that each person say a little about why he or she is here and what they hope to get from the experience. John Marvin, a tall man in his mid-forties, introduces himself. He is a stockbroker with Neuberger and Berman in New York City. "I'm on the brink of a classic career crisis," he says. "I've set myself a five-year goal of a complete career change. I'm tired of moneygrubbing. Outward Bound is a first step in the process."

Liz Roepke, a trim, blonde-haired woman in her mid-thirties, talks about her marriage. "I've been an appendage of my husband for years. I want to find out if there's such a thing as *me.* When I heard about Outward Bound, it seemed as though it might help."

Ann Rolley is a striking woman in her early forties, well groomed, with a certain elegance about her. Her husband is the manager of a bank in Topeka, Kansas. "Basically, I'm happy with myself and my life," she says. "I expect a little more self-confidence, as the literature says."

A tall, friendly-looking man speaks next. He is a lawyer with a New York firm. "I've kind of forgot about Fred Yonkman in the process of working these past years. I don't expect to get it all glued back together here in seven days, but I'm hoping it may help." He looks around the circle. "I've just got to say this. I'm really impressed with the humanness of you Outward Bound people. It's amazing. Feels just right for Fred Yonkman right now."

Ann Rolley interjects, "I couldn't agree more. Last year I took a seminar at the Menninger Clinic. It took eight days and eight evenings to get to the level of intimacy that we seem to have arrived at after just one day. That says a lot about the atmosphere you all are generating."

A small, slightly nervous lady speaks next. "I was recently separated after thirteen years of marriage to a wonderful man. It's left me afraid of developing close relationships. Possibly Outward Bound will be a nice midway." After a moment, she adds, "And if I'm going to be on my own, I want to know I can do it."

George Davis, a brisk man of thirty-nine, is the president of the New Balance Athletic Shoe Company. "I appear to be one of the few people here without a really clear reason," he says. He considers for a moment. "I wouldn't mind taking a good look at myself while I'm here"—he gives a little laugh—"the only thing is, I might not like what I see."

Denny Kelso, the instructor, talks about his career plans. "I'm not absolutely sure about the profession of lawyering. I'm looking forward to spending time talking with some of you pros and finding out a bit more." There is a sense of steady dependability to Denny. A steadfastness that engenders trust. When he speaks, he is purposeful, calm, looks you straight in the eye. Beneath the composed exterior lurks a fun-loving side that shows.

John Erkkila says that he is *not* in transition, that he is happily married, with a family. "Part of me, though, likes to live in situations of flux and transition. That's why I keep coming back to Outward Bound. For me, the experience in the north woods is a spiritual one; it regenerates me."

The meeting breaks up with everyone aware that for the next few days they

Arnie balancing his way on the ropes course.

Arnie's nemesis, the high Burma bridge.

are going to *experience* an Outward Bound course. Judging from comments at the meeting, the majority of the group see the seminar as being a potential contribution to their lives and want the experience.

The next morning is spent at the ropes course. There is the usual degree of nervousness on some of the obstacles, but only one person has real trouble. He is a big, genial bear of a fellow named Arnie Shore, who wears a full black beard and looks to be in his early thirties. Arnie is the executive director of the Russell Sage Foundation in New York City. Part of his purpose here is to gather background experience for a survey of research data that he is compiling on Outward Bound. He has been contracted by OBI to collect all the studies that have been done on Outward Bound and carry out a thorough summary and analysis of them. He has told the group that he has a problem with heights.

The high point of the Minnesota ropes course is a zip wire. A cable runs in a graceful arc from the top of a high tree, some sixty feet up, to the ground. A sliding pulley runs on the cable. Each person hangs from the pulley (clipped in for safety) and slides down. To get to the top of the zip wire, a Burma bridge has to be crossed. This is constructed of three horizontal strands of rope, one for the feet and one for each hand. Despite much encouragement from Derek and from the group, Arnie is unable to pluck up his nerve and cross the bridge. The height is just too much for him.

The ropes course. The big swing.

Introductory activities over, the groups pack and prepare for the canoe expedition that constitutes the main part of the program.

Our group has been christened Wahsuhmowin, an Indian name. Arnie Shore, Ann Rolley, John Marvin, and George Davis are part of the group. The other five are Ulrich (Uli) Pendl, five feet four inches of irrepressibility, a mischievous banker from New York who attended Salem School as a boy and studied under Kurt Hahn; Chester Braman, vice-president of the Graniteville Company in New York; Gerry Hoades, a tall, smiling woman from Scarsdale, New York, who had listed tennis coach as her occupation on the Outward Bound application form; Sarah Graydon, a doctor's wife from Connecticut; and Hilary Maddox, a film maker from New York checking out the possibility of making a documentary film about the women's experience at Outward Bound. All in all, a diverse and enthusiastic group.

During the first section of the expedition the group will travel in two North canoes. These giants, modern Fiberglas facsimiles of the birch canoes used by the voyagers a century ago measure some twenty-five feet in length, and each

Evening calm on Basswood Lake.

can transport six to eight people with gear. The canoe is wide enough for two people to sit abreast and have enough elbow room to paddle. The bow and stern of the canoe rise in the curving, upswept beaks that give the North canoes their characteristic appearance.

The canoes and gear are loaded onto the trailer, and the group packs into the Outward Bound van.

By midafternoon we are paddling north following a broad lake, Pipestone Bay. Initially paddling is clumsy; both sides need to co-ordinate if the canoe is to follow a straight path. The afternoon's journey involves negotiating a narrow waterway between Pipestone Bay and the next large open water, Basswood Lake. The waterway is a narrow course with rapids, jutting rocks, and some shallows. The canoes are beached. The gear is unloaded and carried around the rapids. Derek gathers the group together. He is wearing only a pair of shorts, enjoying the water and the sun.

"It's going to be a problem moving the North canoes through this stretch," he says, gesturing toward the channel.

"We need to keep the canoes close in to the right bank. As you can see, the water is shallow in places. We are all going to have to wade along, holding the canoe, and haul it through the shallow sections."

Glances are exchanged. This means getting wet. Nothing out of the ordinary for Outward Bound.

First the canoe is paddled in deep water around a small spit until its bow comes close to the first rocks. Derek is the first over the side. The water is waist-deep. The others follow with varying degrees of alacrity.

Sarah Graydon is wearing a little sun hat, looking very composed. As she lowers herself gingerly over the side and into the water, she gives a snort and comments, "Gawd, they'd never believe this back in Connecticut." She takes a couple of tentative steps and without warning sinks to her neck. She is clutching the side of the canoe. Her sun hat slips awry.

Derek looks over his shoulder and grins. "Gotta watch it," he chuckles. "Gets deep in places."

Sarah grunts noncommittally, straightens her hat, and with a determined expression on her face plows along beside the canoe, splashing water.

It takes half an hour to half float, half haul the twenty-five-foot boat through the channel. It is an exasperating business; feet catch and slip on hidden underwater rocks.

Basswood Lake is an expansive body of water, ten miles long and up to a mile wide in places. It feels good to have the canoes surging forward again across the open water after the struggles with the shallows.

As the evening light caresses the surface of the lake, the canoes are beached on a small wooded island. The low sun—made hazy by its journey through ever increasing layers of the earth's atmosphere as it approaches the horizon—sparkles. The surface of the lake is still, just enough movement to make the light rays dance.

Derek hustles, issuing brisk commands. "Attend to communal chores first.

Hauling the North canoes through the shallows.

Pitch the tents. Unpack the food. Light the fire. See to your personal needs last." Instructions have not been given (intentionally, one suspects) on how to pitch the tents.

John Marvin, Chester Braman, and George Davis struggle with a pyramid-shaped tent. Somehow the aluminum poles go outside the tent. Chester, tallest of the three, is able to perform the crucial task of reaching to the apex and hitching the lines that suspend the tent. It takes half an hour for everyone to figure which pole goes where and which cord ties what.

The night is calm. Some people, eschewing the claustrophobic tent interiors, throw their sleeping bags in the open air, down by the water's edge. The somnolent lapping of the lake against the sloping shore is a lullaby for tired bodies.

Sigurd Olson, the naturalist, calls this area "the singing wilderness." He writes:

> The singing wilderness has to do with the calling of the loons, northern lights, and the great silences of a land lying northwest of Lake Superior. . . . I have heard

it on misty migration nights when the dark has been alive with the high calling of birds, and in rapids when the air has been full of their rushing thunder. I have caught it at dawn when the mists were moving out of the bays, and on cold winter nights when the stars seemed close enough to touch. But the music can even be heard in the soft guttering of an open fire or in the beat of rain on a tent, and sometimes not until long afterward when, like an echo out of the past, you know it was there in some quiet place or when you were doing some simple thing in the out-of-doors.

Tonight the singing wilderness sighs gently. There is a murmur in the air, a just perceptible breeze that rises on the lake and wafts to our island. It moves through the trees softly, a rustle that hovers on the threshold of perception. The night insects hum. The cadence of the water against the shoreline rocks is muted. The cool air brings sleep.

White-water rapids are the agenda next morning. The group is met by two of Derek's instructors, who have with them a number of two-person aluminum Grumman canoes. The rapids are frisky but not severe. It is a lighthearted, fun-filled morning. Arnie is laughing, wielding his paddle with enthusiasm, if not dexterity, as he maneuvers at speed between rocks. Sarah earns a cheer from the group when she pilots her craft with precision and aplomb through a tricky section.

We are back in the two North canoes, again heading northeast along Basswood Lake, when a stiff breeze blows up. Both Derek and John Rhoades captain their craft into shore and forage for branches. Two stout timbers for each canoe are found. They are lashed in place as masts, and sails are improvised from the tent rain flies. With their broad red sails and upturned bows, the North canoes look like Viking galleys. The sails work; the canoes run before the wind. The crew alternate between dozing and handling the lines from the sails.

Night is spent camped on an island at the north end of Basswood Lake.

After dinner the group gathers to discuss progress. Derek starts the ball rolling with general remarks about the purpose of the seminar, reiterating that it is designed as an Outward Bound experience rather than a guided tour. "On the whole," he concludes, "it's going well. However, you are going to have to become better organized. A lot of time is being wasted preparing camp in the evening and getting away the next morning. It cuts into our discussion time, which is an important part of the process."

Uli Pendl responds. "Let me tell you, there are times when I have been very frustrated these past two days." Uli speaks with a noticeable Germanic accent, a certain autocratic manner. He does not mince his words. "The course has been too damn crammed with activity. There is not time to just appreciate our surroundings. It's do this, do that all the time."

John Rhoades answers. "Hey, Uli," he says in a conciliatory voice, "it's part of the Outward Bound process. You know that as well as anyone." (Uli has been on a previous OBI seminar.)

Uli is majestically imperious to conciliation. "So," he says. "So? The Outward Bound process. It is not everything, is it?" Uli likes playing devil's advocate.

White water at Basswood.

He has what you might call a very positive concept of himself. "A horrendous self-confidence," in his own words.

George Davis adds, "It's clear to me that one of the problems is delegation. There are certain things that need doing. If we delegate responsibilities, they'll get done more efficiently."

Arnie Shore has emerged as the natural leader of the group. He is analytic and diplomatic in his comments. "There has been a certain jerkiness," he says. "It's like the progress of a canoe. When the people on each side paddle in unison, with each person pulling his weight, the canoe goes forward smoothly. If certain people slack, or if there is a lack of co-ordination, progress becomes jerky. The canoe veers side to side. Time and energy are wasted." The analogy is an appropriate one for the surroundings. He continues. "It bothers me that we seem to have so little time for group discussion."

Other people make comments, and there is general agreement on the group's lack of organization.

John Rhoades summarizes. "What I'm hearing is that there is frustration because of lack of organization. Also some people are feeling the need for some quiet time. And that we need space for more group discussion."

On this note the meeting breaks up. It is significant that neither Derek nor John has offered solutions to the problems. The Outward Bound process continues.

An improvised sail on the North canoe.

Next morning the North canoes are exchanged for aluminum Grummans. The northward trek is to continue. The map shows a striking change in the topography. The open expanse of Basswood gives way to myriad small lakes, a patchwork quilt of land and water. From the group's point of view the most interesting symbols on the map are thin red lines with a red capital *P* next to them. *P* stands for "portage." The waterways become discontinuous, and in order to continue the northward journey, the canoes and gear will have to be carried over the portages.

The flotilla of five canoes heads on. There are eleven people in the group. Four canoes have two people each, one has three.

Paddling these light craft is an art. They are open canoes, the basic Canadian touring design, about twelve feet long. The two occupants kneel, one in the bow and one in the stern (a passenger sits in the center section), and paddle on opposite sides. They can alternate sides as muscles tire. The person in the stern uses a J stroke, drawing the paddle straight back through the water and then curving and pushing it out to the side at the conclusion of the stroke, to counteract the tendency of the paddle to cause the canoe to turn. This helps keep the canoe moving in a straight line.

There is a stage that comes in canoeing when both paddlers work in instinctive co-ordination. The canoe flows along the surface of the water sensitive to the paddler's every touch, exquisitely responsive. A breath of wind, a lapping wave, a movement from the other paddler and a correction is made without thinking.

The portages of the north woods are well-trodden tracks that have been tamped by feet throughout the years. On arriving at a portage, the canoes are first

beached and emptied. One person carries the gear stowed in the traditional Duluth packs; the other person carries the canoe. (On long or difficult portages both may carry the canoe.) The canoe is lifted and balanced on one's thighs at its center, the lifter in a bent-knees squat, one hand grasping the near gunwale and one the far gunwale. With a slight bounce, the knees are straightened, and the canoe is lifted smoothly overhead and lowered onto the shoulders. One's head is now inside the upside-down canoe. Two shoulder pads on a cross brace called a *yoke* make the burden more comfortable. When the length of the canoe is tilted, down behind and up in front, the carrier can see where he or she is going. Then, like a Chinese coolie wearing a large aluminum hat, the portager sets off. The person carrying the gear can keep a light hand on the low rear end of the canoe to aid stability. Balance and maintaining an even forward momentum are the keys to successful portaging.

It is the longest and hardest day yet, a continuous alternation between paddling and portaging. The paddling legs are cool and refreshing and enhanced by a sense of mystery. The islands through which we thread our way are low-lying and thickly wooded, with undulating shorelines. The waterways, sometimes as narrow as fifty feet, meander their way through. It is not always clear where the water ends or exactly where a portage starts. We feel our way with the tingle of excitement that must have been felt (though an order of magnitude more) by the early explorers.

Portage follows portage follows portage. It is hot and sticky in the trees. Carrying the canoes on the longer portages can be brutally hard work, particularly if there is a steep uphill section. I am astonished at the goodwill and enthusiasm that our middle-aged, East Coast "softies" (a term which they themselves use in good-natured self-deprecation) bring to the task. They seem positively to relish the physical exertion.

Derek and John are keeping a careful eye on the endeavors. One of the basic tenets of Outward Bound is the systematic application of *controlled* and *understandable* stress. The destination for the day, Kahshahpiwi, some ten miles to the north of last night's camp, has been selected to provide just that. It is up to Derek and John to monitor the group's progress, to make sure that the difficulties are coped with sensibly, to make sure that weaker members of the group are not taxed beyond prudent limits. This *controlled* stress, coupled with Outward Bound's deliberate involvement of participants in situations of risk, gives the program its special qualities. Seeing our group paddle and portage their canoes through the Quetico brings home again how much civilized adults relish these experiences once they have crossed that initial barrier of apprehension that invariably precedes involvement.

Kahshahpiwi is reached in the late evening. It is a long, narrow lake with steep cliffs rising on its western shore.

The following morning the group hikes up to the cliffs, temporarily abandoning the waterways, for a traditional Outward Bound land activity, high rappel. The descent down the rock face is such that the rappeller's body dangles way out in midair, spinning slowly, feet away from the rock, a vertiginous descent.

Arnie is appropriately apprehensive. I am sure that he is thinking back to his experience on the ropes course as he awaits his turn. Derek is standing by the edge, supervising. He peers over, sees that the last person has reached the ground, and turns to Arnie.

"Ready?"

Arnie fiddles with his nylon-webbed diaper seat, checks the knots, and steps forward. Derek ties the safety rope with a bowline knot around Arnie's waist. He notices that Arnie is taking deep breaths.

"Relax," Derek encourages. "It's just like making love. Lie back and enjoy it."

Arnie rolls his eyes heavenward but manages a grin.

Derek clips the figure of eight descendeur into Arnie's diaper with a carabiner, with the rappel ropes already running through it. The descendeur is aluminum, about six inches long. It acts as a friction brake, allowing a controlled slide down the ropes.

"All right," says Derek, checking over the system, "right hand clasps the rappel ropes in front; left hand takes them behind."

Arnie follows instructions.

"Now," says Derek, "lean back."

Arnie leans back tentatively, putting his weight on the ropes. He is about two feet from the edge of the cliff, a hundred-foot vertical drop. He glances over his shoulder.

"I'd suggest that you don't look down," says Derek, standing very close to Arnie, one hand encouragingly on the ropes near Arnie's hand. "You are going to have to take a couple of steps back, first. Pull some slack rope through as you do."

Arnie slowly begins to inch his way to the edge, pulling rope up with his rear hand as he does so. The drop yawns below his heels as he finds himself at the moment of truth.

The other members of the group are watching his progress intently. From the expressions on people's faces they are silently trying to will him over. It is a moment of intense quiet and concentration.

Derek says nothing, just stands close, one hand on the rappel ropes, stabilizing them, paying close attention to Arnie's every move.

Arnie hesitates momentarily on the edge. His breath is coming in short gasps. Bearing in mind the ropes course, a betting man would probably gamble that he will chicken out at the last moment.

With a decisive motion Arnie steps back, leans out, and is over the edge and sliding down, almost before we know what has happened. Later he was to say, "I knew if I hesitated, if I didn't do it straight off, that I probably wouldn't do it at all."

The group whoops with delight.

"All right, Arnie!"

"Sock it to 'em."

Rock-climbing on a lakeside cliff.

"Great going!"

Arnie makes it to the bottom in a controlled, graceful slide. Afterward he grins, pleased as punch with himself. "Once I got going, I even kind of enjoyed it."

Later that day I spend a few minutes talking with Arnie about the research project that OBI has contracted him to do.

"What aspects of Outward Bound are you going to be looking for?" I ask.

We are sitting on some sloping, waterworn rocks at the lake's edge.

Arnie's forehead wrinkles. "It is not a research project per se," he answers. "As you know, there exists a sizable body of research literature that has been assembled on Outward Bound over the past twenty years or so, studies of self-concept, of social relationships in Outward Bound, of the effects of stress and risk taking. And more esoteric notions, too—moral development, anxiety, motivation, for example. My task is not to do more original research. It is to pull together all the existing studies, summarize them, analyze them."

"*All* the existing studies?" I ask. "That's quite a task."

Arnie smiles. "Well we're only human, of course. But we do intend to be quite comprehensive." He pauses. "It's not as bad as it seems. I do have staff people at the foundation to help with the legwork."

"What, mainly, are you going to be looking for?"

"Well, in general terms, an answer to the question, 'What do we know about Outward Bound?'"

Next day I leave Derek's and John's group and transfer to accompany Denny

Kelso's and John Erkkila's group for the return journey. They, too, have arrived at Kahshahpiwi and have done the high rappel. They are in good spirits. Harriet Schupf (the woman who at the first meeting told of her divorce after thirteen years of marriage) had been the first one off the high rappel, earning everyone's applause.

The journey back to Homeplace turns into an adventure. It is decided that an evening paddle in the North canoes will lend a little variety. We embark at 6 P.M., but as dusk descends, a stiff breeze rises. We continue to paddle as it grows dark, and the wind builds. We are retracing our steps southward, crossing the broad expanse of Basswood Lake again. The wind is behind us, helping our progress, lifting the waves into whitecaps. Ominous dark clouds obscure the stars. By 10 P.M. the wind is a howl, and the canoes are plowing along through a blackness in which only Denny and John know the bearings. At eleven o'clock Denny decides it's time to call it quits. It is difficult to imagine these large craft overturning, but if in the dark they did—unpleasant circumstances to contemplate.

Denny and John (eyes like bats) guide the canoes to an island. An impromptu bivouac is made on an uncomfortable, sloping, wooded hillside. For some of the group it is a long night.

Morning brings a cold gray dawn. The canoes are launched, and a brisk paddle loosens stiff bodies.

The final challenge of the expedition involves portaging the six-hundred-pound North canoes past a half-mile shallow channel. It is hard, grunting work, and

the distance seems more like a mile. Both canoes are carried and relaunched on the other side.

Before embarking again, Denny gathers the group together at the water's edge.

"The expedition is almost over," he says. He points across the lake. "There is our takeout point, less than half an hour's paddle away now."

Twelve pairs of eyes follow his gesture. It is an emotional moment. In the bustle of activity of the past few days there has been a sense of timelessness. We have been immersed in a world that has completely occupied our senses and awareness. Later Fred Yonkman (the lawyer from Greenwich) was to comment that it was the first time in years that he had not thought of business, not seen newspapers or television, and not thought of friends or family. Now, abruptly, life as usual is close at hand.

Denny breaks a leafy branch from a bush and then walks knee-deep into the water. He gestures to the group to come close. Following his example, everyone wades into the water and stands around him in a circle. Denny has the capacity to be quite solemn when occasion demands. This is such an occasion.

"When the *manger du lard*, the neophyte voyageurs, had crossed the Height of Land portage," he says, "the old-timers initiated them into the ranks of the true voyageurs, the *hommes du nord*, by sprinkling them with water from a cedar bough and reciting the voyageurs' verse."

Denny dips the branch into the water and, as he recites, moves around the circle, sprinkling each person's head.

> *As a voyageur, I promise that*
> *I shall never tire,*
> *I shall always sing,*
> *I shall love the pays d'en haut*
>   *for the rest of my days*
>
> *I shall share all that I have*
>   *with my fellow voyageur,*
> *And, I shall never kiss the spouse*
> *Of another voyageur—*
> *Without the spouse's permission!*

Amid laughter, the bough is thrown ceremoniously into the lake. Twelve *hommes du nord* climb into the canoes and paddle the last half hour across Basswood Lake.

After the solitude of the north woods Homeplace is a bustle of activity. Showers, saunas, a last friendly game of volleyball, the predeparture activities.

Derek's plan for the trip has worked out well. The group feels that in the six-day time period they have been stretched and have actually *experienced* some facets of Outward Bound.

When we are all seated in a circle for a final group meeting, Derek asks a question.

"I know we've only been out for a week, but I'm interested to know if any of your self-perceptions have changed?"

Sarah Graydon is the first to answer. "Yes," she says. "I learned that I *can* do more than I thought. For example, I did badly on the first rappel we did."

"How do you know you did badly?" asks Derek.

"Easy," responds Sarah with a grin, "because I did better on the second one. That seems to be a characteristic of Outward Bound. Progress tends to be very tangible. It's very clear to you when you achieve something."

Arnie Shore interjects. "I have to agree with that. I surprised myself at the high rappel at Kahshahpiwi. It makes me feel a little differently now about the ropes course and the Burma bridge."

Derek looks thoughtful after this remark but doesn't say anything.

Arnie continues. "One of the factors was the high level of trust engendered by the staff. Derek and John, you are two of the few people in this world I would trust anywhere, more even than my lawyer or doctor."

Ann Rolley, somehow managing to look as sedately elegant as at the start of the program, says, "I think I'm a little braver. But I haven't grown"—a smile—"my pants are falling off. I must have lost four inches from my waist. My fifteen-year-old son canoes. Once he tried to teach me. He ended up saying, 'Forget it.' I can't wait to tell him what I've done."

Harriet Schupf asks *the* question. "The simple things of paddling, packing,

Crossing a stream. Three people, working together, support each other.

finding sleeping space satisfied me physically and intellectually, which came as a surprise to me. What I need to find out is, can I carry this over to my normal life?"

John Erkkila responds. "Well," he says, "I can't really answer that question. We're not trying to teach a philosophy per se at Outward Bound, but we are trying to encourage people to capitalize on their own resources and develop attitudes of introspection and self-evaluation."

Fred Yonkman has found the experience particularly stimulating emotionally. He is one of those men whose emotions are near the surface. "I just don't understand it. It's been one of the most incredible family feelings I ever had. I can't believe that it developed in such a short time." He wipes his eyes with the back of his hand. "Darn it, I'm going to cry again if I don't watch out."

On this warm note the meeting breaks up.

The thoughtful look on Derek's face as Arnie talked of having different feelings about the Burma bridge was purposeful. Just before the group departs, Derek and Arnie return to the ropes course. Arnie is jubilant when this time he is able to take those steps across the Burma bridge, sixty feet up, and ride the zip wire back to the ground.

His success is shared by everyone and lends a note of final enthusiasm to "See you later" and "Keep in touch" as the group climbs into the Outward Bound vans to depart.

Three months later I hear from Arnie again. The letter, dated November 22, is short, and I include it here in its entirety.

Dear Bob,

I read your letter as a request for a spontaneous account of how OB has affected me, not a carefully constructed analysis. In this spirit, I have several reactions which I should like to share.

I like to believe that I am adaptive. The Outward Bound course gave me a sense that this was true but that there was a great deal more to being adaptive. I learned as a consequence of the course that situations defined as conventionally difficult provided an opportunity for gaining something more if only I decided not merely to come to grips with the situation but to attempt to utilize the situation to advantage. The particular instances to which this principle apply might seem trivial. Nonetheless, the most troublesome issues to my mind are those which reoccur with regularity and about which one often has an upset feeling. To wit, I jog back and forth to the parking lot which houses my car a mile or so from my house not merely to get the car but to enjoy the distance; I walk back and forth to work, not merely to get there and to get home but to partake of the relaxation of relatively slow, repetitive movement; I go to the laundry piled heavy with clothes not just to get them washed but to find again and again that it's fun to carry more with one hand than one thought possible. Another form of adaptation is, I think, more creative. That is, faced with the problem of how to sleep three extra in my parents' house without disrupting their routine, I found myself fashioning beds in the OB style—with alacrity, style, and insufficient wherewithal.

About the program I remember the heights most. I have feared high places for a long time. I am still not comfortable in them, but now I deal with them less fearfully and almost with enjoyment. The most rewarding moment for me, then, was the rappel and the return to the ropes course, where I finally ascended the wooden ladder to the Burma bridge and took my turn on the slide. The most frustrating moment was listening to some of my coparticipants as they evaluated, reorganized, and otherwise mutilated the OB concept in a round-the-fire chat rather than decide to give themselves over to the experience and leave go of their corporate-managerial baggage just long enough not to be in charge. In those frightening few moments I experienced a glimpse into the social concrete in which my acquaintances and soon-to-become friends were rooted. I felt fear and frustration and some pity.

Just the other day I spent a glorious and busy three days climbing in the White Mountains with one of the members of the other group. As I write this letter I ache and feel good all over. You see, I think I'll be doing more of those wonderfully crazy activities which lead where I've never been.

Sincerely,
ARNOLD SHORE

It is a long way from the north woods to the streets of New York City. It takes a fair leap of the imagination to think that six days there with Outward Bound could have much impact on a professional of Arnie's caliber. But there it is. Not earth-shattering changes, little things. But little things are the fabric of all our lives. On the one hand, going for the car, doing the laundry, going to work each day are not the stuff of drama, but they are the components of which the lives of the majority of us are composed. The fact that six days at Outward Bound has inspired Arnie Shore to feel differently about these basic chores back in New York three months later is as eloquent a testimony to the transfer potential of Outward Bound as I can imagine. Not quite as dramatic, perhaps, as Suejee pedaling her bike in one go over her nemesis hill in Montreal, but in its very simplicity equally convincing.

After his experience at Minnesota Arnie moved ahead with his project to assemble, summarize, and analyze extant research studies on Outward Bound. Almost a year later I received in the mail a fat tome, two inches thick, entitled *Outward Bound: A Reference Volume.* In his preface he writes, "I am not an unabashed admirer of Outward Bound; I am, instead, an unabashed advocate of the need to know more about Outward Bound, of the need to relate research to programmatic interests, and of the need to maintain the highest standards in our intellectual reflections on this extraordinary educational and experimental innovation."

At the present time, some forty years after Lawrence Holt and Kurt Hahn conceived of Outward Bound in wartime Great Britain, it is an undeniable fact that Outward Bound is still an imperfectly understood educational process, even by the people closest to, and most involved in, the program.

Once, on an Outward Bound river-rafting trip down the upper Colorado, Alden Dunham, executive director of higher education for the Carnegie Foundation, asked Joe Nold, then director of the Colorado Outward Bound School, when Outward Bound was going to take steps to validate itself as an educational process, rather than as a religion. At the time, I suspect, Nold did not have a good answer to the question.

Personally (speaking as one with a respectable background of formal training in educational research), the fact that scientific studies of Outward Bound have yielded inconclusive data comes as no surprise to me.

In his study, Arnie Shore looks at some fifty studies in depth and appends a bibliography listing fifteen hundred sources relating either directly or indirectly to Outward Bound. (I strongly recommend that those with analytic questions relating to the Outward Bound process use Shore's work as a starting point.)

Although most of the studies reviewed are generally positive about the impact of Outward Bound on participants, Shore concludes (mainly because of methodological deficiencies in a large number of the studies) that "overall, the research literature of Outward Bound is weak."

It has been my objective in presenting Outward Bound to give an avenue of access in thinking about Outward Bound that *complements* the research data. As I think back through the months that comprised my odyssey to Outward Bound schools across America, I have no personal doubt about the value and validity of Outward Bound for the vast majority of participants.

I have, throughout these pages, given some of my insights on the Outward Bound process. Of these, in terms of the potential effect on any particular individual, I have to say that that person's *psychological readiness for change*, his or her openness to the potential of the program, seems to me the major determining factor influencing outcomes. The other factors—the particular instructor, the environment, the degree of acceptable risk encountered, the amount of understandable stress in the program, the composition of any particular Outward Bound group, and the degree to which transfer is facilitated when participants return home—are all important. But pre-eminently the individual's responsiveness to Outward Bound's special experience is the key.

The incidents I have recounted in these pages—the people, the places, the situations—are all true. The dialogues are as accurate as a notebook and a keen ear have been able to make them. Nothing has been made up, no fiction, no overdramatizing of events; in Outward Bound there is no need. I make no apologies for the plethora of description, for somewhere in these data lies the heart of Outward Bound.

Outward Bound is a fascinating phenomenon, one that *works*, despite a lack of precise intellectual understanding. Each course is to some degree an act of faith on the part of both instructors and participants.

I would like to say that my journey through the heartlands of Outward Bound has brought me new revelations, new insights into the whys and wherefores of life, but it hasn't, and I'm not disappointed. What it has done is to reaffirm for me the inherent values of the Outward Bound experience. It has put me in touch again with our basic need for adventure. It has proven to me once more the degree to which the human organism thrives when stretched and challenged. And it has reminded me that the wilderness is a special and appropriate place for these activities.

In the Gila Wilderness of New Mexico I watched Jeanette, at the point of collapse, stagger to the top of Granny Mountain. After the course she wrote to say: "It's exciting now to find out there's no reason why I can't do anything I want to." In North Carolina it was intriguing to watch Art Duel, the society lawyer, come to terms with the fact that at forty he had less physical confidence than he thought. I remember Suejee at Hurricane Island, clenching her fists in frustration at the edge of the jump into the ocean and later writing to say, "The me that looked out at the world was friendlier, more relaxed, and also braver and less paranoid of life." In Washington I tramped the North Cascades with the Sleazy Mothers, as grimy and noisy a bunch of ragamuffins as one would ever meet in the high mountains, and was impressed with their thoughtful letters written months after the program had ended. In the Colorado mountains in winter I observed Scott fight a battle involving his continuance in the program and his efforts to not add one more to his list of failures—and succeed. At Minnesota a group of over-thirty adults, well established in professions and careers, found that Outward Bound had something for them, too.

When I think of Outward Bound, I think of these people and all the others who in the last forty years have shared the Outward Bound experience. I think of the Colorado Rockies, the great deserts of the Southwest, the gorges and hills of North Carolina, the coast of Maine, the "singing wilderness" of the north woods, and the high snow peaks of the North Cascades. I think of companionship, of warmth, of laughter, of tenderness, of caring. I think of relationships with a group of very special people. This to me is the *essence* of Outward Bound.

THE DARTMOUTH
OUTWARD BOUND CENTER

Chapter Seven

THE DARTMOUTH
OUTWARD BOUND CENTER

Dartmouth College has a long tradition of academic excellence and also a history of involvement in the out-of-doors. In 1969 the Dartmouth Outward Bound Center was chartered by Outward Bound, Inc.

One of the main goals of the Dartmouth Outward Bound Center is to incorporate Kurt Hahn's philosophy of adventure learning within the academic, residential, and social life of Dartmouth College. Central to the Dartmouth concept is Hahn's educational prescription:

> I regard it as the foremost task of education to ensure the survival of these qualities: an enterprising curiosity, an undefeatable spirit, tenacity in pursuit, readiness for sensible self-denial and, above all, compassion.

In a variety of ways the center integrates Outward Bound ideas and activities in an ongoing manner into the daily life of the college. Outward Bound on campus provides real-life experiences to complement work in the classroom. One of the characteristics of the Dartmouth Outward Bound program is community-service activities in the local neighborhood, an important attribute for a college located in a rural setting.

Dartmouth differs from the six other chartered Outward Bound schools in that a large proportion of its activities are centered on the Dartmouth campus for students enrolled at the college or are outreach programs with other institutions in the immediate locality. The Dartmouth Outward Bound Center offers only a relatively small number of programs open to the general public.

There are two main on-campus programs at Dartmouth: the Living/Learning Term and Outward Bound laboratories. The Living/Learning Term is an eleven-week residential experience for ten to twelve undergraduates. The program begins with a wilderness expedition. On return to campus the group resides communally in a house near campus. Each student enrolls in a normal academic load at the college, with one course selected to be taken by all members of the group. The core academic experience has included anthropology, dance, drama, education, English, environmental studies, geography, history, psychology, sociology, and speech.

An expedition through the Presidential Range on the Dartmouth Adult Leadership Program.

In addition to academic work and sharing the running of the house Living/ Learning students share outdoor-skills weekends. They also organize and conduct activities with local young people and the elderly.

Characteristically the Dartmouth program displays its own Outward Bound ropes course built atop a high wooded hill in Hanover, featuring a fourteen-foot-high wall that can be surmounted only by a group working in close co-operation. There is also a range of rope swings, ladders, and bridges that take students sixty feet off the ground.

The hills and forests of New Hampshire provide arenas for rock-climbing, canoeing, rappelling, orienteering, and solo. The nearby Presidential Range provides demanding terrain for mountain expeditions, including trips to the summit of Mount Washington, with ascents and descents via the spectacular Tuckerman Ravine.

Among more unusual Dartmouth activities have been groups spending thirty-six hours living, eating, and sleeping in a tree; forty-eight hours incarcerated in a maximum-security prison; and twenty-four hours in a pitch-black abandoned bomb shelter learning to cope with sensory deprivation. The totality of these experiences in the Dartmouth Living/Learning Term is an experience in community living, integrating Outward Bound with academic work. In 1969, when the program started, it was as an experiment; today it is a firmly established offering in the college program and a fundamental component of the Dartmouth Outward Bound Center.

Outward Bound laboratories are the second central feature of the on-campus

Tuckerman Ravine in the summer.

The ropes course. Agility and trust. (Photograph by Bob McArthur)

Rock-climbing at Dartmouth. (Photograph by Bob McArthur)

Dartmouth program. They are weekend experiences designed in co-operation with individual faculty members to complement classroom learning in their courses. As an example of this laboratory approach, Outward Bound was integrated into a Dartmouth academic course, Sociology/Psychology 27. The course was designed as a human relations learning experience with a focus on both interpersonal and intergroup relations. Bob Kleck from the Psychology Department and George Theriault of the Sociology Department jointly taught the course.

Both George and Bob placed emphasis on the intellectual aspect of the course, on learning *about* individual and group behavior. They both expressed concerns that the Outward Bound component might detract from intellectual learning. Bob especially was concerned that the addition of Outward Bound might place the emphasis too heavily on the affective component to the detriment of the intellectual process.

During the first few weeks the group engaged in conventional group dynamics, then in a group project in the aesthetic realm, and finally, in an intensive five-day Outward Bound experience.

The Outward Bound component began with a blindfolded ride. The group was left in the woods not far from Walden Pond late in the afternoon and told that they had been dropped behind enemy lines without food. They could not engage any people or use roads or trespass on private property. They were to remain at the drop-off point until noon the following day, when they were to set off on a course, following map and compass, for Misery Mountain, where they would find a food cache. The route traversed a swamp with waist-deep water (iced over in spots). From Misery Mountain the route continued to Zilch Pond (unnamed on the map), where they would find a trading post. During the expedition they were given a list of thirteen items to search for. At the trading post the items were exchanged for food.

After the expedition phase the group was again blindfolded and transported to the nearby Carroll School. They were led, still blindfolded, to a circular stairwell leading thirty-five feet into the ground. They entered the silo, the top was put in place, and they were permitted to remove their blindfolds. Total blackness. They were told they were in the shaft of a World War II bomb shelter; they were to explore the shelter and make use of any artifacts they discovered.

The first part of the experience consisted of exploration of the bomb shelter, in which the group discovered three rooms, a maze, various passageways, a red light, an open socket, some candles, food, half as many sleeping bags as there were people, a stove, a flashlight, a jigsaw puzzle, some coins, an intercom, some buckets, and finally, some matches. The second phase consisted of living together in the shelter (without watches or other kinds of lights) for a period of forty-eight hours.

At the conclusion of the experience the group was met by George at the door, and after a hearty lunch all traveled back to Hanover in the same van, discussing the experiences en route.

Three class sessions following the Outward Bound experience focused on those group dynamics evoked by the experience.

Perhaps the most widely accepted value of the experience was the opportunity to see members of the group in a different context. Prior to the OB trip knowledge of each other had, by and large, been limited to classroom behavior. In at least three marked instances (which surprised the group) traits of individuals were revealed that would not have been emphasized without the field experience.

The lack of imposed leadership (on the part of the OB staff) created an atmosphere enabling the group to interact in a new context. Leadership characteristics were not pre-empted by OB staff and constituted one of the most volatile of the group dynamics throughout the trip.

The group reached its most intense impasse (according to testimony) during the bomb shelter experience. The issue apparently arose over the matter of stress, some feeling they were not under enough and others feeling any more stress would be undesirable.

The OB experience seemed to contribute significantly to the cohesiveness of the group in the final stages of the course. Some journals indicated that not all participants experienced highs and that significant learning did occur in areas of self-perceptions, interpersonal relations, and the understanding of group development.

In addition to Sociology/Psychology 27, other Outward Bound laboratory sessions have been incorporated into courses in economics, education, environmental studies, geography, government, and business administration.

The main outreach elements of the Dartmouth Outward Bound program are a series of projects involving youthful offenders, work with local schoolchildren, and a mental health project in which professional staff team with undergraduates to provide Outward Bound activities for selected inpatients of the Dartmouth–Hitchcock Mental Health Center. The following account was written by Kristi Kistler, Peter Bryant, and Gary Tucker, members of the mental health project:

In 1975 . . . two members of the Dartmouth Outward Bound Center and an activities therapist and a staff psychiatrist at the Dartmouth–Hitchcock Mental Health Center undertook a five-week experimental therapeutic project with seven disturbed adolescents and young adults ranging in age from 16 to 23. Five were diagnosed as psychotic, and two had characterological problems. All had been hospitalized at least once, and some as many as six times, for periods ranging from two weeks to several months. Some had been in treatment for six years. At the time of the project, four patients were in the day hospital, one was in out-patient treatment, and two were inpatients at the mental health center.

A major task was to modify Outward Bound methodology for use with patients. The goals of the project were to help patients develop a sense of self-worth and resourcefulness; to develop trust in themselves and their capabilities, as well as trust in others; to foster communication and compassion within the group; to improve physical conditioning and coordination; to experience a shared adventure that was both fun and demanding; to learn outdoor-living skills; and to complete a time-limited task that would provide a sense of success and pride.

(Photograph by Bob McArthur)

The group met once a week for approximately two hours except for the last week; that meeting lasted four consecutive days and included an overnight camping trip. At the first meeting patients and staff got acquainted.

Subsequent sessions were devoted to outdoor exercises with ropes and practice in tying knots; balance exercises, rock-climbing, and rappelling; preliminary planning for the overnight trip; and instruction in building a shelter, fire-building, menu-planning, and packing gear. Each session ended with a discussion of what had been learned that day and the accompanying feelings.

During the early sessions it was apparent that the patients lacked initiative, but they all participated enthusiastically in activities suggested by the staff. They also tended to make unrealistic plans, such as climbing very large, faraway mountains. However, their ideas were tempered by reality as they participated in specific activities and became aware of their own generally poor physical conditioning. That awareness prompted some of them to start an early-morning daily exercise program.

It was impressive to observe the extent to which the patients were capable of complex psychomotor skills, particularly . . . knot-tying and rappelling. All patients seemed able to grasp these skills with only slight difficulty, even those on heavy medication. The fact that staff and patients participated equally in all activities led to a growing feeling of trust, communication, and mutual support within the group. Individual anxieties and concerns were replaced by group concerns and group commitments.

The key element that nurtured continued participation was the balance between challenge and success. Although the patients needed to be challenged, they were apt to withdraw from participation if the situation was too threatening or demanding. Therefore, in each session the staff attempted to build on the skills and level of risks of the preceding one.

The camping trip began with a breakfast meeting at the mental health center. The group traveled by car to a small mountain that could easily be ascended. Group members carried all their gear in backpacks. After an initial orientation and discussion of practical aspects of camping and a compass exercise, the hike began. The group easily climbed the peak by noon and descended to another camp, where tents were put up for the overnight stay and the evening meal was prepared. The next morning they bushwhacked to another peak, with each patient taking turns leading the group by compass. The group descended rapidly and returned home.

Staff felt the project had a number of beneficial effects, among them the fact that the participants themselves considered it a successful experience. The project provided a common ground on which a disparate group of people could relate to each other and work together in solving problems. Group members derived considerable support and comfort from each other, and some were enabled to undertake tasks they might not otherwise have attempted. Group support continued to be evidenced after the conclusion of the project; several weeks later, when one of the group had to be hospitalized at the state hospital, several group members supported and cared for her while she was awaiting transfer there.

Staff believe the project's success centered on two important factors. All the patients were involved in an ongoing treatment relationship, and thus the project was not simply an isolated event. In addition, the project was not promoted as a treatment activity but as an opportunity for patients to do something "normal." The graduated and tailored format of the sessions allowed for the development of relationships between group members and the building of skills and confidence.*

Based on the success of this and other projects, in 1978 the Dartmouth Outward Bound Center initiated a three-year project in co-operation with the Dartmouth–Hitchcock Mental Health Center. The project design included a continuing series of inpatient programs, the development of a series of outpatient programs, and a systematic research effort aimed at assessing more accurately the impact of Outward Bound on this particular population.

In addition to these on-campus and local outreach projects the Dartmouth Outward Bound Center offers some programs to the general public, including bicycling in northern New England, a college "winterim" program, two ten-day courses for adult women, and a leadership-training program for adults interested in leading Outward Bound activities. The Adult Leadership Program (ALP) is designed for those with previous experience of Outward Bound activities who plan to instruct.

Leadership is an ambiguous concept. Despite lack of definition we have acknowledged the instructor's central role in affecting outcomes. Typically he or she moves from a highly involved, directive role in the early stages of a program and progressively withdraws to the point where the students are making all of the decisions themselves. This process is characterized by three prime factors: the nature of the leader (instructor), the nature of the group, and the particular situation.† The instructor's job of weaning students from dependence is made difficult by the fact that the Outward Bound situation typically encourages *dependence*. The activities are challenging, unfamiliar to the students, and the instructor is a powerful figure in the student's perception. It is difficult for the student not to regard the instructor as the unquestionable authority and to resist exerting self-reliance.

A competent Outward Bound leader must be closely in touch with her or his students—aware of their backgrounds, their skills, their emotional states, and their progress hour to hour, day to day during the course. Part of this is intuitive; part, the result of an explicit process of checking expectations, asking questions, and continually monitoring the group's progress.

The instructor will impart some skills directly: safety and technical skills and also the guidance necessary to ensure that the course elements unfold in the desired progression.

The nondirective involvement of the instructor in the later stages of a program does not imply an abrogation of responsibility. Rather, the instructor needs to engineer situations, define boundaries, and frequently observe the progress of students through the situations as a basis for informed later discussion. Nondirective does not mean noninvolved. In fact intelligent nondirective involvement with a group is one of the more sophisticated skills in the instructor's repertoire.

---

* This account is from Kistler, Bryant, and Tucker, "Outward Bound: Providing a Therapeutic Experience for Troubled Adolescents," *Hospital and Community Psychiatry* 28, no. 11 (November 1977).

† Much of this and the following information on leadership is drawn from Robert McArthur's paper, "Leadership Training for Outward Bound Activities."

One of the characteristics that sets Outward Bound apart from recreational adventure activities is the conscious attempt to interpret these activities as metaphors for self-knowledge. The instructor plays a crucial role in assisting the student in making sense of the activities and relating them meaningfully to the broader scheme of things.

The skills a competent Outward Bound instructor needs—knowledge of the students, direct instruction on safety and technique, skillful nondirective participation, and guidance in interpretation of the experience—are major focuses for the Dartmouth ALP.

In the early stages of the twenty-eight-day ALP program, participants function as members of a small group engaged in a wide variety of skills-training activities under the direction of a senior Outward Bound instructor. These include the range of outdoor skills: camping, map and compass, ropes, rock-climbing, emergency care, initiatives, search and rescue, woodcraft, and adventure playground planning and construction. In addition a good deal of emphasis is placed on group process skills. Midway through the program the group undertakes a four-day expedition, traversing the Presidential Range as the conclusion of the first major phase of the program.

During the second phase ALP participants design and operate a series of experiences for young people in the Hanover area. These include devising a search and rescue exercise for Dartmouth College undergraduates and organizing a ropes course, introductory rock-climbing, initiative exercises, and log cabin construction for forty youngsters at a local summer camp. Additionally an adventure playground (a series of balance and agility exercises using swings and other activities from the Outward Bound ropes course) is designed and constructed. ALP participants carry out these responsibilities under the observation of the Outward Bound staff members and receive regular feedback and evaluation of their efforts.

Lowering a Stokes litter and "victim" down a steep cliff on the Adult Leadership Program. (Photograph by Bob McArthur)

Transporting an injured person on an improvised litter during a practice evacuation. (Photograph by Bob McArthur)

Evening in the Presidential Range.

So, in its broad outlines the Dartmouth ALP is divided into two main phases: the initial stage, in which Outward Bound staff teach skills and technique, and the second stage, in which participants act as instructors, designing and carrying out Outward Bound activities for young people in the Dartmouth area.

Bob McArthur, director of the Dartmouth program and the ALP course, points to a trade-off in the outcomes of the ALP course in comparison with a regular Outward Bound course. The ALP course "dealt with social skills and teaching skills with greater effectiveness than the area of self-knowledge," he writes in his report on the program. "One of the key criticisms of staff and some students on the course was the lack of stress within the course to test individual emotional and physical limits." The laboratory nature of the course and the emphasis on teaching teaching skills had reduced the opportunities of the course for the kind of personally challenging experiences that Outward Bound specializes in. Given the ALP's goal of developing leadership skills, this is undoubtedly a worthwhile trade-off.

The program at the Dartmouth Outward Bound Center differs in some respects from the offerings of the other six Outward Bound schools. The Living/Learning Term and the laboratories are integrated with the academic curriculum of the college, as the mental health program is integrated with the ongoing activities of the Dartmouth–Hitchcock Mental Health Center. These ongoing core projects give the Dartmouth Center its special qualities. Among the other offerings the bicycle-based Outward Bound course is unique among American Outward Bound schools, as is the ALP program. At the six other Outward Bound courses the standard course is the typical main bill of fare, with experimental and innovative courses occasionally being developed from that base. At Dartmouth the reverse is true; innovative and experimental programs are the norm, and standard Outward Bound courses open to the general public are offered only on a limited basis. Perhaps the program at the Dartmouth Center, as much as anything, lends credence to the notion that Outward Bound truly is a *process*, a dynamic educational system that is far more than the sum of the adventurous activities through which it finds expression.

APPENDIX

OUTWARD BOUND®, Inc.

NATIONAL OFFICE

Outward Bound, Inc.
384 Field Point Road
Greenwich, CT 06830
(203)661-0797

OUTWARD BOUND SCHOOLS

Colorado Outward Bound School
945 Pennsylvania Street
Denver, CO 80203
(303)837-0880

Dartmouth Outward Bound Center
P.O. Box 50
Hanover, NH 03755
(603)646-3359

Hurricane Island Outward Bound School
P.O. Box 429
Rockland, ME 04841
(207)594-5548
[For information, call *toll free*
(800)243-8520]

Minnesota Outward Bound School
308 Walker Avenue South
Wayzata, MN 55391
(612)473-5476

North Carolina Outward Bound School
P.O. Box 817
Morganton, NC 28655
(704)437-6112

Northwest Outward Bound School
0110 S.W. Bancroft Street
Portland, OR 97201
(503)243-1993

Southwest Outward Bound School
P.O. Box 2840
Santa Fe, NM 87501
(505)988-5573

INDEX

A

Aberdovey program (Wales), 151
Acceptable risk, 81
Accident statistics, 82
Activities, discussion of, 21. *See also* types of activities
Adam (magazine), 48
Adult Leadership Program (ALP), 250, 258–63
All-women's group programs, 133
Alpine expedition, 27, 150, 191
Anguilla rostrata (eels), 115
Antarctic, 27
Appalachia, topography of, 43
Arctic, 27
Australia, ix, 151
Austria, 151

B

Backpacks, 6–7, 47
Bald Island, 136
Barnes, Pat (Cub), 186, 187, 191–92, 194, 198, 203–4
Basswood Lake, 225, 227, 237
Belaying process, 76
Berkley, Sara, 9, 12, 14, 16, 18, 19, 29
Berry, Wendell, 67
Biggs, Tom, 154, 177
Birch, James, 175

Birth Canal (obstacle on the ropes course), 85
Bouldering, 73, 74
Boundary Waters Canoe Area, vii
Bowline knot, 106
Braman, Chester, 224, 226
Brennan, Jim, 11, 15–46, 47, 49, 57, 59
Bryant, Peter, 255–58
Bull Sluice Rapid, 59–62, 63
Bunting, John, 56, 59, 62, 63, 64
Butter Island, 138

C

Calkins, Barbara, 194, 195, 210
Calm Before the Storm Rapids, 63
Canada, ix
Canoe expedition, 224–40
    application of controlled and understandable stress, 233
    communal chores, 225–26
    improvised sail, 229
    lakeside rock-climbing, 235
    map symbols, 232
    portages, 232–33, 237–40
    return journey, 237–40
    types of canoes used, 224–25, 227, 232
    See also Minnesota Outward Bound School
Carabiners, 85
Careinides maenas (crabs), 114
Cargo net (obstacle on the ropes course), 86
Cascade Mountains, 147, 151, 156

Charles, Prince, 150
Chattooga River raft expedition, 50–64
  ferry position, 53
  gorge region, 52
  negotiating the rapids, 53–64
  safety drill, 56
  section IV region, 56–59
  tongue formation, 53
Chimneys Cliff, 69, 78, 82
Chocolate Glacier, 154
Choya cactus, 17
Cochran, Jock, 183–84, 186, 187, 190, 191,
  193, 197, 202
Collins, Joe, 3–5, 9, 12, 14, 17, 19
Colorado Outward Bound School, ix, 179–
  211, 265
  introductory ski courses, 182–83
  ski expedition, 179–205
  walk-jog exercise, 182
Community building, viii
Confidence, experiencing, 131
Cool Glacier, 154, 162, 164
Corkscrew Rapids, 63
Crack in the Rock Rapids, 63
Crevasse rescue practice, 167, 168
Curly (North Carolina participant), 44, 59–
  60, 62, 75, 81, 83–84, 92

D

D'Amberosio, Ernie, 187, 205
Dangle Rock, 72
Dartmouth College, ix, 249, 259
Dartmouth-Hitchcock Mental Health Center,
  255–58, 263
Dartmouth Outward Bound Center, ix, 247–
  63, 265
  Adult Leadership Program (ALP), 250,
    258–63
  experience and class sessions, 254–55
  Living/Learning term, 249–50, 263
  outreach elements of, 255–58
  Outward Bound laboratories, 251–55
  rock-climbing, 253
  ropes course, 251, 252, 259
Davis, George, 221, 224, 226, 229
Dawn Trader (boat), 95–116, 132, 133–42, 143
  beginning the voyage, 102–3
  capsize drill, 137

Dawn Trader (boat) *(Continued)*
  final expedition, 133–45
  foul weather gear, 105–7
  helmsperson, 98–99, 102, 108
  knot tying, 106
  length of, 109
  monkey line, 106
  oars and oar clashes, 105–6, 111
  raising the main sprit, 132, 136
  sailing positions, 99, 100–1, 108
  Spectacle Island landing, 112–16
  See also Hurricane Island Outward Bound
    School
Delinquent youth programs, x–xi
Deliverance (motion picture), 49
Deliverance Rock Rapids, 63
Dennett, Bill, 100, 101, 102, 105, 109, 115,
  123, 126, 128, 134, 138–40, 142
Dennis, Patrick (Pat), 101, 111, 138, 139
Dependence experience, 24
Dick's Creek Falls Rapid, 53–54
Doran, Maureen, 100, 110, 132, 133
Double fisherman's knot, 106
Duel, Art, 44, 46–50, 53, 57–60, 62, 65, 66,
  69–71, 74, 75, 78, 83–87, 88, 131, 209,
  245
Dunham, Alden, 243–44

E

Eagle Island, 136
Eiger Mountain, 182
El Capitan, 182
Emerald Peak, 195, 196, 197
England, viii–ix, x, 44, 150, 151, 172, 215,
  243
Erkkila, John, 217, 221, 237, 242
Eskdale Outward Bound School (England),
  215
Eye of the Needle Rapids, 54

F

Ferry position, 53
Finucayne, Jim, 46, 55, 59, 63–65, 71, 75,
  76, 81–83, 87–91, 92
Fire fighting, viii
Flea's Leap (activity), 134, 143

Forward (nautical term), 95

Freeman, Herman, 44, 46, 57, 59–60, 62, 64–66, 67, 71, 72, 78–80, 83, 84, 92, 93, 209

Froelicher, F. Charles, ix

G

Gibbons, Euell, 113, 114, 115, 126

Gila River, 6, 7, 8, 10–11, 18, 43
   negotiating an obstacle, 15

Gila Wilderness Area of New Mexico, vii, 3–42, 43, 49, 67, 245
   canyon walls, 6
   desert inhabitants of, 7
   Granny Mountain hike, 8–26
   location of, 7
   marathon runs, 31, 38
   Miller Spring camping site, 18–19
   rope climbs, 30–31, 42
   See also Southwest Outward Bound School

Ginger Cake Mountain, 69

Glacier Peak, 153, 154, 156 57, 173

Glacier Peak climb, 154–68
   beginning of, 160
   crevasse rescue practice, 167, 168
   ice pick practice, 164–68
   planning, 157–59
   at the summit, 162–64
   See also Northwest Outward Bound School

Glacier Peak Wilderness Area, 154

Goldsmith, Ken, 25

Gordonstoun (school), viii–ix, 150, 151

Granny Mountain, 81, 245

Granny Mountain hike, 8–26

Grant, Glen, 195, 200

Gray, Ron, 9, 12, 16, 19, 21, 25, 29, 39, 40, 42

Graydon, Sarah, 224, 225, 241

Great Britain, *see* England

Greiner, Teresa, 195, 196

Guinness Book of World Records, 215

H

Hahn, Kurt, vii, viii, 150–51, 203, 224, 243
   background of, viii–ix
   philosophy of, 26, 249

Hammond, Drew, 44–57, 59, 63–69, 71, 72–78, 83–85, 87, 89–91, 93

Hawksbill Mountain, 69

Heacock, Susan, 100, 102, 115

Herr, Bruce, 56, 59–60, 64

Hillary, Sir Edmund, 84

Himalayan Mountains, 27

Hitler, Adolf, viii

Hoades, Gerry, 224

Hogan, Jim, ix

Holt, Lawrence, ix, 150, 151, 243

Honeycomb Glacier, 168

Honeycomb High Route, 168

Hong Kong, ix, 151

Hospital and Community Psychiatry, 254

Hotchkiss, John, 153, 154, 156, 157, 164, 171, 173, 177

Humpback Mountain, 69

Hurricane Island Outward Bound School, ix, xi, 48, 95–145, 245, 265
   age range, 101
   Dawn Trader voyage, 95–116, 132, 133–42, 143
   final expedition, 133–42
   high rappel at, 124–25
   morning meeting, 117
   morning run and dip tradition, 120–21
   solo experience, 126–28
   "watch," 123

I

Igloo building, 193–95, 196

Independence Pass, 187

Indian eggs (cactus), 18

Instructors, 24–25, 81, 129–31, 145, 258–59
   intuitive level of, 130
   See also names of instructors

Intimacy experience, 24

J

Jawbone Rapids, 63

Jeanette (Gila Wilderness participant), 14–16, 17, 18, 19, 21, 25, 36, 40–41, 42, 245

Jimbo (instructor), 8, 12, 13, 14, 17, 19, 21, 25, 28, 29–30, 31, 42, 43, 45, 81
Jonas Ridge Mountain, 69

K

Kahler, Mike, 47, 58, 59, 63, 65, 71, 80–81, 82
Kahshahpiwi, 233–37, 241
Kelso, Denny, 217, 221, 237, 240
Kenya, ix, 151, 215
Keyhole Rapid, 56
Kilimanjaro, 215
Kistler, Kristi, 255–58
Kleck, Bob, 254
Knot tying, 106
Koehler, Paul, 157, 159, 171, 173–74, 175

L

Lake Creek, 190
Lake Creek skiing, 185
Langehop, Tom, 100, 102, 108, 110, 113, 115, 126, 132, 133, 138, 140
Laurel Knob Mountain, 69
"Leadership Training for Outward Bound Activities" (McArthur), 258
Lewis, C. S., 100
Linvell Gorge, 69, 78, 168
Living/Learning Term (Dartmouth Outward Bound Center), 249–50, 263
Log-crossing exercise, 45–46, 81
London *Times*, viii–ix
Lutkin, Emily, 44, 45, 46, 47, 50, 59, 65–67, 69, 71, 78, 83, 92, 93

M

McArthur, Robert, 258, 261, 262
Maddox, Hilary, 224
Malaysia, 151
Mantelshelf move (rock-climbing), 75–76
Map reading, 9
Marvin, John, 220, 224, 226
Mateuse, Ron, 182, 183, 184, 187, 190–93, 197–200, 203, 207
Meyers, Dan, 44

Michalets, Ellen, 44, 46, 48, 50, 54, 55–56, 59, 63, 68, 72, 75, 78, 81, 82, 84
Miller, Ingrid, 183, 185, 187, 189–90, 196, 204–5, 207, 210
Miller Spring (camping site), 18–19
Miner, Joshua L., ix
Minnesota Outward Bound School, ix, x, 100, 104, 115, 213–45, 265
  base camp, 213, 215
  canoe expedition, 224–40
  rope-climbing, 223, 235
Misery Mountain, 254
Missouri Basin, 191, 192–93, 196, 203, 207
Missouri Gulch, 202
Missouri Mountain, 191, 197, 202
Monroe Island, 103, 105, 107
Moritz, Fritz, 150, 151, 160, 163, 164, 166
Mountaineer's ice ax, 164–65
Mount Rainier, 164
Murray, Doyle, 156, 177

N

Napeequa Valley, 168–72
  purification ritual, 170–72
  solo experience, 168–72
  See also Northwest Outward Bound School
Narrows Rapids, 54
National Outdoor Leadership School (NOLS), 163
Nazi party, 151
Netherlands, 151
New York *Times*, 39
New Zealand, ix, 151
Nigeria, 151
Nold, Joe, 244
North Carolina Outward Bound School, ix, 39, 43–93, 131, 209, 265
  Chattooga River raft expedition, 50–64
  hiking, 64
  log-crossing exercise, 45–46, 81
  marathon, 84
  overnight solo experience, 66–71
  rock-climbing, 72–84, 92
  rope-course, 85–92
  Table Rock climb, 82–84, 92
North Carolina Outward Bound School Safety Policy, 82

North Cascade Mountains, 173, 174, 187, 245
  crevasse rescue practice, 167
Northwest Outward Bound School, ix, 147–77, 265
  Glacier Peak climb, 154–68
  hikes, 153
  ice pick practice, 164–68
  Napeequa Valley destination, 168–72
  solo experience, 168–72
Norway, 151
Nystrom, Scott, 188–89, 190, 191–93, 197–98, 202, 205, 207, 209–11, 245

O

Olson, Sigurd, 226–27
One-Inch Journey, The (Berry), 67
Outward Bound:
  alumni (U.S.), ix
  average age of students, x
  beginnings of (in U.S.), ix–x
  Colorado, ix, 179–211, 265
  Dartmouth, ix, 247–63, 265
  dropouts, 58
  in England, viii–ix, x, 44, 150, 151, 172, 215, 243
  essence of, 244–45
  final goal of, vii–viii
  first course, ix
  Hurricane Island, ix, xi, 48, 95–145, 245, 265
  marine bootcamp image, 104
  Minnesota, ix, x, 100, 104, 115, 213–45, 265
  North Carolina, ix, 39, 43–93, 131, 209, 265
  Northwest, ix, 147–77, 265
  number of schools, ix
  publicity materials, 58–59
  second goal of, viii
  Southwest, ix, 3–41, 265
  traditional twenty-six-day program, 26–27
Outward Bound: A Reference Volume (Shore), 243
"Outward Bound: Providing a Therapeutic Experience for Troubled Adolescents" (Kistler, Bryant, and Tucker), 258

Outward Bound, Inc. (OBI), 215, 217, 227, 236, 249, 265
Outward Bound Trust (London), ix
Owls Head, 103, 105, 106
Owls Head Bay, 103

P

Passages: Predictable Crises of Adult Life (Sheehy), x, 39–40
Peavey, Dan, 9, 17, 18, 25, 36–39
Pendl, Ulrich (Uli), 224, 227–29
Penobscot Bay, 107
Peyton, Anne, 95, 96, 97–103, 105–9, 111–13, 116, 120, 122, 128, 130, 132–34, 136, 138, 140, 141
Philip, Prince, 150
Pine Creek, 191
Piñon pine *(Pinus edulis)*, 13
Piolet ancre technique, 165
Pipestone Bay, 225
Pisgah National Forest, 69
PolarGuard sleeping bags, 179
Pooley, Bonnie, 100–1, 108, 128, 129
Presidential Range, vii, 250
Pritchard, Derek, 213–17, 220, 223, 225–27, 229, 234, 237, 240–41
Pritchard, Mrs. Pat, 220
"Problem of Individual Change in Outward Bound, The" (Rhoades), 217
Program effectiveness, judging, 40
Ptarmigan Glacier, 154
Purification ritual, 170–72

Q

Quetico Provincial Park, 215
Quiet Rock, 220
Quon, Pierre, 98
Quon, Suejee, 97–98, 99, 100, 110, 112, 113, 116, 120–23, 125–27, 134, 138–40, 142–45, 243, 245

R

Raft expedition, *see* Chattooga River raft expedition

Rhoades, John, 217, 227, 229, 233, 237, 241
Rhodesia, 151
Ridge hiking, in Zion National Park, 22–23
Rock-climbing, 72–84, 92, 235, 253
Rock Jumble Rapids, 63
Rockland harbor, 99, 103, 138, 141
Roepke, Liz, 220
Rohit, Desai, 100
Roller Coaster Rapids, 54
Rolley, Ann, 220, 224, 241
Ropes course and rope-climbing, 30–31, 42, 85–92, 134, 235, 251, 252, 253

S

Salem School (Germany), 151
Sauk River, 147
Scholarships, x
Schupf, Harriet, 237, 241–42
Screaming Left Falls Rapids, 63
Second Ledge Rapids, 54
Self-confidence, vii–viii
Self-limitations, recognition of, 131–32
Seven Foot Falls Rapids, 63
Sheehy, Gail, 39–40
Sheep Island, 103
Shore, Arnold, 221–24, 227, 229, 234, 236, 241, 242–43, 244
Shortoff Mountain, 64–65, 70
Shoulder Bone Rapids, 63, 64
Simmons, Leslie, 217
Singapore, ix, 151
Singing Wilderness, The (Olson), 226–27
Sitkum Glacier, 154
Ski expedition, 179–205
    approaching the summit, 189, 190, 208
    cabin quarters, 192
    camp skills development, 186–87
    crocodile formation, 188
    igloo building, 193–95, 196
    introductory courses, 182–83
    Piepes transmitter, 190
    wax used, 184, 188
    See also Colorado Outward Bound School
Sleeping bags, 47, 111, 115–16, 179, 203
Social science methodology, 129–30

Social service, concept of (as an educational vehicle), 151
Sock-em-Dog Rapids, 63
Solo experience, 66–71, 109, 126–28, 168–72, 175, 187, 203–4
    as a meditative experience, 66
South Africa, 151
Southwest Outward Bound School, ix, 3–41, 265
    Granny Mountain hike, 8–26
    program effectiveness, 40
    rhythm of the desert, 8
    traditional twenty-six day program, 26–27
    tribes, 7
    See also Gila Wilderness Area of New Mexico
Spectacle Island, 112–16
Square knot, 106
Stanger, John, 177
Steinhart, Pat, 186, 187, 194, 197–98, 202, 207, 210
Stekoa Rapids, 63
Strunk, Jay, 44, 46, 51–52, 53, 58, 59, 63, 64, 71, 72, 83, 92–93
Suiattle Glacier, 168
Superior National Forest, 215
Swayzee, Gregg, 150, 154, 165, 174–75
Swimmer's Rapid, 55

T

Table Rock Mountain, 43, 69, 82–84, 92–93
Taft, Henry W., 217
Tenpeak Mountain, 168
Theriault, George, 254
Thomas, Jim, 101, 113, 128
Tongue formation, 53
Trail maintenance, viii
Tucker, Gary, 255–58
Tuckerman Ravine, 251
Turkey Park, 29

U

Udall, Randy, 179–82, 193–95

V

Vertical ice-climbing technique, 206
Viebranz, Curt, 100–5, 107–9, 111–13, 115–
    16, 120, 122, 123, 128, 134, 138–39, 140

W

Walk-jog exercise, 182
Wall (problem-solving exercise), 135
Warner, Anne, 100, 105, 110, 128
Welsh program, ix, 151
West Africa, ix
West Germany, 151
White Chuck Glacier, 154, 156, 159, 164
White Pass, 147, 156
White River, 147
Wild Way to Eat, A (Gibbons), 113, 114,
    115, 126

Women, x, 44, 104
Woodall Shoals Rapids, 63

Y

Yellow Dog (instructor), 150–54, 156–57,
    159–60, 162–66, 168–69, 170–71, 172
Yoke (cross brace), 233
Yonkman, Fred, 220, 240
Yosemite Valley, 182

Z

Zambia, 151
Zilch Pond, 254
Zion National Park, 34–35
    climbing a desert spire, 35
    ridge hiking in, 22–23

Robert Godfrey is a professional photographer and free-lance writer. He served for a number of years as an instructor for Outward Bound and more recently has been involved in an advisory capacity. He is the author of *Climb!*, a history of climbing and mountaineering in Colorado, and the director of the film *Free Climb*. He holds a doctorate in counseling psychology and research and statistical methodology.